MW01002629

A Short History
of The Church
of Jesus Christ
of Latter-day Saints

TRUTH
RESTORED

by Gordon B. Hinckley
of the Council of the Twelve Apostles
of The Church of Jesus Christ
of Latter-day Saints

©1947, 1979 Corporation of the President, The Church
of Jesus Christ of Latter-day Saints

First printed in Missionary Reference Set edition, September 1988

ISBN 0-87579-169-7

All rights reserved
Printed in the United States of America

CONTENTS

The Prophet Joseph Smith

1 GENESIS

WESTERN New York in the early nineteenth century was essentially frontier territory, a place of opportunity to those for whom the tremendous task of clearing and breaking the virgin land held little fear. Among these were Joseph and Lucy Mack Smith and their eight children, who in 1816 came to the vicinity of Palmyra, not far from Rochester.

They were a typical New England family of English and Scottish extraction who prized the independence their fathers on both lines had fought for in the American Revolution of 1776. And they were religious folk who read the Bible and had family prayer, although like many of their kind they belonged to no church.

This condition among the people of the frontier areas of America became a matter of serious concern to religious leaders, and a crusade was begun to convert the unconverted. It was carried over a vast area from the New England states to Kentucky. In 1820 it reached western New York. The ministers of the various denominations united in their efforts, and many conversions were made among the scattered settlers. One week a Rochester paper noted: "More than 200 souls have become hopeful subjects of divine grace in Palmyra, Macedon,

Manchester, Lyons and Ontario since the late revival commenced." The week following it was able to report "that in Palmyra and Macedon . . . more than four hundred souls have already confessed that the Lord is good."[1]

Joseph's Story

Under the impetus of this revival, four of the Smith family—the mother and three children—joined the Presbyterian Church. Joseph Jr., then fourteen years of age, also felt a strong desire to affiliate himself with a church. But he wanted to be right in so important a step, and he became deeply distressed that, although the various ministers had been united in their efforts when the revival commenced, they disagreed sharply among themselves when the converts began to file off to the various congregations. The more he listened to the conflicting arguments, the more confused he became. He reasoned that all of them could not be right, and the question as to which was recognized by God as His church greatly troubled him. In a simple, straightforward account, he tells of the course he took and of the remarkable events which followed:

"While I was laboring under the extreme difficulties caused by the contests of these parties of religionists, I was one day reading the Epistle of James, first chapter and fifth verse, which reads, *If any of you lack wisdom, let him ask of God, that giveth to all men liberally, and upbraideth not; and it shall be given him.*

"Never did any passage of scripture come with more power to the heart of man than this did at this time to mine . . . I reflected on it again and again, knowing that if any person needed wisdom from God, I did; for how to act I did not know, and unless I could get more wisdom than I then had, I would never know; for the teachers of religion of the different sects understood the same passages of scripture so differently as to destroy all confidence in settling the question by an appeal to the Bible.

"At length I came to the conclusion that I must either remain in darkness and confusion, or else do as James directs, that is, ask of God. I at length came to the determination to 'ask of God,' concluding that if he gave wisdom to them that lacked wisdom, and would give liberally, and not upbraid, I might venture.

"So, in accordance with this, my determination to ask of God, I retired to the woods to make the attempt. It was on the morning of a beautiful, clear day, early in the spring of eighteen hundred and twenty. It was the first time in my life that I had made such an attempt, for amidst all my anxieties I had never as yet made the attempt to pray vocally. . . .

"Having looked around me, and finding myself alone, I kneeled down and began to offer up the desire of my heart to God. I had scarcely done so, when immediately I was seized upon by some power which entirely overcame me, and had such an astonishing influence over me as to bind my tongue so that I could not speak. Thick darkness gathered around me, and it seemed to me for a time as if I were doomed to sudden destruction.

"But, exerting all my powers to call upon God, . . . and at the very moment when I was ready to sink into despair and abandon myself to destruction — not to an imaginary ruin, but to the power of some actual being from the unseen world, who had such marvelous power as I had never before felt in any being—just at this moment of great alarm, I saw a pillar of light exactly over my head, above the brightness of the sun, which descended gradually until it fell upon me.

"It no sooner appeared than I found myself delivered from the enemy which held me bound. When the light rested upon me I saw two Personages, whose brightness and glory defy all description, standing above me in the air. One of them spake unto me, calling me by name and said, pointing to the other—*This is my Beloved Son. Hear Him!*

"My object in going to inquire of the Lord

The grove where the First Vision was received

was to know which of all the sects was right, that I might know which to join. No sooner, therefore, did I get possession of myself . . . than I asked the Personages who stood above me in the light, which of all the sects was right—and which I should join.

"I was answered that I must join none of them, . . . that: 'they draw near to me with their lips, but their hearts are far from me, they teach for doctrines the commandments of men, having a form of godliness, but they deny the power thereof.' "[2]

As might be expected, so unusual a story caused considerable excitement. In good faith he spoke of it to one of the preachers who had been engaged in the revival. The boy was taken aback when the man treated the story with contempt, telling him that such things were of the devil, that all visions and revelations had ceased with the apostles, "and that there would never be any more of them." Nor was this the end of the matter for the young boy. He soon found himself singled out for ridicule; and men, who ordinarily would have paid little attention to such a young lad, took pains to revile him. It was a source of great sorrow to him. He continues:

"It was, nevertheless, a fact that I had beheld a vision. I have thought since, that I felt much like Paul, when he made his defense before King Agrippa, and related the account of the vision he had when he saw a light and heard a voice; but still there were but few who believed him; some said he was dishonest, others said he was mad; and he was ridiculed and reviled. But all this did not destroy the reality of his vision. He had seen a vision, he knew he had, and all the persecution under heaven could not make it otherwise; and though they should persecute him unto death, yet he knew, and would know to his latest breath, that he had both seen a light and heard a voice speaking unto him, and all the world could not make him think or believe otherwise.

"So it was with me. I had actually seen a light, and in the midst of that light I saw two Personages, and they did in reality speak to me; and though I was hated and persecuted for saying that I had seen a vision, yet it was true; and while they were persecuting me, reviling me, and speaking all manner of evil againt me falsely for so saying, I was led to say in my heart: Why persecute me for telling the truth? I have actually seen a vision; and who am I that I can withstand God, or why does the world think to make me deny what I have actually seen? For I had seen a vision. I knew it, and I knew that God knew it, and I could not deny it, neither dared I do it; at least I knew that by so doing I would offend God and come under condemnation."[3]

On the great problem that had perplexed him, Joseph Smith's mind was now settled. He joined none of the churches that had sought his interest. And more important, he had learned that the promise of James was true: One who lacked wisdom might ask of God, and obtain, and not be upbraided.

2 AN ANGEL AND A BOOK

Life for Joseph Smith was never the same once he had told the story of his vision. For one thing, that remarkable experience had left an indelible impression upon him. The knowledge he had thus received placed him in a unique position. Nevertheless, his manner of living was not greatly different from that of the ordinary farm boy of his day, except that he was often made an object of ridicule. But he continued to work on his father's farm, to work for others in the area, and to associate with companions of his own age. Those acquainted with him describe him as a strong, active boy of cheerful disposition, who enjoyed wrestling and other sports. The story of his life and experiences at this time is again best told in his own words:

"I frequently fell into many foolish errors, and displayed the weakness of youth, . . . which, I am sorry to say, led me into divers temptations, offensive in the sight of God. In making this confession no one need suppose me guilty of any great or malignant sins. A disposition to commit such was never in my nature. . . .

"In consequence of these things I often felt condemned for my weakness and imperfections; when, on the evening of [September 21, 1823], after I had retired to my bed for the night, I betook myself to prayer and supplication to

Almighty God for forgiveness of all my sins and follies, and also for a manifestation to me, that I might know of my state and standing before him; for I had full confidence in obtaining a divine manifestation as I previously had done.

"While I was thus in the act of calling upon God, I discovered a light appearing in my room which continued to increase until the room was lighter than at noonday, when immediately a personage appeared at my bedside, standing in the air, for his feet did not touch the floor.

"He had on a loose robe of most exquisite whiteness. It was a whiteness beyond anything earthly I had ever seen; nor do I believe that any earthly thing could be made to appear so exceedingly white and brilliant. His hands were naked, and his arms also, a little above the wrist; so, also, were his feet naked, as were his legs, a little above the ankles. His head and neck were also bare. I could discover that he had no other clothing on but this robe, as it was open, so that I could see into his bosom.

"Not only was his robe exceedingly white, but his whole person was glorious beyond description, and his countenance truly like lightning. The room was exceedingly light, but not so very bright as immediately around his person. When I first looked upon him I was afraid; but the fear soon left me.

"He called me by name and said unto me that he was a messenger sent from the presence of God to me, and that his name was Moroni; that God had a work for me to do; and that my name should be had for good and evil among all nations, kindreds, and tongues, or that it should be both good and evil spoken of among all people."

An American Scripture

"He said there was a book deposited, written upon gold plates, giving an account of the former inhabitants of this continent, and the source from whence they sprang. He also said that the fulness of the everlasting Gospel was contained in it as delivered by the Savior to the ancient inhabitants [of America];

"Also that there were [deposited with the plates] two stones in silver bows—and these stones, fastened to a breastplate, constituted what is called the Urim and Thummim. . . . The possession and use of these stones were what constituted 'seers' in ancient or former times; and . . . God had prepared them for the purpose of translating the book.

"After telling me these things, he commenced quoting the prophecies of the Old Testament. . . . [Joseph then lists some of the passages of scripture quoted by Moroni.]

"Again, he told me, that when I got those plates of which he had spoken . . . I should not show them to any person; neither the breastplate with the Urim and Thummim; only to those to whom I should be commanded to show them; if I did I should be destroyed. While he was conversing with me about the plates, the vision was open to my mind that I could see the place where the plates were deposited, and that so clearly and distinctly that I knew the place again when I visited it.

"After this communication, I saw the light in the room begin to gather immediately around the person of him who had been speaking to me, and it continued to do so until the room was again left dark, except just around him; when, instantly I saw, as it were, a conduit open right up into heaven, and he ascended till he entirely disappeared, and the room was left as it had been before this heavenly light had made its appearance.

"I lay musing on the singularity of the scene, and marveling greatly at what had been told me by this extraordinary messenger; when, in the midst of my meditation, I suddenly discovered that my room was again beginning to get lighted, and in an instant, as it were, the same heavenly messenger was again by my bedside.

"He . . . again related the very same things which he had done at his first visit, without the least variation. . . . Having related these things, he again ascended as he had done before.

"By this time, so deep were the impressions made on my mind, that sleep had fled from my eyes, and I lay overwhelmed in astonishment at what I had both seen and heard. But what was my surprise when again I beheld the same messenger at my bedside, and heard him rehearse or repeat over again to me the same things as before; and added a caution . . . that Satan would try to tempt me (in consequence of the indigent circumstances of my father's family), to get the plates for the purpose of getting rich. This he forbade me. . . .

"After this third visit, he again ascended into heaven as before, and I was again left to ponder on the strangeness of what I had just experienced; when almost immediately after the heavenly messenger had ascended from me the third time, the cock crowed and I found that day was approaching, so that our interviews must have occupied the whole of that night.

"I shortly after arose from my bed, and, as usual, went to the necessary labors of the day;

but, in attempting to work as at other times, I found my strength so exhausted as to render me entirely unable. My father, who was laboring along with me, discovered something to be wrong with me, and told me to go home. I started with the intention of going to the house; but, in attempting to cross the fence out of the field where we were, my strength entirely failed me, and I fell helpless on the ground, and for a time was quite unconscious of anything.

"The first thing that I can recollect was a voice speaking unto me, calling me by name. I looked up, and beheld the same messenger standing over my head, surrounded by light as before. He then again related unto me all that he had related to me the previous night, and commanded me to go to my father and tell him of the vision and commandments which I had received. . . .

"I returned to my father in the field and rehearsed the whole matter to him. He replied to me that it was of God, and told me to go and do as commanded by the messenger. I left the field, and went to the place where the messenger had told me the plates were deposited; and owing to the distinctness of the vision which I had had concerning it, I knew the place the instant that I arrived there."[1]

The Hill Cumorah

About four miles south of Palmyra is a hill of considerable size, rising abruptly on the north side and tapering to the south with a long slope. On the west side, not far from the top, as Joseph had seen it in vision, was the weathered surface of a rounded stone, the edges of which were covered with earth.

Eagerly he removed the earth so that he

might get a lever under the edge. Lifting the rock, he looked into a box formed by a stone in the bottom with other stones cemented together to form the sides. There, indeed, was the treasure!—a breastplate, two stones set in silver bows, and a book of gold leaves bound together with three rings.

Anxiously he reached down to take them, but immediately felt a shock. He tried again, and received another paralyzing shock. Yet again he reached, and this time the shock was so severe as to render him weak and powerless. In his frustration he called out, "Why can I not obtain this book?"

"Because you have not kept the commandments of the Lord," answered a voice at his side. The boy turned, and there stood the same messenger with whom he had conversed during the night. Guilt overwhelmed him, and Moroni's solemn caution flashed through the boy's mind that Satan would try to tempt him because of the indigent circumstances of his father's family, but that the plates of gold were for the glory of God, and he must have no other purpose in mind in relation to them.[2]

Thus rebuked, he was told that he would not receive the plates at that time, but that he would undergo four years of probation, and that during that period he should come to the hill each year on this same day.

"Accordingly," he writes, "I went at the end of each year, and at each time I found the same messenger there, and received instructions and intelligence from him at each of our interviews, respecting what the Lord was going to do, and how and in what manner his kingdom was to be conducted in the last days. . . .

Monument to the angel Moroni on the crest of the Hill Cumorah

"At length the time arrived for obtaining the plates, the Urim and Thummim, and the breastplate. On the twenty-second day of September, one thousand eight hundred and twenty-seven, having gone as usual at the end of another year to the place where they were deposited, the same heavenly messenger delivered them up to me with this charge: that I should be responsible for them; that if I should let them go carelessly, or through any neglect of mine, I should be cut off; but that if I would use all my endeavors to preserve them, until he, the messenger, should call for them, they should be protected."[3]

Troublemakers

Joseph soon learned why Moroni had charged him so strictly to guard the record taken from the hill. No sooner was it rumored that he had the plates, than efforts were made to seize them from him. To preserve them, he first carefully hid them in a hollow birch log. Then he locked them in a chest in his father's home. Later they were buried beneath the hearthstone of the family living room. A cooper's shop across the street was their next hiding place. All of these and other stratagems were employed to keep the plates safe from neighborhood mobs who raided and ransacked the Smith home and surrounding premises, and even employed a diviner in their zeal to locate the record.

On two different occasions Joseph was shot at, and it soon became apparent that he could find no peace in the neighborhood of Palmyra. Some months prior to the time he received the plates he had married Emma Hale of Harmony Township, Pennsylvania. He had met her nearly two years earlier when he boarded at her father's home while working in the vicinity for a Mr. Josiah Stoal. And when in December 1827 an invitation came from his wife's parents to live in their home at Harmony, Joseph accepted in the hope that he could find there the peace needed for the work of translation.

Once comfortably settled, he commenced work on the record. It was a strange volume, approximately six inches in width by eight inches in length, and six inches thick. The golden pages, or plates, were not quite so thick as common tin, and were bound together by three rings on one side. Approximately one-third of the plates could be turned freely, similar to the pages of a loose-leaf book, but the remaining two-thirds were "sealed" so that they could not be examined. Beautiful engravings, small and finely cut, were found on the plates.

Joseph began his work by copying onto paper several pages of the strange characters. Some of these he translated by means of the Urim and Thummim, the "interpreters" which he had received with the plates.

Not far from Joseph's New York home lived a prosperous farmer by the name of Martin Harris. He had heard much of Joseph's experiences, and in contrast with most of the people of the community, he had shown a friendly interest in them. In February 1828, Mr. Harris called on Joseph.

He was shown the pages of transcribed characters with some of the translations that had been made from them. They greatly interested him, and he asked permission to borrow them. Joseph consenting, he took them to New York City, and, according to his testimony, "presented

"Reformed Egyptian" characters as they appeared on the gold plates

the characters which had been translated, with the translation thereof, to professor Charles Anthon, a gentleman celebrated for his literary attainments.

"Professor Anthon stated that the translation was correct, more so than any he had before seen translated from the Egyptian. I then showed him those which were not yet translated, and he said that they were Egyptian, Chaldaic, Assyriac, and Arabic; and he said they were true characters, . . . and that the translation of such of them as had been translated was also correct.

"I took the certificate and put it into my pocket, and was just leaving the house, when Mr. Anthon called me back, and asked me how the young man found out that there were gold plates in the place where he found them. I answered that an angel of God had revealed it unto him.

"He then said to me, 'Let me see that certificate.' I accordingly took it out of my pocket and gave it to him, when he took it and tore it to pieces, saying that there was no such thing now as ministering of angels, and that if I would bring the plates to him he would translate them. I informed him that part of the plates were sealed, and that I was forbidden to bring them. He replied, 'I cannot read a sealed book.'

"I left him and went to Dr. [Samuel] Mitchell, who sanctioned what Professor Anthon had said respecting both the characters and the translation."[4]

Some years later when he was approached by an avowed detractor of Joseph Smith, Professor Anthon denied ever having commented with favor upon the characters or the translation. Yet the fact remains that Martin Harris was so impressed by the experience that he returned to

Joseph Smith and then immediately proceeded to Palmyra to put his affairs in order so that he might assist with the translation.

He arrived back in Harmony on April 12, 1828. Work on the translation was begun and carried forward, although there were frequent interruptions. By June 14, 1828, Martin Harris had recorded 116 pages of manuscript from Joseph's dictation.

During this period, Mrs. Harris had asked her husband to bring the manuscript home so that she might see it. Martin asked Joseph for this privilege, but Joseph denied him. Refusing to accept the decision, Martin continued pleading until, eventually, he was permitted to take the manuscript, provided he show it to none other than members of his immediate family. Martin agreed, but when he returned to his home he yielded to pressure from others who were curious, and evidently the work was stolen from him.

Joseph Smith realized too late that he had made a serious mistake in permitting the translation to get out of his hands. He knew that he had done wrong, and he suffered great mental anguish. This was a lesson he never forgot; nor did Martin Harris ever forget it, for he was never again permitted to assist with the translation. The lost portion was not redone, since it was evident to Joseph that his enemies could alter the original and publicly belittle him.

For the remainder of that year and the following spring he was prevented from doing any further work with the plates. Most of his time was spent in farming his own land and working for others.

On April 5, 1829, there came to his door a

young man by the name of Oliver Cowdery. He was a stranger to Joseph, but he knew the Smith family, having boarded with them while teaching school in the vicinity of their home the previous season. He had heard the unusual story of the golden plates and was determined to investigate it first hand. Two days following his arrival he commenced writing as Joseph read aloud the translation of the record.

They found an unusual story. It concerned the descendants of a family who left Jerusalem about 600 B.C. The father, Lehi, had been inspired to flee the city, which was doomed to the sorrowful destruction which came shortly thereafter. Building a ship, the family crossed the ocean and landed somewhere on one of the American continents.

From this family sprang two nations known as the Nephites and the Lamanites. For the most part, the Nephites were a God-fearing people, while the Lamanites were generally indolent, quarrelsome, and wicked. The Nephites had among them the history of Israel up to the time the family had left Jerusalem, and with this they kept a record of their own nation as well as translations of writings from other civilizations they encountered.

Their history records that prophets and priests taught them principles of righteousness and administered to them the ordinances of salvation. Most remarkable of all, the Savior visited these people following his resurrection in fulfillment of his statement recorded in the Gospel of John: "Other sheep I have, which are not of this fold: them also I must bring, and they shall hear my voice, and there shall be one fold, and one shepherd."[5] He taught them the

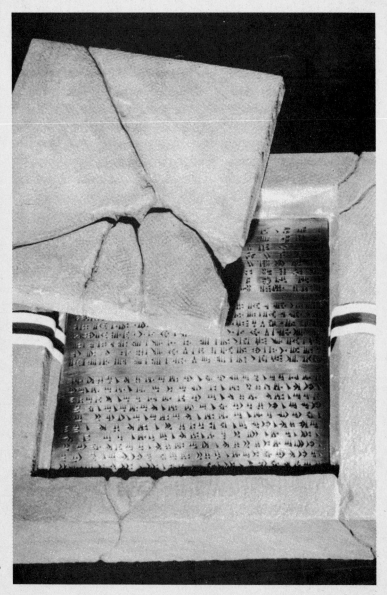

Evidence that men wrote anciently on metal plates is found on these gold tablets of King Darius of Persia, which date back to 521-486 B.C.

principles he had taught in Palestine and set up his church among them, giving its leadership authority identical to that which he conferred upon the Twelve Apostles in Jerusalem.

Following the teachings of Christ, these people lived in peace and happiness for generations. But as the nation grew prosperous it became wicked, despite the warnings of the prophets. Among these prophets was Mormon, who in his day kept the chronicles of the nation. From these extensive records he had compiled on plates of gold an abridged record. This he had given to his son, Moroni, who survived the destruction of the Nephite nation at the hands of the Lamanites. Moroni, prior to his death, buried the record in the Hill Cumorah, where Joseph Smith received it some fourteen centuries later. A remnant of the Lamanite nation is found today among the American Indians.

3 THE POWER OF GOD AMONG MEN

AMONG the doctrines taught in the ancient record was that of baptism for the remission of sins. Joseph Smith had never been baptized, for he had not become a member of any church. As he and Oliver discussed the matter, he resolved to inquire of the Lord concerning the ordinance.

They retired to the seclusion of the woods along the banks of the Susquehanna River. It was the 15th day of May 1829. While they were engaged in prayer a light appeared above them, and in it a heavenly messenger descended. He announced himself to them as John, known in scripture as John the Baptist.

The Priesthood Restored

He said he had come under the authority of Peter, James, and John, Apostles of the Lord, who held the keys of the priesthood, and that he had been sent to confer upon them the priesthood of Aaron with authority to administer in the temporal affairs of the gospel. He then laid his hands upon their heads and ordained them, saying, "Upon you my fellow servants, in the name of Messiah I confer the Priesthood of Aaron, which holds the keys of the ministering of angels, and of the gospel of repentance, and of baptism by immersion for the remission of sins."[1]

Joseph Smith and Oliver Cowdery received the Aaronic Priesthood in 1829 from the resurrected John the Baptist

He then instructed them that with the authority of the priesthood they had received they should baptize each other by immersion. Joseph first baptized Oliver in the nearby river, and Oliver then baptized Joseph. Again men had been baptized under proper authority and in similar manner as when Jesus had gone to John in the River Jordan "to fulfill all righteousness."[2]

It was not long thereafter that another remarkable and even more significant event occurred. It took place "in the wilderness between Harmony, Susquehanna county [Pennsylvania], and Colesville, Broome county [New York], on the Susquehanna river." The ancient Apostles Peter, James, and John appeared to and conferred upon Joseph Smith and Oliver Cowdery the higher powers of the priesthood and they became "apostles and special witnesses" of Christ. With this ordination there was restored to earth the same authority to act in God's name that had been enjoyed in the primitive Church.[3]

Witnesses

In June 1829 the work of translation was completed. About three months of diligent labor had been devoted to the task, although Joseph had possessed the plates for almost two years. During all of this time he had exercised every precaution to safeguard them, lest he lose them. No one was permitted to see them.

But in the course of translation he had discovered that the record itself stated that "three witnesses shall behold it, by the power of God, besides him to whom the book shall be delivered; and they shall testify to the truth of the book and the things therein.

"And there is none other which shall view it, save it be a few according to the will of God, to bear testimony of his word unto the children of men; for the Lord God hath said that the words of the faithful should speak as it were from the dead."[4]

As we have seen, among those who had materially assisted in the work were Martin Harris and Oliver Cowdery. Another young man, David Whitmer, had also been of service, though only for a brief period. When these three learned there were to be witnesses, they asked for the privilege.

Joseph inquired of the Lord and subsequently announced to the three that if they would humble themselves, theirs might be the privilege of seeing the ancient record and the responsibility of testifying to the world of what they had seen.

On a summer day in the year 1829, Joseph Smith, Oliver Cowdery, Martin Harris, and David Whitmer retired to the woods near the Whitmer home in southern New York state. In the broad light of day they knelt in prayer, Joseph praying first, followed by the others in succession. But when all had prayed, no answer was received. They repeated the procedure again without result. After this second failure, Martin Harris suggested that he withdraw from the group because he felt that it was he who stood in the way of their receiving a manifestation. With Joseph's consent, he left.

The three again knelt in prayer, and presently they beheld a light above them in the air. An angel stood before them. He held the plates in his hands and deliberately turned them leaf by leaf so that the men might see the engravings thereon. They then heard a voice above them saying, "These plates have been revealed by the power of God, and they have been translated by the power of God. The translation of them which you have seen is correct, and I command you to bear record of what you now see and hear."[5]

Joseph then left Oliver and David and went to find Martin Harris. He discovered him fervently engaged in prayer and joined him in an earnest petition to the Lord. That petition was rewarded with an experience similar to the one had by the others.

These men wrote the following signed declaration, which appeared in the first edition of the Book of Mormon, and which has appeared in every subsequent edition:

"Be it known unto all nations, kindreds, tongues, and people, unto whom this work shall come: That we, through the grace of God the Father, and our Lord Jesus Christ, have seen the plates which contain this record, which is a record of the people of Nephi, and also of the Lamanites, their brethren, and also of the people of Jared, who came from the tower of which hath been spoken. And we also know that they have been translated by the gift and power of God, for his voice hath declared it unto us; wherefore we know of a surety that the work is true. And we also testify that we have seen the engravings which are upon the plates; and they have been shown unto us by the power of God, and not of man. And we declare with words of soberness, that an angel of God came down from heaven, and he brought and laid before our eyes, that we beheld and saw the plates, and the engravings thereon; and we know that it is by the grace of God, the Father, and our Lord Jesus Christ, that we beheld and bear record that these things are true. And it is marvelous in our eyes.

Nevertheless, the voice of the Lord commanded us that we should bear record of it; wherefore, to be obedient unto the commandments of God, we bear testimony of these things. And we know that if we are faithful in Christ, we shall rid our garments of the blood of all men, and be found spotless before the judgment-seat of Christ, and shall dwell with him eternally in the heavens. And the honor be to the Father, and to the Son, and to the Holy Ghost, which is one God. Amen." [Signed by Oliver Cowdery, David Whitmer, and Martin Harris.]

In addition to the three witnesses, there were eight others who saw the plates. Their experience, however, was different. It happened

Oliver Cowdery   *Martin Harris*   *David Whitmer*

The three special witnesses who bore testimony of the authenticity of the Book of Mormon

only a day or two after the three had been shown the record by the angel.

Joseph Smith invited eight men to view the plates. They gathered about him, and he showed them the record. Again, it was in the broad light of day. Each handled the strange volume with complete liberty to leaf through the unsealed portion and closely examine the engravings. It was a simple, matter-of-fact experience in which all participated together. Their testimony on the matter follows. It also has appeared in all editions of the Book of Mormon.

"Be it known unto all nations, kindreds, tongues, and people unto whom this work shall come: That Joseph Smith, Jun., the translator of this work, has shown unto us the plates of which hath been spoken, which have the appearance of gold; and as many of the leaves as the said Smith has translated we did handle with our hands; and we also saw the engravings thereon, all of which has the appearance of ancient work, and of curious workmanship. And this we bear record with words of soberness, that the said Smith has shown unto us, for we have seen and hefted, and know of a surety that the said Smith has got the plates of which we have spoken. And we give our names unto the world, to witness unto the world that which we have seen. And we lie not, God bearing witness of it." [Signed by Christian Whitmer, Jacob Whitmer, Peter Whitmer, Jun., John Whitmer, Hiram Page, Joseph Smith Sr., Hyrum Smith, and Samuel H. Smith.]

Scores of writings deal with the statements of these two sets of witnesses. For more than a century various explanations have been offered in an attempt to account for their testimonies on some basis other than the one the witnesses declared to be the case. In the last analysis, all of the circumstances—the fact that both experiences took place in the broad light of day, that there were two widely different types of experiences, that all concerned were mature men of demonstrated judgment—these facts, together with the future acts and declarations of these parties, all point to the conclusion that the situations in each case were just as they said they were. There was no collusion, no chicanery, no juggling. In each case it was a sober, factual experience that no participant ever forgot or denied.

All of the three witnesses left the church founded through Joseph Smith. Two of them took a strong position in opposition to him. But not one of them ever denied his testimony concerning the Book of Mormon. In fact, each, on more than one occasion up to the time of his death, reaffirmed that testimony.

Martin Harris and Oliver Cowdery returned to the Church after years of disaffection, but even when they were outside the organization, they boldly declared the validity of the statement published over their names in the Book of Mormon. David Whitmer never came back into the organization, but repeatedly took the same stand as his associates had taken, and shortly before his death he published a pamphlet denying statements made in the *American Cyclopedia* and the *Encyclopaedia Britannica* to the effect that the witnesses had repudiated their testimony.

Of the eight witnesses, three left the Church, but none of them ever denied his testimony.

The Book Published

With the completion of the translation, its publication was made possible through the assistance of Martin Harris, who pledged his farm to guarantee the printing costs. The work was done by Egbert B. Grandin of Palmyra, New York, who printed five thousand copies for $3,000. The volume contained more than five hundred pages and was called the Book of Mormon because the ancient prophet-leader Mormon had

The eight witnesses who bore testimony that they saw and held in their hands the gold plates from which the Book of Mormon was translated

been its principal editor. It issued from the press in the spring of 1830.

As it was circulated and read, another type of witness to its validity appeared, perhaps more powerful than the testimony of those who had seen the plates. In the book itself are found these words: "When ye shall receive [read] these things, I would exhort you that ye would ask God, the Eternal Father, in the name of Christ, if these things are not true; and if ye shall ask with a sincere heart, with real intent, having faith in

The Grandin Press, on which the first edition of the Book of Mormon was printed

Christ, he will manifest the truth of it unto you, by the power of the Holy Ghost."[6]

The majority of the early converts came into the Church through reading the Book of Mormon. Thousands gave their lives because of their beliefs. Since its first publication, the book has been translated into more than two dozen languages, and it has affected the lives of men and women in many lands. The sufferings they have endured and the works they have accomplished are, perhaps, the strongest of all testimonies for the reality of the gold plates and their translation into the Book of Mormon — the book which has become in this generation another witness for Christ.

4 THE CHURCH ORGANIZED

NOT long after his ordination under the hands of Peter, James, and John, it was made known to Joseph Smith that the Church of Jesus Christ should again be set up in the earth. This event formally occurred the following spring in the home of Peter Whitmer in Fayette Township, Seneca County, New York.

On Tuesday, April 6, 1830, six men gathered in the Whitmer home. There were others present, but these six participated in the actual organization proceedings. Their names were Joseph Smith, Jr., Oliver Cowdery, Hyrum Smith, Peter Whitmer, Jr., Samuel H. Smith, and David Whitmer. They were all young men, their average age being twenty-four. All had been baptized previously.

The meeting was opened with "solemn prayer." After that Joseph asked those present if they were willing to accept him and Oliver Cowdery as their spiritual leaders. All agreed. Then Joseph ordained Oliver to the office of elder in the priesthood, and Oliver in turn ordained Joseph. The sacrament of the Lord's supper was administered, and then Joseph and Oliver laid their hands on the heads of the others present and confirmed them members of the Church and bestowed upon them the gift of the Holy Ghost. Next, some of the brethren were ordained to different priesthood offices.

While the meeting was in session, Joseph received a revelation in which he was designated "a seer, . . . a prophet, an apostle of Jesus Christ."[1] Since that time he has been referred to by the Church as "the Prophet." The Church was also instructed at this time to keep a record of all

The Church of Jesus Christ of Latter-day Saints was organized on April 6, 1830, in a log house which stood on the David Whitmer farm.

of its proceedings, a practice since carefully adhered to.

The Name of the Church

The new organization was designated by revelation as "The Church of Jesus Christ," to which the phrase "of Latter-day Saints" was later added. This is worthy of note. The Church was not named for Joseph Smith or for any other man. Nor was it named for any peculiarity of government or function, as has been the case with many religious societies. It was the Church of Jesus Christ restored to earth in "the latter day," and it was so designated.

Another matter of interest is the manner in which the officers of the Church were selected. Joseph Smith had been divinely chosen to lead the work, but his position as leader was subject to the consent of the members. Ever since that first meeting in 1830, the members of the Church have convened periodically to "sustain" or vote on those chosen to direct the affairs of the Church. No man presides without the consent of the membership.

A meeting was called for the following Sunday, and on this occasion Oliver Cowdery delivered the first public discourse in the newly founded Church. Six more individuals were baptized at the close of this meeting, and a week later seven more were added to the rolls. When the first general conference was held the following June, the membership totaled twenty-seven souls, and at the close of the conference eleven more were baptized in Seneca Lake.

In this same month, the first missionary activity was begun. Samuel H. Smith, the twenty-two-year-old brother of the Prophet, filled his knapsack with copies of the Book of Mormon and set off on a journey through neighboring towns to acquaint people with the recently published scripture. After walking twenty-five miles the first day, he approached the proprietor of an inn for a night's lodging. When the innkeeper learned of Samuel's mission, he ordered him out. The young elder slept out of doors that night.

The next day he called at the home of a Methodist minister, the Rev. John P. Greene, who was preparing to leave on a tour of his circuit. The minister was not interested in reading the book himself, but indicated that he would take the volume and keep a subscription list of any who cared to purchase a copy. Samuel returned home feeling that his efforts had been fruitless; it was unlikely that a Methodist minister would urge his flock to purchase the Book of Mormon.

But a strange thing happened. Mrs. Greene picked up the volume and became greatly interested in it. She urged her husband to read it, and both later joined the Church. This same copy fell into the hands of Brigham Young of Mendon, New York. This was his first contact with the Church. Some two years later, after careful study and investigation, he was baptized.

The book, as it was circulated by Samuel Smith and others who followed him, had a similar effect on many other future leaders of the Church. Parley P. Pratt, a Campbellite minister, chanced to read a borrowed copy and soon forsook his old ministry to join the ranks of the newly organized Church. He took the volume to his brother Orson, later renowned as a scientist and mathematician, who soon thereafter threw all of his energy into promoting the new cause. Willard Richards, a Massachusetts physician, re-

marked after reading one page of the volume,
"God or the devil has had a hand in that book,
for man never wrote it."² He read it through
twice in ten days and joined the cause.

And so the influence of the volume increased. From it, the members of the Church
received the nickname—and it is only a
nickname—by which they have since been popu-
larly known—Mormons. However, in their em-
phasis on this scripture of the western
hemisphere, they have not diminished their
advocacy of the Bible, which they regard as the
word of God. These companion volumes stand
hand in hand as two witnesses of the reality and
divinity of the Lord Jesus Christ.

Persecution

More often than not the work was bitterly
denounced in that day of religious bigotry.
Shortly after the organization of the Church,
Joseph Smith was arrested while conducting a
meeting in Colesville, New York. He was charged
with being "a disorderly person, setting the country in an uproar by preaching the Book of
Mormon." The testimony introduced was as ridiculous as the charge, but no sooner was he
acquitted by the judge than he was arrested on
another warrant of the same nature and dragged
off to another town to stand trial, again to be
acquitted. Thus began the persecution that was
to harass him to his death.

A Mission to the Lamanites

The second general conference of the
Church was held in September, 1830. Among
matters of business was the call of Oliver Cowdery to undertake a mission "into the wilderness,
through the western states, and to the Indian
territory." Peter Whitmer, Parley P. Pratt, and

Ziba Peterson were later called to accompany him. This mission charted much of the future history of the Church.

In October the four men left their families and set out on foot. Near the city of Buffalo they met with members of the Catteraugus Indian tribe, to whom they told the story of the Book of Mormon, explaining that it contained a history of their forefathers. Many appeared interested, and the missionaries left copies of the book with those who could read.

Elder Pratt, prior to his conversion to Mormonism, had been a lay preacher of the Church of the Disciples, founded by Alexander Campbell. He was now anxious to discuss Mormonism with his former associates, and the missionaries therefore traveled to northern Ohio where lived a large group of Mr. Campbell's followers. Elder Pratt particularly sought out Sidney Rigdon, one of the leading ministers of the faith.

Mr. Rigdon cordially received the missionaries, but was skeptical of the story they told. Nevertheless, he permitted them to preach to his congregation, and he agreed to read the Book of Mormon. He was baptized shortly thereafter and became an ardent worker in the cause of Mormonism. Elder Pratt described the situation with the statement that "faith was strong, joy was great, and persecution heavy."[3]

A Harvest of Souls

Within three weeks 127 souls had been baptized. Before the missionaries left in December, a thousand members had been added to the Church.

One of the recent converts, Dr. Frederick G. Williams, accompanied the missionaries west from Ohio. They spent several days among the

Wyandot Indians who lived in the western part of the state and then continued their journey to St. Louis, walking most of the way.

Of the journey west from St. Louis, Elder Pratt writes: "We travelled on foot for three hundred miles through vast prairies and through trackless wilds of snow—no beaten road; houses few and far between; and the bleak northwest wind always blowing in our faces with a keenness which would almost take the skin off the face. We travelled for whole days, from morning till night, without a house or fire, wading in snow to the knees at every step, and the cold so intense that the snow did not melt on the south side of the houses, even in the mid-day sun, for nearly six weeks. We carried on our backs our changes of clothing, several books, and corn bread and raw pork. We often ate our frozen bread and pork by the way, when the bread would be so frozen that we could not bite or penetrate any part of it but the outside crust."[4]

Arriving at Independence, Jackson County, Missouri, the elders made preparations to visit the Indians in the adjoining frontier area. They met with the chief of the Delawares, who received them kindly and listened with great interest to the story of the Book of Mormon. However, their opportunities to preach were soon limited. Government agents, at the behest of intolerant religionists, ordered the missionaries from the Indian lands. Four of them remained in Missouri for some time, while Elder Pratt returned to New York to report their labors.

The First Move Westward

When Elder Pratt reached Kirtland, Ohio, he was surprised to find Joseph Smith there, and to

Joseph Smith tells a group of Indians the story of their progenitors as found in the Book of Mormon

learn that the New York members of the Church planned to move to Ohio in the spring. Persecution in New York had increased, and the success of the missionaries in their travels had pointed the way to the future destiny of the Church in the West.

The second annual general conference was called for June 1831, in Kirtland, Ohio. By that time, most of the New York members had moved west, and the congregation present at the conference numbered two thousand. The Church had made substantial growth since the original six members met to effect the organization on April 6, 1830.

At this conference several men were ordained to the office of high priest for the first time in the Church. Also, twenty-eight elders were called to travel to western Missouri, going in pairs and preaching as they went. The Prophet pointed out that it had been revealed to him that the Saints would there establish Zion.

These missionaries, including Joseph Smith, traveled "without purse or scrip," preaching with power as they went, constantly adding to the numbers of the Church. They arrived in Jackson County, Missouri, about the middle of July, and were followed by the entire company of Saints from Colesville, New York, who had settled temporarily in Ohio and then moved on west as a body. At a place called Kaw Township, on a portion of the present site of Kansas City, they commenced a settlement under the direction of the Prophet and Sidney Rigdon.

The first log for the first house was laid by twelve men representing the twelve tribes of Israel. The land was dedicated for the gathering of the Saints, and those present covenanted "to receive this land with thankful hearts" and pledged themselves "to keep the law of God," and to "see that others of their brethren keep the laws of God."[5]

Thus was established the first Mormon settlement in Missouri. Later in the summer, Joseph Smith, Sidney Rigdon, and other leading elders returned to Kirtland, Ohio. For the next seven years the activities of the Church were divided between these two locations a thousand miles apart—Kirtland, Ohio, near the present site of Cleveland; and Jackson County, Missouri, near the present Kansas City.

5 MORMONISM IN OHIO

THOSE years during which the activities of Mormonism were largely centered in Ohio and Missouri were among the most important and the most tragic in the history of the movement. During this time, the basic organization of Church government was established; many fundamental and distinguishing doctrines were pronounced by Joseph Smith; the work spread abroad for the first time; and, concurrent with this development, the Church was subjected to intense persecution, which cost the lives of many and from which all of the Saints suffered seriously.

While events of historical importance were going on in both locations contemporaneously, communication between the two groups was limited because of difficulties of transportation, although officers of the Church traveled from one location to the other as necessity required. For the sake of clarity, this chapter will deal with events in Ohio from 1831 to 1838, and the chapter following will treat the Missouri story for the same period.

The Holy Bible

One of the projects undertaken by Joseph Smith before his removal to Ohio was a revision of the English Bible. He did not discredit the

King James translation, but he knew, as has since been more generally recognized, that certain errors and omissions in that record had led to numerous difficulties among the sects of Christendom. He had received his first understanding of this from Moroni, who, on his initial visit in 1823, had quoted to Joseph Smith from the scripture a text altered somewhat from the language of our Bible.

Upon his arrival in Ohio, Joseph continued with this labor, working as time permitted. The changes he made indicate some interesting interpretations of parts of the scripture.

Doctrinal Standards

Inevitably, as the Church grew, various questions and problems arose. Joseph sought the Lord for guidance — and received it. Most of the revelations which have since regulated the Church were received during this Ohio-Missouri period.

These revelations deal with a great variety of subjects — the age for baptism, the organization and machinery of ecclesiastical government, the call of missionaries to special labors, counsel on diet and rules for healthful living, a prophecy on the wars that would afflict the nations, the glories of the kingdoms in the life to come, and a variety of other matters. They reflect the breadth of the gospel, and the breadth of the Prophet's thinking. Only a few can be mentioned in this brief writing.

The question as to when an individual should be baptized has been a source of endless discussion among Christian peoples. In the second or third century, the practice of baptizing infants was inaugurated and has since continued, although without scriptural warrant. In fact, one of the fundamental purposes of baptism—the remission of sins—indicates that the recipient must be capable of repentance and of leading a better life. The Book of Mormon clearly teaches against the baptism of infants as a denial of the mercy of Christ, and in November 1831, Joseph received a revelation establishing eight years as the age at which children should be baptized.

On February 16, 1832, Joseph Smith and Sidney Rigdon beheld a vision of the eternal glories. In the record of this experience they bear testimony of the reality and personality of the Savior: "And now, after the many testimonies which have been given of him, this is the testimony, last of all, which we give of him: That he lives!

"For we saw him, even on the right hand of God; and we heard the voice bearing record that he is the Only Begotten of the Father—That by him, and through him, and of him, the worlds are and were created, and the inhabitants thereof are begotten sons and daughters unto God."[1]

They then describe something of the kingdom of eternity which they saw. Men in the hereafter will not be assigned arbitrarily to heaven or hell. The Savior had said, "In my father's house are many mansions,"[2] and Paul had written of a "glory of the sun, and another glory of the moon, and another glory of the stars."[3] In the hereafter, according to the Prophet's teaching, there are various gradations of exaltation. All men will be resurrected through the atonement of Christ, but they will be graded in the life to come according to their obedience to the commandments of God.

Such teachings, flying in the face of traditional Christianity, were bound to stir the indignation of the intolerant. On the night of March 24, 1832, a mob broke into Joseph Smith's home, seized him while he slept, dragged him from the house, beat him severely, choked him into unconsciousness, and then tarred and feathered him, leaving him to die. But he regained consciousness and painfully made his way back to the house. The next day being Sunday, he preached a sermon, and among his congregation were some of the mobsters of the night before. At the conclusion of the meeting he baptized eleven people.

On the same night, Sidney Rigdon was also mobbed. He was dragged by the heels for some distance with his head bumping over the frozen ground. For days he lay in a delirium, and for a time it appeared that he would lose his life, but he eventually recovered.

A Prophecy on War

On Christmas day of this same year, 1832, Joseph Smith made a remarkable prophecy, opening with the words, "Thus saith the Lord." He prophesied that war would come upon the earth, "beginning at the rebellion of South Carolina. . . . and the time will come that war will be poured out upon all nations." He indicated that the southern states would be divided against the northern states, and that the southern states would call upon Great Britain. The time would come when Great Britain would "call upon other nations, in order to defend themselves against [yet] other nations; and then war shall be poured out upon all nations. . . . And thus, with the sword and by bloodshed the inhabitants of the earth shall mourn."[4]

Twenty-eight years later, in December 1860, South Carolina seceded from the Union. On

April 12, 1861, Fort Sumter in Charleston Bay was fired on, and the tragic Civil War began. The forces of the southern states were marshalled against those of the northern states, and the southern states in turn called upon Great Britain. Of the wars since that time, in which Britain has called upon other nations, and of the mourning and bloodshed of the inhabitants of the earth, nothing need be said in this writing. It is a matter of history known to all.

A Word of Wisdom

In February 1833, another interesting revelation was received and proclaimed to the people. It is found in section 89 of the Doctrine and Covenants and is known in Mormon literature as the Word of Wisdom. It is essentially a code of health. In it the Saints are warned against the use of tobacco, alcoholic beverages, "hot drinks," and the intemperate eating of meat. The abundant use of grains, fruits, and vegetables is advocated. A promise of "wisdom and great treasures of knowledge," together with blessings of health, is given those who obey these principles. It is an unusual document whose principles have been confirmed by modern nutritionists and medical scientists. The application of its teachings has had a salutary effect upon the physical welfare of those who have followed them.

Education

In this same period, Joseph Smith organized the "School of the Prophets." Through revelation he had been instructed that those who were to go forth to teach the glad tidings of the restoration of the gospel should first prepare themselves "by study and by faith."[5] This did not mean that those engaged in the ministry of the Church should be trained in seminaries for this purpose, choosing the vocation as one might choose the profession of doctor or lawyer. Each man holding the priesthood had the responsibility of learning enough of the work to enable him to expound and defend the doctrine.

It had been made clear by the Prophet that education was a concern of religion. Among his teachings was the principle that "the glory of God is intelligence."[6] Further, "Whatever principle of intelligence we attain unto in this life, it will rise with us in the resurrection."[7] The broad development of the mind was a rightful concern of the Church, and for this purpose a "School of the Prophets" was established. Not only were classes in theology taught, but a renowned linguist was retained to teach Hebrew. This was a remarkable innovation in adult education on the Ohio frontier, and it was the forerunner of the extensive Mormon education system.

Church Organization Completed

At the time the Church was established, its affairs were under the direction of a presiding elder. But through revelation, other offices were added as the membership increased. Three distinct offices were established in the Aaronic Priesthood—teacher, deacon, and priest. On February 4, 1831, Edward Partridge was named "bishop unto the Church," and on January 25, 1832, Joseph Smith was sustained as President of the High Priesthood. Two counselors were later appointed to serve with him, and these three constituted what has since been known as the First Presidency of the Church.

In February 1835, a Council of Twelve Apostles was chosen, and "seventy" were called to assist the Twelve. In 1833 the father of the Prophet was ordained Patriarch to the Church, which office, the Prophet explained, corresponded to the ancient office of evangelist.

With all of these offices in the priesthood set up and filled, there was again to be found on earth the same basic organization which had existed in the primitive Church, with Apostles, seventy, elders, high priests, teachers, deacons, evangelists, and bishops.

In November 1833, Brigham Young and Heber C. Kimball, two men who were later to play an important part in the affairs of Mormonism, left their homes in Mendon, New York, and traveled to Kirtland to meet Joseph Smith for the first time. They found the Prophet in the woods chopping and hauling wood. There began a long and devoted friendship between Joseph Smith and the man who was to succeed him as President of the Church. When that succession took place, Heber C. Kimball was to stand beside Brigham Young as his counselor in the First Presidency.

The First Temple

One of the outstanding achievements during the Kirtland period of Church history was the construction of a temple of God.

On May 4, 1833, a committee was appointed to take up a subscription for the building of the temple. It should be noted that these people had little in the way of financial resources. The leaders among them had been devoting their time and energies to missionary labors. Moreover, they had recently moved from New York to Ohio, and their means had largely been exhausted in the purchase of lands. Nevertheless, they had received what they regarded as a command-

The Kirtland Temple, first temple built by the Church

ment to build a sacred house, and they set upon their task.

The question arose as to the plan and the type of materials to be used. Some thought that the building should be of frame construction or even of logs, as was generally the custom on the frontier. But Joseph told them that they were not building a house for a man, but for the Lord. "Shall we," he asked, "build a house for our God, of logs? No, I have a better plan than that. I have a plan of the house of the Lord, given by himself; and you will soon see by this, the difference between our calculations and his idea of things."[8] He then gave them the plan. This was a Saturday night, and on the following Monday work was begun.

For three years the Saints labored with all their strength and means to complete the building. The men worked on the walls while the women spun wool and wove it into cloth for clothing. Of these trying days, Joseph's mother writes: "How often I have parted every bed in the house for the accommodation of the brethren, and then laid a single blanket on the floor for my husband and myself, while Joseph and Emma slept upon the same floor, with nothing but their cloaks for both bed and bedding."[9]

In dimension the temple was 59 by 79 feet, 50 feet to the square, and 110 feet to the top of the tower. The walls were built of quarried stone, and the interior was finished with native woods, beautifully worked. No effort was spared to create a house worthy of Deity.

After surveying the building as it stood in 1936, a writer said: "The workmanship, moldings, carvings, etc., show unusual skill in execution. Many motives are used in the various parts, varying in outline, contour and design, but blended harmoniously. . . . It is not probable that all of the workmen engaged on the building were skilled artisans, and yet the result is so harmonious as to raise the question if they may not have been inspired as were the builders of the cathedrals of old."[10]

A Modern Pentecost

The building was completed and ready for dedication March 27, 1836. This was an important day—the climax of three years of toil and sacrifice—and the Saints gathered from far

49

and near. About a thousand of them were able to crowd into the building, and an overflow meeting was held in the schoolhouse.

The services lasted most of the day, from nine in the morning until four in the afternoon, with only a brief recess. The Prophet offered the prayer of dedication, which of itself is an impressive piece of literature. The sacrament of the Lord's supper was then administered.

Since all who desired to participate could not be accommodated at the dedicatory exercises, the services were repeated, and for several days various types of meetings were held in the building, and many spiritual manifestations were experienced. The Prophet compared it with the Day of Pentecost.

The most significant of these experiences occurred on Sunday, April 3. Joseph and Oliver Cowdery were engaged in prayer at the pulpit of the temple, which had been separated from the remainder of the hall by means of curtains. When they had risen from prayer, they beheld a vision, recorded in the Doctrine and Covenants:

"The veil was taken from our minds, and the eyes of our understanding were opened.

"We saw the Lord standing upon the breastwork of the pulpit, before us; and under his feet was a paved work of pure gold, in color like amber.

"His eyes were as a flame of fire; the hair of his head was white like the pure snow; his countenance shone above the brightness of the sun; and his voice was as the sound of the rushing of great waters, even the voice of Jehovah, saying:

"I am the first and the last; I am he who liveth, I am he who was slain; I am your advocate with the Father."[11]

Exodus from Ohio

As the Church grew in numbers and spiritual strength, the forces working against it became more vigorous. Early in the year 1837, a bank was formed in Kirtland, among whose officers were the authorities of the Church. It was only a short time after this that a wave of depression spread over the nation. During the months of March and April, business failures in New York alone passed one hundred million dollars. The Kirtland institution failed along with others, and some of the members of the Church who lost their money in the disaster also lost their faith. It was a dark period in the history of Mormonism.

In the midst of this trouble, elders were called to go to Great Britain to open missionary work there. Heber C. Kimball was appointed to head this mission, and Orson Hyde, Dr. Willard Richards, and Joseph Fielding were called to accompany him. They were to meet John Goodson, Isaac Russell, and John Snyder in New York City, and then proceed to their field of labor.

On June 13, 1837, the Kirtland men left their homes. They had little money and experienced considerable difficulty in reaching Liverpool, where they landed on July 20, 1837. From Liverpool they traveled to Preston, a manufacturing town some thirty miles north, where Joseph Fielding's brother was pastor of Vauxhall Chapel. The missionaries were extended an opportunity to speak in the chapel on the following Sunday. Thus began the work of the Church in the British Isles, which in the years immediately following resulted in the baptism of thousands, many of whom immigrated to the United States and became leaders in the cause.

Meanwhile, in Kirtland, mobbings and the

destruction of property by bands of bigoted religionists increased. The Prophet could find no
peace, and on January 12, 1838, accompanied by
Sidney Rigdon, he left for Missouri, never again
to return to Kirtland, where so large and
important a part of his work had been done.

6 THE CHURCH IN MISSOURI

WE return to the year 1831. Western Missouri was then a beautiful prairie country of rolling hills and wooded valleys. Its rich soil, pleasing contour, and tolerable climate made it a land of great opportunity. It was only sparsely settled; for instance, Independence, the seat of Jackson County, had only a courthouse, two or three general stores, and a few homes, most of them log cabins.

Joseph Smith indicated to his people that in this area, midway between the Atlantic and the Pacific, they should build their Zion, a city of God.

Their missionaries to the Indians had returned with reports of the nature of the country, and in July 1831, the first group of Saints arrived in western Missouri. About sixty of them had come in a body from Colesville, New York. Twelve miles west of Independence, in what is now part of Kansas City, they laid the foundations of a settlement.

The City of Zion

Other members of the Church soon followed. Joseph Smith, who was then in Missouri, declared that they should acquire by purchase sufficient land that they might live together as a people. He pointed out the site on which they should build a beautiful temple, dedicated to

God as his holy house. This should become the crowning glory of the city of Zion.

The Prophet also designed the city. His was a novel and significant concept in civic planning. There would be none of the slums and blighted areas so characteristic of the cities of that day. Nor, on the other hand, would the farmer's family live isolated and alone. This city was to be a mile square, divided into blocks of ten acres with streets 132 feet wide. The center blocks were to be reserved for public buildings. Barns, stables, and farms were to be on the lands adjoining the city. "The tiller of the soil as well as the merchant and mechanic will live in the city," the Prophet said. "The farmer and his family, therefore, will enjoy all the advantages of schools, public lectures and other meetings. His home will no longer be isolated, and his family denied the benefits of society, which has been, and always will be, the great educator of the human race, but they will enjoy the same privileges of society, and can surround their homes with the same intellectual life, the same social refinement as will be found in the home of the merchant or banker or professional man.

"When this square is thus laid off and supplied," the Prophet continued, "lay off another in the same way . . . and so fill up the world in these last days."[1]

Although there was no opportunity to put the plan in all of its details into operation, its basic principles made possible successful Mormon colonization in the West years later. The common practice of the time was for each man to settle on a large tract of land where he was isolated from his neighbors. But the Mormons undertook the pioneering of new country in groups, building communities in which homes were maintained near church, school, and social centers, with the farms being located outside the town.

Among the first undertakings in the new settlement was the establishment of a printing press for the publication of a periodical, *The Evening and Morning Star,* as well as other literature. Appointed as editor of the *Star* was William W. Phelps, who, prior to his conversion to Mormonism, had served as editor of a paper in New York. He was a man with considerable literary ability, and his journal soon became a significant force in the community.

The Beginning of Trouble

With bright prospects before them, the Saints set to with a will to build their Zion. But they soon found themselves in serious difficulties. The old settlers resented their religion and their industry. Two ministers were particularly active in creating opposition. The Mormons were pictured as "the common enemies of mankind."[2] Another source of friction was their differences in politics. Most of the Mormons were from the northeastern, anti-slavery states, while Missouri was linked with the South as a pro-slavery state. These and similar differences were enough to arouse the antagonism of the old settlers.

The first real indication of trouble occurred one night in the spring of 1832 when a mob broke windows in a number of Mormon homes. In the autumn of that same year, haystacks were burned and houses were shot into. These acts were but the beginning of a storm of violence that was eventually to sweep the Mormons from the state of Missouri.

In July of 1833 the old settlers, who had

been agitated by troublemakers, met in Independence for the purpose of finding means to get rid of the Mormons, "peaceably if we can, forcibly if we must."[3] There was no suggestion that the Mormons had violated any law, simply that they were an evil which had come into their midst, and which had to be removed at all costs. They demanded that no Mormons should henceforth be permitted to settle in Jackson County, that those residing there should promise to move from the county, that they should cease printing their paper, and that other businesses should cease their operations. An ultimatum to this effect was drawn up, and a committee of twelve was detailed to present it to the Mormons.

The meeting was recessed for two hours to allow the committee to present the manifesto and return with an answer.

When notice was served on the Mormons, they were in no position to give an answer. The demands were entirely without legal warrant. The Saints had purchased the ground on which they lived; they had broken no law and had not been accused of breaking any. They were stunned by the whole affair, and they requested three months to consider the matter. This was promptly denied. They then asked for ten days, and were told that fifteen minutes was time enough. Obviously they could not agree to the terms presented them.

Mobocracy

The committee returned to the meeting and reported. The result was a resolution to destroy the printing press. Three days later a mob of five hundred men rode through the streets of Independence, waving a red flag and brandishing pistols, clubs, and whips. They destroyed the press and swore that they would rid Jackson County of the Mormons. Every plea for mercy and justice was met with scoffing. In an effort to save their associates, six of the leading elders of the Church offered themselves as ransom for the Saints. They indicated their willingness to be scourged or even put to death if that would satisfy the mob.

With an oath they were answered that not only they, but all of their associates would be whipped and driven unless they left the county.

Realizing their helplessness, the Mormons agreed under duress that they would evacuate by April 1834. With this understanding the mob dispersed. But it was only a matter of days until they were again breaking into homes and threatening the Saints. Knowing there was no security for them, the Mormons appealed to the governor of the state. He replied that they should take their case to the local courts. Such a suggestion was ridiculous in view of the fact that the judge of the county court, two justices of the peace, and other county officers were leaders of the mob. Nevertheless, the Mormons engaged counsel to present their case.

As might have been expected, the court procedure was without effect, unless it served further to incite the mob. On October 31 a reign of terror commenced. Day and night, armed men rode through the streets of Independence setting fire to houses, destroying furniture, trampling cornfields, whipping and assaulting men and women.

Not knowing where to turn, the inhabitants fled north to the desolate river bottoms. Their trail over the frozen, sleet-covered ground was marked by blood from their lacerated feet. Some lost their lives as a result of exposure and hunger. Fortunately, their brethren in Ohio, on learning of their troubles, brought aid and comfort as rapidly as possible. By the time they arrived, more than two hundred homes had been destroyed. Even more tragic, their dream of Zion had been shattered.

In Upper Missouri

The Saints found temporary refuge in Clay County across the Missouri River opposite Jackson County. To sustain themselves and their families, they worked for the settlers of the area, doing all kinds of labor, from wood chopping to teaching school. Temporary log houses were con-

The visitor's center at Independence, Missouri

structed, in which they lived under wretched conditions until they were able to secure themselves more permanently.

To the northeast of Clay County was a wild, largely unbroken prairie country. They saw in it a land of opportunity, and others saw in it a place to put the Mormons where they would be by themselves.

In December 1836, the Missouri legislature created Caldwell County with the thought that it should become a "Mormon county." With characteristic enterprise, the Saints purchased the land and proceeded to lay out cities and farms. Their chief settlement was Far West, and another major colony was planted to the north at Diahman. Two years after the creation of the county, Far West had a population of five thousand, with two hotels, a printing office, blacksmith shops, stores, and 150 houses. Much of this growth had resulted from an influx of Church members from Ohio, including Joseph Smith, who, as we have seen, left Kirtland in January 1838.

The Financial Law of the Church

During this period of intense activity, the Prophet pronounced as a revelation the law of tithing, under which all members were to pay one-tenth of their income to the Church for its work.

This was, of course, only a restatement of an ancient law. In fact, as with other matters of Mormon doctrine and practice, the institution of tithing in 1838 was but a restoration of a principle that had been pronounced in Biblical days. It had been the law of God to his people in Abraham's day and in the times of the prophets who had followed him; and now God had declared anew that his people should be tithed and that this should be "a standing law unto them forever."[4]

A Plague of Sorrow

On July 4, 1838, the Mormons in Far West held a celebration in observance of the nation's Independence Day and the freedom which they then enjoyed from mobs. On this same day, they laid the cornerstone for a new temple. It was to be 110 feet long by 80 feet wide, larger than the structure in Kirtland. Band music and a parade, followed by a reverent dedication, made this day a notable occasion.

But these conditions of peace and progress which they celebrated were to be short-lived. Their old enemies, noting the ever-increasing Mormon population, again sowed dissension. It should be remembered that Missouri was then America's western frontier, and the frontier was generally characterized by a spirit of lawlessness, by the bigotry that comes of ignorance and extremely limited social intercourse, and by suspicion and jealousy. In such an atmosphere it was easy to fan latent fires of intolerance and hatred.

Such agitation led to a conflict in the town of Gallatin on August 6, 1838. It was a minor affair, hardly worthy of notice but for the consequences which followed. A non-Mormon candidate for the state legislature stirred up the old settlers, saying that if the Mormons were allowed to vote, the old settlers would soon lose their rights. It was a simple political contest, but when the Mormons went to cast their ballots, they were forcibly prevented from doing so.

An exaggerated report of the affair reached Far West, and a group of Church members went to investigate. No action was taken, and on their way back to Far West they called at the home of Adam Black, a justice of the peace, and obtained from him a certification to the effect that he was peaceably disposed toward the Mormons and would not attach himself to any mob.

But the enemies of the Saints soon made the most of this trip to Gallatin on the part of the Far West group. Several of them, including this same Justice Black, signed an affidavit to the effect that five hundred armed Mormons had gone into Gallatin to do harm to the non-Mormons of the area. This vicious falsehood was like a match to a pile of straw. Rumor chased rumor until a great fabric of imagined grievances had been built up.

To add to the gravity of the situation, an avowed anti-Mormon of Jackson County days, Lilburn W. Boggs, had become governor. To him the mobocrats sent reports that the Mormons were in insurrection, that they refused to submit to law, and that they were preparing to make war on the old settlers.

Again mobs menacingly rode through the Mormon communities, determined to wage "a war of extermination." When a group of peaceful, non-Mormon citizens appealed to the governor, he is reported to have replied, "The quarrel is between the Mormons and the mob, and they can fight it out."[5]

With such license, trouble spread like a prairie fire before a high wind. When the Mormons tried to defend themselves, the governor used it as an excuse to issue an inhumane and illegal order of extermination — "The Mormons must be treated as enemies, and must be exterminated or driven from the state if necessary for the public peace."[6]

On the 31st day of October, a mob-militia approached the town of Far West. Colonel George M. Hinkle, who led the defenders of the city, requested an interview with General Samuel D. Lucas, commanding the militia. During his interview he agreed to surrender the Mormon leaders without consulting these men. This treachery resulted in the delivery of Joseph Smith, Hyrum Smith, Sidney Rigdon, Parley P. Pratt, and Lyman Wight.

A court-martial was held that night, and the prisoners were sentenced to be shot at sunrise on the public square of Far West. General A. W. Doniphan was ordered to carry out the execution.

To this order Doniphan indignantly replied: "It is cold-blooded murder. I will not obey your order. My brigade shall march for [the town of] Liberty tomorrow morning at 8 o'clock; and if you execute these men, I will hold you responsible before an earthly tribunal, so help me God."[7]

Doniphan was never called to account for this insubordination which saved the Prophet's life. As for the Mormon leader and his fellow prisoners, they were placed in a cramped, dark jail, where they languished for more than five months.

Greatly outnumbered and denied any semblance of legal protection, fifteen thousand members of the Church fled their Missouri homes and property then valued at a million and a half dollars. Through the winter of 1838-39 they painfully made their way eastward toward Illinois, not knowing where else to go. Many died from exposure or from illness aggravated by it. Joseph Smith was in prison, and Brigham

Young, a member of the Council of the Twelve Apostles, directed this sorrowful migration, which was to prove to be the forerunner to a yet more tragic movement a scant eight years later, and of which he was to serve as leader.

7 NAUVOO THE BEAUTIFUL

THE people of Quincy, Illinois, received the Mormon refugees with kindness. However, it became quickly apparent to Brigham Young and others that some provision must be made for the settlement of this large group of exiles so that they might again undertake productive enterprise.

On April 22, 1839, Joseph Smith and those who had been imprisoned with him in Liberty, Missouri, arrived in Quincy. Their guards had let them go, and they had made their way to the Illinois side of the Mississippi. The following day a conference was called by the Prophet, and a committee was detailed to investigate the purchase of lands. On May 1 the initial purchase was completed, and other purchases were subsequently made until extensive holdings were secured on both the Iowa and Illinois sides of the river.

The principal location was the site of Commerce, Illinois, about forty-five miles north of Quincy. At this point the river makes a broad bend, giving the land on its east bank the appearance of a promontory. At the time of the purchase, one stone house, three frame houses, and two blockhouses constituted the village.

It was an unhealthy place, so wet that a man

had difficulty walking across most of it, and teams became mired to their hips. Of the place and its purchase the Prophet later said, "Commerce was unhealthful, very few could live there; but believing that it might become a healthy place by the blessing of heaven to the Saints, and no more eligible place presenting itself, I considered it wisdom to make an attempt to build up a city."[1]

The Prophet's faith in the future of this site is evident from the name he gave it—Nauvoo, derived from the Hebrew and meaning "the beautiful location."

A Manifestation of God's Power

The swamps were drained, and a city was platted with streets crossing at right angles. But the work of building moved slowly. The people were prostrate, exhausted from the trials through which they had passed. Their energies were depleted, and they became easy victims of malaria.

On the morning of July 22, Joseph, who was sick himself, looked about him only to see others sick. The house in which he lived was crowded with them, and tents sheltering other invalids stood in his dooryard. Wilford Woodruff recounts the events which followed the Prophet's appraisal of this discouraging situation:

"He [Joseph] called upon the Lord in prayer, the power of God rested upon him mightily, and as Jesus healed all the sick around Him in His day, so Joseph, the Prophet of God, healed all around on this occasion. He healed all in his house and dooryard; then, in company with Sidney Rigdon and several of the Twelve, went among the sick lying on the bank of the river, where he commanded them in a loud voice, in the name of Jesus Christ, to rise and be made whole, and they were all healed. When he had healed all on the east side of the river that were sick, he and his companions crossed the Mississippi River in a ferry boat to the west side. . . . The first house they went into was President Brigham Young's. He was sick on his bed at the time. The Prophet went into his house and healed him, and they all came out together.

"As they were passing by my door, Brother Joseph said: 'Brother Woodruff, follow me.' These were the only words spoken by any of the company from the time they left Brother Brigham's house till they crossed the public square, and entered Brother Fordham's house. Brother Fordham had been dying for an hour, and we expected any minute would be his last. I felt the spirit of God that was overpowering his Prophet. When we entered the house, Brother Joseph walked up to Brother Fordham and took him by his right hand, his left hand holding his hat. He saw that Brother Fordham's eyes were glazed, and that he was speechless and unconscious.

"After taking his hand, he looked down into the dying man's face and said '. . . Do you believe that Jesus is the Christ?' 'I do, Brother Joseph,' was the response. Then the Prophet of God spoke with a loud voice, as in the majesty of Jehovah: 'Elijah, I command you, in the name of Jesus of Nazareth, to rise and be made whole.'

"The words of the Prophet were not like the words of man, but like the voice of God. It seemed to me that the house shook on its foundation. Elijah Fordham leaped from his bed like a man raised from the dead. A healthy color came into his face, and life was manifested in every act. His feet had been done up in Indian meal poultices; he kicked these off, his feet scattered the contents, then called for his clothes and put them on. He asked for a bowl of bread and milk and ate it. He then put on his hat and followed us into the street, to visit others who were sick."[2]

Elijah Fordham lived forty-one years after this experience.

A Mission to England

Even while facing the task of building a city, the Mormons did not neglect the preaching of the gospel. During the summer of 1839, seven members of the Council of the Twelve Apostles left Nauvoo for England. These men were powerful missionaries. The trials through which they had passed had strengthened their convictions concerning the cause with which they were associated, and they won hundreds of converts through the powerful testimonies which they bore.

Wilford Woodruff's efforts were particularly successful. While preaching in Hanley in the Potteries district of England, he felt impressed to leave that area without knowing why. Obedient to this impression, he traveled to a rural section of Herefordshire. At the home of one John Benbow, a prosperous farmer of the district, he received a cordial welcome and the news that a large group of religionists in that area had broken away from their church and had united themselves to study the scriptures and seek the truth.

Elder Woodruff was given an invitation to speak, and other invitations followed. The organization numbered six hundred, including more

The city of Nauvoo, built on a promontory on the Mississippi

than a score of preachers. All of these, with one exception, embraced Mormonism. Before he left the district, eighteen hundred members had been converted to the Church through his efforts.

At a conference held in the British Isles in April 1840, the decision was made to publish an edition of the Book of Mormon, a hymnbook, and a periodical.

An unusual mission undertaken during this period was that of Orson Hyde, upon whom the Prophet had once pronounced the blessing: "In due time thou shalt go to Jerusalem, the land of thy fathers, and be a watchman unto the house of Israel; and by thy hand shall the Most High do a work, which shall prepare the way and greatly facilitate the gathering together of that people."³

In January 1841, Orson Hyde left the States and went to London, where he labored with other missionaries for some months. Then he made his way to Palestine. Early on the Sunday morning of October 24, 1841, he climbed to the top of the Mount of Olives, and there in prayer and with the authority of the priesthood, he dedicated the land of Palestine for the return of the Jews. The prayer reads in part:

"Grant, therefore, O Lord, in the name of Thy well-beloved Son, Jesus Christ, to remove the barrenness and sterility of this land, and let springs of living water break forth to water its thirsty soil. Let the vine and olive produce in their strength, and the fig-tree bloom and flourish. . . . Let the flocks and the herds greatly increase and multiply upon the mountains and the hills; and let Thy great kindness conquer and subdue the unbelief of Thy people. Do Thou take from them their stony heart, and give them a heart of flesh; and may the Sun of Thy favor dispel the cold mists of darkness which have beclouded their atmosphere. . . . Let kings become their nursing fathers, and queens with motherly fondness wipe the tear of sorrow from their eye."⁴

Following the prayer, he erected a pile of stones as an altar and a witness of his act. With his mission completed, he returned to Nauvoo, arriving in December 1842.

A City from the Swamps

Meanwhile, things had been happening in the western Illinois colony. Homes, shops, and gardens rose from what had been the swamps of Commerce. But because of the extreme poverty in which these people found themselves, their problems were seriously aggravated. Several unsuccessful attempts were made to secure compensation and redress for the losses they had suffered in Missouri. The most notable of these was a petition to the Congress of the United States and an interview between Joseph Smith and the President of the United States, Martin Van Buren.

The petition availed nothing, and Mr. Van Buren replied with a statement that has become famous in Mormon history: "Your cause is just, but I can do nothing for you. . . . If I take up with you I shall lose the vote of Missouri."[5]

The governor of Missouri reacted to these efforts by requesting that the governor of Illinois arrest and deliver to him Joseph Smith and five of his associates as fugitives from justice, although two years had elapsed since they had been allowed to escape from imprisonment in Missouri. The Illinois governor honored the requisition, but on a writ of *habeas corpus* Judge Stephen A. Douglas released the defendants. This action, however, only delayed the Missourians in the execution of their avowed purposes.

The Building of the Temple

During this same period, a decision was made to build a temple in Nauvoo. This sacred edifice was to be reserved for special ordinance work, including baptism for the dead.

The doctrine whereby one who has the opportunity to be baptized is saved, while he who does not have the opportunity is damned, has always appeared discriminatory. And yet the scripture reads, "Except a man be born of water and of the Spirit, he cannot enter into the kingdom of God."[6] The law is all-inclusive.

Joseph Smith resolved this question with the doctrine of vicarious baptism for the dead, announcing it as a revelation from God. When performed under proper authority, baptism may be received by living proxies acting in behalf of the dead. Such a practice existed in the primitive Church. This is attested by the words of Paul to the Corinthians: "Else what shall they do which are baptized for the dead, if the dead rise not at all? Why are they then baptized for the dead?"[7]

To provide facilities for such vicarious work, as well as for other sacred ordinances, the Prophet was commanded through revelation to erect a temple. On April 6, 1841, ten thousand members

The Nauvoo Temple, second temple built by the Mormons. This beautiful structure was desecrated by a mob and later destroyed by fire and storm

of the Church assembled for the laying of the cornerstones of this structure. By November 8 the baptismal font was completed, and by October 30, 1842, the building had progressed sufficiently to permit the holding of meetings in some rooms. However, it was April 30, 1846, after most of the Saints had left Nauvoo, before it was completed in detail. The building cost approximately one million dollars, and at the time it was regarded as the finest structure in the state of Illinois.

This magnificent edifice stood on the highest elevation of the city and commanded a view of the entire countryside on both sides of the river. It became the crown of Nauvoo, which in itself was remarkable in contrast with most of the frontier towns of America, and which prior to its evacuation was the largest then in Illinois.

Many distinguished visitors called at Nauvoo during this period of intense activity. In 1843 an English writer described the Mormon community in an article which was widely published:

"The city is of great dimensions, laid out in beautiful order; the streets are wide, and cross each other at right angles, which will add greatly to its order and magnificence when finished. The city rises on a gentle incline from the rolling Mississippi, and as you stand near the temple, you may gaze on the picturesque scenery around; at your side is the temple, the wonder of the world; round about, and beneath, you may behold handsome stores, large mansions, and fine cottages, interspersed with varied scenery. . . . Peace and harmony reign in the city. The drunkard is scarcely even seen, as in other cities, neither does the awful imprecation or profane oath strike upon your ear; but, while all is storm, and tempest, and confusion abroad respecting the Mormons, all is peace and harmony at home."[8]

Colonel Thomas L. Kane visited Nauvoo three years later. His description is particularly interesting:

"Ascending the upper Mississippi in the Autumn, when its waters were low, I was compelled to travel by land past the region of the Rapids. . . . My eye wearied to see everywhere sordid, vagabond and idle settlers, a country marred, without being improved, by their careless hands.

"I was descending the last hillside upon my journey, when a landscape in delightful contrast broke upon my view. Half encircled by a bend of the river, a beautiful city lay glittering in the fresh morning sun; its bright, new dwellings, set in cool green gardens, ranging up around a stately dome-shaped hill, which was covered by a noble marble edifice, whose high tapering spire was radiant with white and gold. The city appeared to cover several miles; and beyond it, in the background, there rolled off a fair country, chequered by the careful lines of fruitful husbandry. The unmistakeable marks of industry, enterprise and educated wealth everywhere, made the scene one of singular and most striking beauty."[9]

Visitors who came to Nauvoo were impressed with the man under whose direction this remarkable city had risen from disease-ridden swamps. The Prophet at this time was at the zenith of his career. Many of those who knew him during this period have left descriptions of him. He was well-built, about six-feet tall, and weighed approximately two hundred pounds. His eyes were blue, his hair brown and wavy, his skin clear and almost beardless. He was a man of great energy and dignified bearing.

After visiting him, the Masonic grand master of Illinois wrote: "On the subject of religion we widely differed, but he appeared to be quite as willing to permit me to enjoy my right of opinion as I think we all ought to be to let the Mormons enjoy theirs. But instead of the ignorant and tyrannical upstart, judge my surprise at finding him a sensible, intelligent companion and gentlemanly man."[10]

One of the most distinguished men to visit Joseph Smith during this period was Josiah Quincy, who had been mayor of Boston. Out of his impressions of the Prophet he later wrote:

"It is by no means improbable that some future textbook . . . will contain a question something like this: What historical American of the nineteenth century has exerted the most powerful influence upon the destinies of his countrymen? And it is by no means impossible that the answer to that interrogatory may be thus written: *Joseph Smith, the Mormon Prophet. . . .*

"Born in the lowest ranks of poverty, without book-learning and with the homeliest of human names, he had made himself at the age of thirty-nine a power upon earth. Of all the multitudinous family of Smith, from Adam down (Adam of the 'Wealth of Nations' I mean) none has so won human hearts and shaped human lives as this Joseph."[11]

Such was the reaction of strangers who came to Nauvoo and called upon its most prominent citizen.

In 1839 the Mormons had purchased land so swampy that a horse had difficulty walking across it. By 1844 they had built on this same ground a city without equal on all of the American frontier. Sturdy brick homes, some of which are still occupied, broad farms and orchards, shops, schools, and a magnificent temple — with twenty thousand citizens, gathered not only from the eastern states and Canada, but from the British Isles as well — This was Nauvoo — the Beautiful!

8 THE MARTYRS

ON the evening of May 6, 1842, former-governor Lilburn W. Boggs of Missouri was sitting in his home when an unknown assailant fired a pistol through the window and seriously wounded him. The pistol was found on the grounds, but the would-be assassin was not apprehended. It was feared for a time that Boggs would die, but he eventually recovered.

Because he had taken a prominent part in expelling the Mormons from the state, it was soon rumored that they were responsible for the deed. The ex-governor, without any apparent foundation for his act, made an affidavit accusing Orrin Porter Rockwell, a member of the Church, of the crime. He followed this with a second affidavit charging Joseph Smith as accessory-before-the-fact. The governor of Missouri was then asked to requisition the governor of Illinois to deliver Joseph Smith and Rockwell to a representative of the state of Missouri.

A warrant was issued, and the men were arrested; but they were released after trial on a writ of *habeas corpus*. The plans of the Missouri enemies of the Prophet had gone awry, but they were not to be frustrated so easily.

Enemies from Within

In 1840 a Dr. John C. Bennett had allied

himself with the Mormon cause. He was a man gifted in many ways, educated and capable, but apparently lacking in principle. Because of his abilities he was given a number of important responsibilities, but when he became involved in moral offenses he was chastised by Joseph Smith. He retaliated by leaving Nauvoo and publishing a book against the Church. He then got in touch with enemies of the Church in Missouri, thus adding fuel to the smoldering fire of hatred. The result of this was another plot for the arrest of Joseph Smith. But, again, this came to nothing.

There was another group in Nauvoo, however, whose efforts were to meet with greater success. Six men — William and Wilson Law, Frances M. and Chauncey L. Higbee, and Charles A. and Robert D. Foster — had been disfellowshipped from the Church, whereupon they determined to retaliate against the Prophet.

Added to these difficulties was the political situation. The Mormons voted for men whose policies they thought would lead to the greatest good, sometimes the candidates of one party and sometimes those of another. In the presidential campaign of 1844, disagreeing with the policies of both major parties, they steered a middle course by nominating Joseph Smith as a candidate for the office of president of the United States, with Sidney Rigdon as a candidate for the vice-presidency. The Mormon leader issued a statement of his views on government which attracted the attention of many. Among other things, he advocated that the government solve the slave problem by purchasing the negroes, thus freeing the slaves and compensating their owners — a policy which if followed might have saved the treasure and lives later sacrificed in the Civil War. He further suggested that prisons be made schools where offenders might be taught useful trades and thus become valuable members of society.

To further acquaint the people of the nation with the Prophet's views, a number of men left Nauvoo to campaign for his candidacy. It was while these men were absent from Nauvoo that the Prophet's troubles reached a climax.

On June 10, 1844, the six men named above published a libelous paper called the *Nauvoo Expositor*. It caused a great stir because it openly maligned prominent citizens of the community.

The people were incensed. Since the Illinois legislature, in the charter given Nauvoo, granted the city the authority "to declare what shall be a nuisance, and to prevent and remove the same,"[1] the city council met for some fourteen hours, took evidence, read the law on the subject of nuisances, consulted the charter granted by the legislature to determine their rights and obligations, declared the publication a nuisance, and ordered the mayor, who was Joseph Smith, to abate it.

He in turn issued an order to the city marshall to "destroy the printing press from whence issues the *Nauvoo Expositor,* and pile the type of said printing establishment in the street, and burn all the *Expositors* and libelous handbills found in said establishment."[2] The marshall carried out the order and so reported.

Its publishers immediately used this as a pretext for accusing Joseph Smith and his brother Hyrum of violating the freedom of the press. They were arrested, tried, and acquitted. But ever since, the action has been denounced by scores of writers. A careful analysis of the law then in effect, however, has led a distinguished legal authority to conclude: "Aside from damages for unnecessary destruction of the press, for which the Nauvoo authorities were unquestionably liable, the remaining actions of the council, including its interpretation of the constitutional guarantee of a free press, can be supported by reference to the law of their day."[3]

But the fire of hatred, which had been fanned so long, now burst into fury. Rumors flew throughout western Illinois. The Prophet's enemies reached Governor Thomas Ford with exaggerated stories, and the governor requested that Joseph and Hyrum meet him in Carthage, where feeling against the Smiths was particularly strong. He added, "I will guarantee the safety of all such persons as may be brought to this place from Nauvoo either for trial or as witnesses for the accused."[4]

To this, Joseph Smith, sensing the real importance of the situation, replied: "We dare not come, though your Excellency promises protection. Yet, at the same time, you have expressed fears that you could not control the mob, in which case we are left to the mercy of the merciless. Sir, we dare not come, for our lives would be in danger, and we are guilty of no crime."[5]

The Prophet knew whereof he spoke. Though he had been arrested and acquitted thirty-seven times, the last entry in his journal, written at this time, reads: "I told Stephen Markham that if I and Hyrum were ever taken again we should be massacred, or I was not a prophet of God."[6]

He thought of escaping to the West, but some of those close to him advised him to go to

Carthage and stand trial. To his brother, he said, "We shall be butchered."[7] Nevertheless, on the morning of June 24, 1844, the prophet and several associates set out for Carthage. Pausing near the temple, they looked at the magnificent building and then at the city, which only five years previous had been little more than swampland. To the group with him Joseph said, "This is the loveliest place and the best people under the heavens; little do they know the trials that await them."[8]

Further on he made another significant remark: "I am going like a lamb to the slaughter; but I am calm as a summer's morning; I have a conscience void of offense towards God, and towards all men. I shall die innocent, and it shall

Carthage Jail

yet be said of me—he was murdered in cold blood."[9]

When they arrived in Carthage they were arrested on a charge of treason and committed to jail on a false mittimus. When the illegality of this action was protested to Governor Ford, he replied that he did not think it his duty to interfere, as they were in the hands of the law. He thereupon turned the matter over to the local magistrate, who happened to be one of the leaders of the mob, and suggested that he use the Carthage Greys to enforce the incarceration.[10]

Joseph Smith secured an interview with the governor, who promised him that he would be protected from the mobs, which by this time had gathered in Carthage. Moreover, the governor assured him that if he, the governor, went to Nauvoo to investigate matters for himself, as Joseph Smith had requested him to do, he would take the Prophet with him.

Notwithstanding these promises, Governor Ford went to Nauvoo on the morning of June 27, leaving Joseph and Hyrum Smith, and Willard Richards and John Taylor incarcerated in Carthage jail, with a mob militia encamped on the town square.

The day was spent by the prisoners in discussion and the writing of letters. To his wife Joseph wrote: "I am very much resigned to my lot, knowing I am justified, and have done the best that could be done. Give my love to the children . . . and all who inquire after me. . . . May God bless you all."[11] The letters were sent with visitors who left at one-thirty in the afternoon.

As the day wore on, a feeling of depression came over the group. At the request of the

Prophet, John Taylor sang "A Poor Wayfaring Man of Grief," a song dealing with the Savior, which had been popular in Nauvoo.

A poor, wayfaring man of grief
Has often crossed me on my way,
Who sued so humbly for relief
That I could never answer, Nay.

I had not power to ask his name;
Whither he went, or whence he came;
Yet there was something in his eye
That won my love, I knew not why.

Once when my scanty meal was spread
He entered — not a word he spake!
Just perishing for want of bread;
I gave him all; he blessed it, brake.

* * * *

In prison I saw him next — condemned
To meet a traitor's doom at morn;
The tide of lying tongues I stemmed,
And honored him 'mid shame and scorn.

My friendship's utmost zeal to try
He asked, if I for him would die;
The flesh was weak, my blood ran chill,
But the free spirit cried, "I will."

Then in a moment to my view,
The stranger started from disguise:
The tokens in his hands I knew;
The Savior stood before mine eyes.

He spake — and my poor name he named —
"Of me thou hast not been asham'd;
These deeds shall thy memorial be;
Fear not, thou didst them unto me."

Not long after the song was finished, "there was a little rustling at the outer door of the jail, and a cry of surrender, and also a discharge of three or four firearms followed instantly. The doctor glanced an eye by the window, and saw about a hundred armed men around the door.... The mob encircled the building, and some of them rushed by the guard up the flight of stairs, burst open the door, and began the work of death."

Hyrum was struck first. He fell to the floor

The watch that saved John Taylor's life

exclaiming, "I am a dead man." Joseph ran to him, exclaiming, "Oh, dear brother Hyrum." Then John Taylor was hit, and he fell to the floor seriously wounded. Fortunately, however, the impact of one ball was broken by the watch in his vest pocket. This saved his life.

With bullets bursting through the door, Joseph sprang to the window. Three balls struck him almost simultaneously, two coming from the door and one from the window. Dying, he fell from the open window, exclaiming, "O Lord, my God!"

Dr. Richards escaped without injury, but the Church had lost its Prophet and his brother, the Patriarch. The deed was completed in a matter of seconds.[12]

Sorrow and Hope

When news of the murder of Joseph and Hyrum Smith reached Nauvoo, a pall of gloom settled over the city. The next day the bodies of the dead were taken to Nauvoo. Thousands lined the streets as the cortege passed. The brothers were buried on the following day.

Meanwhile, the inhabitants of Carthage had fled from their homes in fear that the Mormons would rise en masse and wreak vengeance. But there was no disposition to return evil for evil. The Saints were content to leave the murderers in the hands of Him who has said, "Vengeance is mine. I will repay."

The mobocrats had thought that in killing Joseph Smith they had killed Mormonism. But in so doing they had understood neither the character of the people nor the organization of the Church. Joseph had bestowed the keys of authority upon the Apostles, with Brigham Young at their head, and the people sustained them in this capacity, although there was some confusion for a time.

Under the leadership of Brigham Young, the progress of Nauvoo continued. It became increasingly clear, however, that there would be no peace for the Mormons in Illinois. The blood of the Smiths appeared only to have made the mob bolder. The law had not punished the murderers; the governor had apparently connived with them. Why should they not carry to completion the work of extermination?

When the shock of the murders eased, depredations against property began again. Fields of grain were burned, cattle were driven off, then houses on the outskirts of the city were destroyed. Under these circumstances, Brigham Young and other leaders of the Church determined to seek out a place where the Saints could live in peace, unmolested by mobs and prejudiced politicians.

Joseph Smith had uttered a remarkable prophecy in 1842 at a time when the Mormons were enjoying peace in Nauvoo. He had said "that the Saints would continue to suffer much affliction and would be driven to the Rocky Mountains, many would apostatize, others would be put to death by our persecutors or lose their lives in consequence of exposure or disease, and some of you will live to go and assist in making settlements and build cities and see the Saints become a mighty people in the midst of the Rocky Mountains."[13]

There, in the vastness of the West, lay their hope for peace. Constantly badgered by threats and mob force, the Church began preparations in the fall of 1845 to leave their fair city and go forth into the wilderness to find a place where they might finally be able to worship God according to the dictates of their consciences.

9 EXODUS

THE exodus of the Mormons from Nauvoo, Illinois, in February 1846, stands as one of the epic events in the pioneer history of the United States. In severe winter weather, they crossed the Mississippi River, their wagons loaded with the few possessions they could take with them. Behind them were the homes they had constructed from the swamps of Commerce during the seven years they had been permitted to live in Illinois. Before them was the wilderness, largely unknown and uncharted.

Because this march was much like the exodus of the Israelites from their homes in Egypt to a promised land they had not seen, the Mormons named their movement "The Camp of Israel."

Brigham Young and the first company ferried across the river on February 4. A few days later the river froze sufficiently to support teams and wagons. Although this weather proved a boon in expediting the movement, it also brought intense suffering. Of the conditions in which these exiles found themselves, one of their group, Eliza R. Snow, wrote:

"I was informed that on the first night of the encampment, nine children were born into the world, and from that time, as we journeyed onward, mothers gave birth to offspring under almost every variety of circumstances imaginable, except those to which they had been accustomed; some in tents, others in wagons—in rain-storms and in snow-storms. . . .

"Let it be remembered that the mothers of these wilderness-born babies were not savages, accustomed to roam the forest and brave the storm and tempest. . . . Most of them were born and educated in the Eastern States—had there embraced the gospel as taught by Jesus and his apostles, and, for the sake of their religion, had gathered with the saints, and under trying circumstances had assisted, by their faith, patience and energies, in making Nauvoo what its name indicates, 'the beautiful.' There they had lovely homes, decorated with flowers and enriched with choice fruit trees, just beginning to yield plentifully.

"To these homes, without lease or sale, they had just bid a final adieu, and with what little of their substance could be packed into one, two, and in some instances, three wagons, had started out, desertward, for—where? To this question the only response at that time was, God knows."[1]

Brigham Young presided over this pilgrim band. They accepted him as prophet and leader, the inspired successor to their beloved Joseph. He, they believed, would direct them to a place of refuge "in the midst of the Rocky Mountains," where Joseph had predicted they would become "a mighty people."

Planting for Other Reapers

After the exiles reached the Iowa side of the Mississippi River, they were organized into companies of hundreds, and standards of conduct were set up. The companies were subdivided into fifties and tens, with officers over each group.

Brigham Young was sustained as "president over the whole Camp of Israel."[2]

They traveled in a northwesterly direction, over the territory of Iowa, through a sparsely settled region between the Mississippi and Missouri Rivers. In the early days of their movement, snow lay on the ground to a depth of six or eight inches, and their canvas wagon covers offered little protection against the cold north winds.

With the coming of spring, the snow melted, making travel even more difficult. There were no roads in the direction the Saints traveled; they had to build their own. At times the mud was so

Crossing the Mississippi

deep that three yoke of oxen were required to pull a load of five hundred pounds. Exhausted by a day of pushing and pulling, chopping wood for bridges, loading and unloading wagons, the travelers would find they had moved only a half dozen miles. Slush and rain made their camps veritable quagmires. Exposure to such conditions, together with improper nourishment, took a heavy toll of life.

Burials along the way were frequent. Crude coffins were fashioned from cottonwood trees, brief services were held, and the loved ones of the deceased turned their faces and their teams westward, realizing they would never pass this way again. One wonders why these people did not become bitter and vindictive, particularly when they remembered their comfortable homes now ravaged and burned by the Illinois mob.

But they lightened their sorrows with self-made pleasures. They had their own brass band, and they made good use of it. The settlers of Iowa were often amazed to see these pioneers clear a piece of land about their camp fires, and then dance and sing until the bugler sounded taps.

It was while traveling under these circumstances that one of their number, William Clayton, composed that epic hymn of the prairie, "Come, Come Ye Saints." Set to an old English air, this song became an anthem of hope and faith for all the thousands of Mormon pioneers. Nothing, perhaps, expresses so well the spirit of this movement.

When food became scarce, the pioneers found it necessary to trade precious possessions — dishes, silverware, lace — brought from the East or across the sea, for a little corn

Come, Come, Ye Saints

William Clayton   **Old English Tune**

Resolutely ♩ = 66

1. Come, come, ye Saints, no toil nor la-bor fear; But with joy wend your way. Though hard to you this jour-ney may ap-pear, Grace shall be as your day. 'Tis bet-ter far for us to strive Our use-less cares from us to drive; Do this, and joy your hearts will swell— All is well! all is well!

2. Why should we mourn or think our lot is hard? 'Tis not so; all is right. Why should we think to earn a great re-ward, If we now shun the fight? Gird up your loins; fresh cour-age take; Our God will nev-er us for-sake; And soon we'll have this tale to tell— All is well! all is well!

3. We'll find the place which God for us pre-pared, Far a-way in the West, Where none shall come to hurt or make a-fraid; There the Saints will be blessed. We'll make the air with mu-sic ring, Shout prais-es to our God and King; A-bove the rest these words we'll tell— All is well! all is well!

4. And should we die be-fore our jour-ney's through, Hap-py day! all is well! We then are free from toil and sor-row, too; With the just we shall dwell! But if our lives are spared a-gain To see the Saints their rest ob-tain, O how we'll make this cho-rus swell— All is well! all is well!

and salt pork. In this way the homes of many Iowa settlers were made more attractive and the Mormons were able to replenish their scant food supplies. Occasionally the brass band traveled out of its way a considerable distance to give a concert in a frontier settlement in order to add to the commissary.

One of the remarkable features of this movement was the building of temporary settlements along the way. The pioneer company occasionally stopped long enough to clear, fence, plow, and plant large sections of ground. The leaders called for volunteers—some to split rails for fences and bridges, others to remove trees, and others to plow and sow. A few cabins were built, and several families were detailed to remain and care for the crops. Then the pioneer company moved forward, leaving the crops for later companies to harvest.

This spirit of mutual service and cooperation characterized the entire movement. Without this, the migration of twenty thousand people through the wilderness could have ended in disaster.

Approximately three and a half months after leaving Sugar Creek, their camp on the west shore of the Mississippi, the pioneer company reached Council Bluffs on the Missouri. Following them, across the entire territory of Iowa, was a slow-moving train of hundreds of wagons. They were to continue to filter out of Nauvoo and move over the rolling Iowa hills all of that summer and late into the year. Here was modern Israel seeking a new promised land!

The Mormon Battalion

On a June morning in 1846, at one of the temporary camps along the trail, the Mormons were surprised by the approach of a platoon of United States soldiers. Captain James Allen had come with a call for five hundred able young men to fight in the war with Mexico.

He was directed on to Council Bluffs to see Brigham Young and other authorities of the Church. It is not surprising that the leaders remarked on the irony of the situation — their country, which had stood by while they, its citizens, had been dispossessed of their homes by unconstitutional mobs, now called upon them for military volunteers.

It is true that the Mormons had petitioned the government for assistance in the form of contracts to build blockhouses along the westward trail. They believed that this would be a service to the thousands of emigrants, Mormon and non-Mormon, who would move west in the years to come. Such blockhouses would afford protection against the Indians and other dangers of the prairie. But a military call for five hundred urgently needed men was hardly the answer they expected. Moreover, the call was highly disproportionate in terms of numbers when compared with the population of the nation as a whole.

Nevertheless, they responded. Brigham Young and others went from camp to camp, hoisting the national flag at each recruiting place. And though this meant leaving families fatherless on the plains, the men enlisted when President Young assured them that their families should have food so long as his own had any.

Captain Allen expressed amazement at the music and dancing on the eve of departure. The recruits were to go to Mexico. Their families now of necessity would be compelled to establish

The Mormon Battalion Monument erected on the Utah state capitol grounds

winter quarters and wait until the following year to go to the Rocky Mountains. When or where they would meet again was an open question. Perhaps it was a statement from Brigham Young that eased the sorrow of departure. He promised the men that "if they would perform their duties faithfully, without murmuring and go in the name of the Lord, be humble, and pray every morning and evening" they would not have to fight and would return home safely.[3]

From Council Bluffs the Mormon Battalion marched to Fort Leavenworth. There they received advance pay for clothing, and a large part of this money they sent back for the relief of their families.

From Leavenworth they marched southwest to the old Spanish town of Santa Fe. Here they were saluted by the garrison under the command of Colonel Alexander W. Doniphan, the man who had saved Joseph Smith's life in Missouri.

From Santa Fe they marched south down the valley of the Rio Grande, but before reaching El Paso they turned to the west, following the San Pedro River.

They then crossed the Gila River, marched to Tucson, followed the Gila to the Colorado, and made their way over the mountains to San Diego, California. Much of the road they made was later followed by the Southern Pacific Railroad.

The story of their historic march is one of suffering from insufficient rations, of killing thirst and desperate attempts to secure water, of exhausting travel through heavy desert sand, and of cutting a road over forbidding mountains. They had left their families in June 1846. They reached San Diego January 29, 1847. The war was over when they reached their post, and they were not obliged to do any fighting. Brigham Young's prophetic promise had been fulfilled.

Upon reaching the Pacific Coast, their commander, Colonel Philip St. George Cooke of the United States Army, congratulated them with a citation, which reads in part as follows:

"The lieutenant colonel commanding, congratulates the battalion on their safe arrival on the shore of the Pacific Ocean, and the conclusion of their march of over two thousand miles.

"History may be searched in vain for an equal march of infantry. Half of it has been through a wilderness, where nothing but savages and wild beasts are found, or deserts where, for want of water, there is no living creature. There, with almost hopeless labor, we have dug deep wells, which the future traveler will enjoy. Without a guide who had traversed them we have ventured into trackless tablelands where water was not found for several marches. With crowbar and pick and axe in hand, we have worked our way over mountains, which seemed to defy aught save the wild goat, and hewed a pass through a chasm of living rock more narrow than our wagons."[4]

But while the members of the Battalion had been serving under their country's flag, those of their people who had remained in Nauvoo were being driven by mobs in defiance of every constitutional guarantee.

The Fall of a City

Although most of the Mormons had succeeded in getting out of Nauvoo before May 1, 1846, the date set by the mob for their complete departure, some of their number had not been so fortunate. By August there remained about one thousand, many of them sick and aged. It was thought that the mob would spare these, at least.

But history bears somber witness of the fact that those who had indulged in such wishful thinking were mistaken. When it became apparent that the mob would not wait, the people of

Nauvoo appealed to the governor for aid. He responded by sending a Major Parker with ten men to represent the militia of the state of Illinois. Major Parker was later succeeded by a Major Clifford.

The mob answered the Major's appeals for a peaceful settlement of the difficulty by attacking him and the Mormons who had volunteered to serve under him. Though greatly outnumbered, the defenders of the city fashioned five old steamboat shafts into cannons and constructed improvised breastworks. In the name of the people of Illinois, Major Clifford requested the mobbers to disperse.

Their answer was an assault on the city. The defenders were able to hold them off for a time, but they were so seriously outnumbered that the Mormons had no choice but to agree to evacuate the city as quickly as they could gather together a few of their possessions.

Even this did not satisfy the mob. While the Mormons were leaving, they were set upon and abused, and their wagons were ransacked for anything of value. Crossing to the Iowa side of the river, they set up a temporary camp. Colonel Thomas L. Kane of Philadelphia, who chanced to see them at this time, later described their situation before the Historical Society of Pennsylvania:

"Dreadful, indeed, was the suffering of these forsaken beings. Cowed and cramped by cold and sunburn, alternating as each weary day and night dragged on, they were, almost all of them, the crippled victims of disease. They were there because they had no homes, nor hospital nor poor-house nor friends to offer them any. They could not satisfy the feeble cravings of their sick:

they had not bread to quiet the fractious hunger-cries of their children. . . .

"These were Mormons, famishing in Lee County, Iowa, in the fourth week of the month of September, in the year of our Lord 1846. The city [which he had just visited],—it was Nauvoo, Illinois. The Mormons were the owners of that city, and the smiling country around. And those who had stopped their ploughs, who had silenced their hammers, their axes, their shuttles and their workshop wheels; those who had put out their fires, who had eaten their food, spoiled their orchards, and trampled under foot their thousands of acres of unharvested bread; these,—were the keepers of their dwellings, the carousers in their temple,—whose drunken riot insulted the ears of their dying."[5]

In these straitened conditions, many would doubtless have starved but for thousands of quail which flew into their camp, and which they were able to catch with their hands. These they regarded as manna from heaven, an answer to prayer.

Fortunately, they were not left in this condition for long. Their brethren, who had gone on ahead, sent back relief wagons and divided with them their own meager stores. Their last picture of Nauvoo, as they tediously made their way over the Iowa hills, was of the tower of their sacred temple, now spoiled and desecrated.

10 TO THE PROMISED LAND

IT was apparent to Brigham Young and the other leaders of the Church that it would be unwise to attempt to reach the Rocky Mountains in the year 1846, since the expedition now had been seriously weakened by the loss of the young men who had marched with the Mormon Battalion. Accordingly, a temporary settlement was established along the Missouri River.

The site, adjoining the present city of Omaha, soon had more of the appearance of a town than a camp. Many of the people got along with dugouts and other crude shelters. However, a thousand sturdy log houses were erected before January 1847.

During all of that winter, feverish activity went on. Anvils rang with the making and repairing of wagons. Available maps and reports were carefully studied, and every preparation possible was undertaken to ensure the success of the move scheduled for the following spring.

The community was not without its pleasures, although comforts were few. Dances were frequently held under the sponsorship of the various quorums of the priesthood. Religious worship was carried on as though the people were permanently settled. Schools for the children were successfully conducted, for the

Monument to the Utah pioneers in the old cemetery at Winter Quarters

education of the young has always been of prime importance in Mormon philosophy.

But often a pupil—sometimes several—did not appear when the school bell rang. A type of scurvy, called black canker, took a sorrowful toll. Lack of proper nourishment, insufficient shelter, extremes of temperature in the lowlands along the river—these made the people easy victims of disease.

In recent years the Church has erected a monument in the old cemetery of Winter Quarters. In heroic size it depicts a mother and father laying a child in a grave they know they never again will visit. Surrounding the monument are the graves of some six hundred of those who died at this temporary encampment on the prairie.

Westward

In the early spring of 1847, plans were completed for the sending of a pioneer company to the Rocky Mountains. Their responsibility was to chart a route and find a place for the thousands who would follow.

On January 14, President Young delivered to the Saints what he declared to be a revelation from the Lord. This became the constitution governing their westward movement. It is an interesting document, reading in part as follows:

"The Word and Will of the Lord concerning the Camp of Israel in their journeyings to the West:

"Let all of the people of the Church of Jesus Christ of Latter-day Saints, and those who journey with them, be organized into companies, with a covenant and promise to keep all the commandments and statutes of the Lord our God.

"Let all the companies be organized with

captains of hundreds, captains of fifties, and captains of tens, with a president and his two counselors at their head, under the direction of the Twelve Apostles.

"And this shall be our covenant — that we will walk in all the ordinances of the Lord. . . .

"And if any man shall seek to build up himself, and seeketh not my counsel, he shall have no power, and his folly shall be made manifest.

"Seek ye; and keep all your pledges one with another; and covet not that which is thy brother's.

"Keep yourselves from evil to take the name of the Lord in vain. . . .

"Cease to contend one with another, cease to speak evil one of another.

"Cease drunkenness, and let your words tend to edifying one another.

"If thou borrowest of thy neighbor, thou shalt return that which thou hast borrowed; and if thou canst not repay then go straightway and tell thy neighbor, lest he condemn thee.

"If thou shalt find that which thy neighbor has lost, thou shalt make diligent search till thou shalt deliver it to him again.

"Thou shalt be diligent in preserving that which thou hast, that thou mayest be a wise steward; for it is the free gift of the Lord thy God, and thou art his steward.

"If thou art merry, praise the Lord with singing, with music, with dancing, and with a prayer of praise and thanksgiving.

"If thou art sorrowful, call on the Lord thy God with supplication, that your souls may be joyful.

"Fear not thine enemies, for they are in mine

hands, and I will do my pleasure with them."[1]

To these general standards of conduct were added other specific rules. Every man was to carry a loaded gun or have one in his wagon where, in case of attack, he could get it at a moment's notice. At night the wagons were to be drawn into a circle to form a corral for the teams. There was to be no travel or work on the Sabbath; both teams and men should rest on that day. Prayer, night and morning, should be a regular practice in the camp.

On April 5 the pioneer company started west. It consisted of 143 men, 3 women, and 2 children, with Brigham Young leading the group. Fortunately, when they had gone only a short distance, Apostles Parley P. Pratt and John Taylor arrived at Winter Quarters from England. They brought with them barometers, sextants, telescopes, and other instruments. In the hands of Orson Pratt, an accomplished scientist, these made it possible for the pioneers to determine the latitude, longitude, temperature, and elevation above sea level of their position each day. Such information was invaluable in the preparation of a guide for those who were to come later.

One of the famous trails of history already existed along the south side of the Platte River. It was to become more heavily traveled in years to come by thousands of emigrants bound for Oregon and California. However, Brigham Young decided against using the Oregon road, and determined to break a new trail on the north side of the river. In so doing, he said, the Mormons would avoid conflict with other westward-bound people and would also have more feed for the cattle of the companies to follow. It is interesting to note that when the Union Pacific Railroad was built some years later, it followed this Mormon road for a considerable distance.

In 1847 great herds of buffalo roamed the plains. It was customary practice among westward-bound emigrants to shoot them simply for sport. But Brigham Young took a different attitude. He advised his people to kill no more than were needed for meat.

A Log of the Journey

For a number of reasons, not the least of which was to prepare a guide for those to come later, the pioneers were interested in knowing the number of miles they covered each day. The first device employed to determine this was a red cloth tied to a wagon wheel. By counting the revolutions of the wheel and multiplying this number by the circumference of the rim, it was possible to determine the distance traveled. But watching the revolutions of a wheel, day in and day out, soon became tedious. There was need for a better way.

Consulting with Orson Pratt, Appleton Harmon solved the problem. Carving a set of wooden gears, he constructed what was called a roadometer. It was a novel device, the forerunner of the modern odometer. Although constructed of wood, it was amazingly accurate.

For the guidance of those who should follow, the pioneer company left letters describing mileage and conditions of the trail. These were tucked in an improvised mail box or were painted on a sun-bleached buffalo skull.

Journals were carefully kept, noting details of the journey. Two excerpts from Orson Pratt's journal serve as illustrations:

"*May 22nd.* — At a quarter past five this morn-

The wooden odometer that measured the daily distance traveled by the pioneer wagons

ing, the barometer stood at 26.623, attached thermometer at 51.5 degrees, detached thermometer 48.5 degrees. A light breeze from the south—the sky partially overspread with thin clouds. . . . Five and a half miles from our morning encampment we crossed a stream, which we named Crab Creek; one and three-quarters mile further we halted for noon. A meridian observation of the sun placed us in latitude 41 deg. 30 min. 3 sec. I intended to have taken a lunar distance for the longitude, but clouds prevented. With our glasses, Chimney Rock can now be seen at a distance of 42 miles up the river. At this distance it appears like a short tower placed

105

upon an elevated mound or hill. Four and a quarter miles further brought us to another place where the river strikes the bluffs; as usual we were obliged to pass over them, and in about two and a quarter miles we again came to the prairie bottoms, and driving a short distance we encamped, having made fifteen and a half miles during the day. For a number of miles past, the formation, more particularly that of the bluffs, has been gradually changing from sand to marl and soft earthy limestone, the nature of which is beginning to change the face of the country, presenting scenes of remarkable picturesque beauty. . . .

"*May 23rd.* — To-day, as usual, we let ourselves and teams rest. The mercury in the barometer is, this morning, much more depressed than what can be accounted for by our gradual ascent; at five o'clock it stood at 26.191, attached thermometer 54.5 deg., detached thermometer 52 deg. A depression of the mercury is said to indicate high winds. To-day several of us again visited the tops of some of these bluffs, and by a barometrical measurement I ascertained the height of one [of] them to be 235 feet above the river, and 3590 feet above the level of the sea. . . . Rattlesnakes are very plentiful here. . . . Soon after dinner we attended public worship, when the people were interestingly and intelligently addressed by President B. Young and others."[2]

The route of the pioneers lay up the valley of the Platte to the confluence of the North Platte and South Platte Rivers. It then followed the North Platte through what is now Nebraska and Wyoming to a point where the Sweetwater River flows into the North Platte. The route then lay

A replica of one of the buffalo skulls left for the guidance of groups who followed the original company of pioneers

along this stream to its headwaters near South Pass, Wyoming.

By June 1 the company had reached old Fort Laramie, where they were surprised to find a group of Church members from Mississippi who had come from the south by way of Pueblo, Colorado, with the purpose of joining the pioneer company and following them to their destination.

On June 27 they moved over South Pass, that place where the Rockies gently slope to the prairie, and over which moved most of the westward-bound emigrants. At South Pass the Mormons met Major Moses Harris, a famous

107

trapper and scout. From him they received a description of the basin of the Salt Lake. His report of the country was unfavorable. Of this interview Orson Pratt wrote:

"We obtained much information from him in relation to the great interior basin of the Salt Lake, the country of our destination. His report, like that of Captain Fremont's, is rather unfavourable to the formation of a colony in this basin, principally on account of the scarcity of timber. He said that he had travelled the whole circumference of the lake, and that there was no outlet to it."[3]

On June 28 they met that wiry veteran of the west, Jim Bridger. Anxious to learn all they could of the country toward which they were traveling, the Mormons accepted his suggestion that they make camp and spend the night with him. He indicated that some good country could be found both to the north and to the south of the basin of the Salt Lake, but he discouraged any plan for establishing a large colony in the basin itself.

On June 30 Samuel Brannan rode into view. He was a member of the Church who, on February 4, 1846, the date of the first exodus from Nauvoo, had sailed from New York with more than two hundred Mormons bound for California by way of Cape Horn. Landing at Yerba Buena, now San Francisco, he had established the first English-language newspaper published there. He left California in April, riding east over the mountains to meet Brigham Young. Enroute he had passed the scene of the Donner Party tragedy of the preceding winter, and gave the Mormons a description of that ill-fated camp in which more than a score of people starved to

Great Salt Lake City as it appeared in 1853

death in the snows of the Sierras. Brannan enthusiastically described for President Young the beauties of California. It was, he indicated, a rich and productive land of great beauty and equable climate, a land where the Mormons could prosper. But President Young could not be dissuaded from the purpose to which he had set himself—God had a place for his people, and there they would go to work out their destiny.

"This Is the Right Place"

As the pioneer company approached the mountains, travel became more difficult. Their teams were jaded, and their wagons were worn. Moreover, the steep mountain canyons, with their swift streams, huge boulders, and heavy tree growth, presented problems very different from those experienced on the plains.

On July 21 Orson Pratt and Erastus Snow, two advance scouts, entered the Salt Lake Valley. Three days later Brigham Young, who had moved more slowly because of illness, rode out of the canyon and looked across the valley. He paused, and then announced, "This is the right place."

This was the promised land! This valley with its salty lake gleaming in the July sun. This treeless prairie in the mountains. This tract of dry land broken only by a few bubbling streams running from the canyons to the lake. This was the object of vision and of prophecy, the land of which thousands yet at Winter Quarters dreamed. This was their land of refuge, the place where the Saints would "become a mighty people in the midst of the Rocky Mountains."

11 PIONEERING THE WILDERNESS

T WO hours after the arrival of the main body of pioneers, the first plowing in the Salt Lake Valley was undertaken. The ground, however, was so dry and hard that the plows were broken. Consequently, one of the canyon streams was diverted and the soil soaked. Thereafter the plowing was easier. On July 24 potatoes were planted and the ground watered. This was the beginning of irrigation by Anglo-saxon people in the West, marking, in fact, the beginning of modern irrigation practice.

Although other seeds were also planted in addition to the potatoes, there was small chance that a crop of any consequence would mature. But it was hoped that at least enough of a crop would develop to provide seed for the following spring.

Brigham Young arrived on Saturday, and on the following day the people met for worship. There they received a statement of the policies that were to prevail in the new colony. President Young declared that no work should be done on Sunday. He promised that if it was, the offender would discover that he would lose five times as much as he gained. No one was to hunt on that day. No man was to try to buy land, but every man would have his land measured out to him

for city and farming purposes. He could till it as
he pleased, but he must be industrious and take
care of it. There was to be no private ownership
of streams of water, and wood and timber were
to be regarded as common property. President
Young also advised the Saints to use only dead
timber for fuel in order to save the live timber
for future use. He promised that if they would
walk faithfully in the light of these laws they
would be a prosperous people.[1]

The First Winter

The next day everyone was busy exploring
the surrounding country to learn of its resources.
Though their faith was strong and their hopes
high, the situation in which these people found
themselves was anything but encouraging. They
were a small group with scant provisions, located
a thousand miles from the nearest settlement to
the east and seven hundred miles from the Pacific Coast. They were unfamiliar with the
resources of this strange new land, which was
untried and different in its nature from that
which they had left.

Yet they began preparations for an extensive
city. Four days after their arrival in the valley,
Brigham Young walked to a spot north of their
camp and proclaimed, "Here is the [place] for
our temple."[2] The city was soon platted around
this site, with streets 132 feet wide. Such width
was considered foolish in those days, but the
foresight in this action has become evident with
the advent of modern traffic. The projected
community was named Great Salt Lake City.

One thing that caught the fancy of the
pioneers as they explored the valley was the similarity between this new-found Zion and the Holy
Land. Twenty-five miles south of their camp was

a beautiful fresh water lake with a river running from it to the Great Salt Lake, another Dead Sea. They named the river Jordan.

Once policies and plans had been decided, Brigham Young and others began the long journey back to Winter Quarters. Those remaining in the valley immediately commenced construction of a fort in which to house themselves as well as the large company expected later in the summer. Most of the families spent the first winter in the fort, although there were a few who ventured to build homes of their own.

Fortunately, that first winter was unusually mild. Nevertheless, the colonists suffered. Food was poor and scarce, as was clothing. Sego roots were dug and thistle tops were boiled for food. In remembrance of the part it played in sustaining life, the sego lily is today Utah's state flower.

No time was wasted in preparing for the future. All through the winter the task of fencing and clearing the land progressed. A common field of five thousand acres was plowed and planted. This was a tremendous accomplishment, considering the tools these people had.

The Coming of the Gulls

In the spring, wide fields of green grain appeared to be ample reward for the labors of the previous fall and winter. Now, these people thought, there would be plenty to eat, both for themselves and for the large number of immigrants expected that summer. Under irrigation, the crops flourished. The future looked bright.

Then one day it was noticed that large crickets were eating the grain. These had been seen by the first men to enter the valley, and the newcomers had noted that some of the natives used them for food. But they had expected nothing of this kind. Each day the situation grew worse. The insects came in myriads, devouring everything before them.

Terror struck into the hearts of the people as they saw their grain fall before the insects. With all their strength they fought them. They tried

Monument on Temple Square honoring the miracle of the sea gulls

burning and drowning. They tried beating them with shovels and brooms. They tried every means they could devise to save their crops. Still the voracious insects came, eating every stalk of grain before them.

Exhausted and in desperation, the Saints turned to the Lord, pleading in prayer for preservation of bread for their children.

Then, to their amazement, they saw great flocks of white-winged sea gulls flying from over the lake to the west and settling on the fields. At first the people thought they were coming to add to the devastation. But the gulls went after the crickets, devouring them, then flying away and disgorging, only to return for more.

The crops of 1848 were saved, and on Temple Square in Salt Lake City stands a monument to the sea gull. In bronze it bears the inscription, "Erected in grateful remembrance of the mercy of God to the Mormon Pioneers."

Gold in California

Brigham Young returned to Winter Quarters on October 31, 1847. On the following December 5, he was sustained as President of the Church. From the time of Joseph Smith's death, Brigham had led the Church in his capacity as President of the Council of Twelve Apostles. He named as his counselors in the First Presidency Heber C. Kimball, who had come into the Church with him, and Dr. Willard Richards.

On May 26, 1848, he left Winter Quarters, never again to return to the East. While he now knew the way, this second journey was more difficult than had been the pioneer trip. The company of which he was leader included "397 wagons with 1229 souls, 74 horses, 19 mules, 1275 oxen, 699 cows, 184 cattle, 411 sheep, 141 pigs, 605 chickens, 37 cats, 82 dogs, 3 goats, 10 geese, 2 beehives, 8 doves, and 1 crow."[3] It was no small task to shepherd such a caravan over a thousand miles of prairie and mountains.

They reached the valley on October 20, 116 days after their departure from Winter Quarters. Meanwhile, something had happened in California that had fired the hearts of the adventurous the world over, and that was to have its effect on the Mormons.

After the Mormon Battalion had been mustered out in California, some of the Battalion men stopped at Sutter's Fort in the Sacramento Valley to work and earn a little money before crossing the mountains to rejoin their families. Six of them, with Sutter's foreman, James W. Marshall, and some Indians, undertook the construction of a sawmill on the south fork of the American River. There, on January 24, 1848, Marshall picked some gold out of the sand in the mill race. Henry Bigler, one of the Battalion men, wrote in his journal that night: "This day some kind of metal was found in the tail race that looks like gold."[4]

This historic entry is the only original documentation of the discovery that sent men rushing over land and sea to California.

But while others were rushing to the American River, the Battalion men completed their contract with Sutter, gathered together what possessions they had, and made their way east over the mountains to the semi-arid valley of the Great Salt Lake, there to undertake with their friends the painful labor of subduing the wilderness.

Meanwhile, the gold fever had infected some of those in the valley who had just passed through a difficult winter. Speaking of this, Brigham Young said:

"Some have asked me about going. I have told them that God has appointed this place for the gathering of his Saints, and you will do better right here than you will by going to the gold mines. . . . Those who stop here and are faithful to God and his people will make more money and get richer than you that run after the god of this world; and I promise you in the name of the Lord that many of you that go thinking you will get rich and come back, will wish you had never gone away from here, and will long to come back, but will not be able to do so. Some of you will come back, but your friends who remain here will have to help you; and the rest of you who are spared to return will not make as much money as your brethren do who stay here and help build up the Church and Kingdom of God; they will prosper and be able to buy you twice over. Here is the place God has appointed for his people. . . .

". . . As the Saints gather here and get strong enough to possess the land, God will temper the climate, and we shall build a city and a temple to the Most High God in this place. We will extend our cities and our settlements to the east and the west, to the north and to the south, and we will build towns and cities by the hundreds, and thousands of the Saints will gather from the nations of the earth. This will become the great highway of the nations. Kings and emperors and the noble and wise of the earth will visit us here, while the wicked and ungodly will envy us our comfortable homes and possessions. Take courage, brethren. . . . Plow your land and sow wheat, plant your potatoes. . . . The worst fear that I have about this people is that they will get rich in this country, forget God and his people, wax fat, and kick themselves out of the Church and go to hell. This people will stand mobbing, robbing, poverty and all manner of persecution, and be true. But my greater fear for them is that they cannot stand wealth; and yet they have to be tried with riches, for they will become the richest people on this earth."[5]

Before the close of the year 1848 the population of the valley had reached five thousand. This heavy influx of immigrants seriously taxed the resources of the community. Hunger and hardship were common that winter, and these circumstances added to the discouragement of many. In the midst of these trying conditions, Heber C. Kimball, speaking before the people in one of their meetings, prophesied that in less than one year there would be plenty of clothing and other needed articles sold on the streets of Salt Lake City for less than in New York or St. Louis.[6]

Such a situation was incredible, but the fulfillment of that prophecy came about, and in remarkable fashion.

Thinking to get rich with the sale of goods in California, eastern merchants had loaded great wagon trains with clothing, tools, and other items for which there would be demand at the gold diggings. But on reaching Salt Lake City they learned that competitors had beaten them by shipping around the Cape.

Their only interest then was to unload what they had for what price they could get and go on to California as quickly as possible. Auctions were held from their wagons on the streets of Salt Lake City. Cloth and clothing sold for less than they could be bought for in New York. Badly needed tools could be had for less than in St. Louis. Fine teams, jaded from the long journey, were eagerly traded for the fatter but less valuable stock of the Mormons. Good, heavy wagons, in great demand in the mountain colony, were traded for lighter vehicles in which the gold seekers could make better time.

Glad Tidings to the World

While eager men were traveling over land and sea to search for gold, the Mormons also sent eager men over land and sea—in search of souls. Missionaries were sent to the Eastern States, to Canada, and to the British Isles. In spite of the prejudices that moved before them, they made substantial headway with the baptism of thousands of souls.

Missionary work in France and Italy was not so fruitful, although some converts were made at first. In the Scandinavian countries, the elders were mobbed and jailed, but a spirit of tolerance gradually developed, and thousands of converts were made in those lands.

These preachers, traveling without purse or scrip, went to Malta, to India, to Chile, and to the islands of the Pacific. Almost everywhere they encountered hatred and the cries of the mob. But in all of these lands they found a few who were receptive to their message.

Once baptized, these converts desired almost invariably to "gather" with others of their faith in the valleys of the Rockies—Zion, they called it. And once there, differences of language and customs were soon lost sight of as men and women from many lands worked together in the building of a commonwealth.

It was inevitable that the boundaries of the Church should extend beyond the valley of the Salt Lake. With thousands of converts coming from the nations, other settlements were founded. At first these were rather close to the mother colony, but soon wagon trains were moving north and south toward the distant valleys. By the close of the third year, settlements extended two hundred miles to the south. By the end of the fourth year, colonies were found over a distance of three hundred miles. Then, in 1851, five hundred of the Saints were called to go to southern California to plant a colony. They there laid the foundations of San Bernardino.

In nearly every case this pioneering entailed great sacrifice. Families were often called to leave their comfortable homes and cultivated fields and go into the wilderness to begin over again. But through their efforts hundreds of colonies were planted over a vast section of the West. Of the extent of this colonization, James H. McClintock, Arizona state historian, wrote:

"It is a fact little appreciated that the Mormons have been first in agricultural colonization of nearly all the intermountain States of today. . . . Not drawn by visions of wealth, unless they looked forward to celestial mansions, they sought, particularly, valleys wherein peace and plenty could be secured by labor. . . .

"First of the faith on the western slopes of the continent was the settlement at San Francisco by Mormons from the ship Brooklyn. They landed July 21, 1846, to found the first English-speaking community of the Golden State, theretofore Mexican. These Mormons established the farming community of New Helvetia, in the San Joaquin Valley, the same fall, while men from

the Mormon Battalion, January 24, 1848, participated in the discovery of gold at Sutter's Fort.
Mormons also were pioneers in Southern California, where in 1851, several hundred families of
the faith settled at San Bernardino.

"The first Anglo-Saxon settlement within the
boundaries of the present State of Colorado was
at Pueblo, November 15, 1846, by Capt. James
Brown and about 150 Mormon men and women
who had been sent back from New Mexico, into
which they had gone, a part of the Mormon
Battalion that marched on to the Pacific Coast.

"The first American settlement in Nevada
was one of the Mormons in the Carson Valley, at
Genoa, in 1851.

"In Wyoming, as early as 1854, was a
Mormon settlement at Green River, near Fort
Bridger, known as Fort Supply.

"In Idaho, too, preeminence is claimed by
virtue of a Mormon settlement at Fort Lemhi, on
the Salmon River, in 1855, and at Franklin, in
Cache Valley, in 1860. . . .

"In honorable place in point of seniority [in
the settlement of Arizona] are to be noted the
Mormon settlements on the Muddy and the
Virgin."[7]

Speaking of the quality of their pioneering,
F. S. Dellenbaugh, great student of the
settlement of the West, wrote:

"It must be acknowledged that the Mormons
were wilderness breakers of high quality. They
not only broke it, but they kept it broken; and
instead of the gin mill and the gambling hall, as
cornerstones of their progress and as examples
to the natives of the white men's superiority, they
planted orchards, gardens, farms, schoolhouses,
and peaceful homes."[8]

12 YEARS OF CONFLICT

Even under the best of circumstances pioneering a wilderness is a wearisome, laborious task. In the Great Basin of the West, it was an unending struggle against drought, Indians, difficult travel conditions, poverty, scarcity of water power, excessive freight rates on merchandise brought overland, crickets, grasshoppers, and crop failures. Tragedies were frequent in the fight to secure a foothold in this vast, forbidding country.

One would think that under such conditions there would be little time for spiritual matters. But the Mormons were ever conscious of the reason they had come to this region. It was not for adventure; nor was it to get rich. They had seen more than enough adventure in Missouri and Illinois, and the lands they had left were far richer than those of the valleys of the mountains. They had come to worship God and to build up his work.

Converts from the Nations

It was not uncommon for men suddenly to be called by the Church to go to distant lands as missionaries. Such labor invariably meant great sacrifice on the part of both the missionary and the family at home. While the father preached the gospel, the mother and children did the heavy chores, though they were frequently assisted by members of the priesthood who took time from their own work.

Converts in large numbers gathered to the colonies in the mountains. To assist the poor, the Perpetual Emigrating Fund Company was formed in 1849, whereby those needing help might borrow money to care for their transportation, the money to be paid back as quickly as possible so that others might be benefited. The fund began functioning in 1850, and within the next thirty years it aided forty thousand people to get to Utah and did a business amounting to $3,600,000.

Before the coming of the railroad, it was impossible to find wagons enough to carry all those who wished to cross the plains. Some of them were so anxious to gather with the Church that they walked, pulling handcarts more than a thousand miles. Most of those who traveled in this way reached the Salt Lake Valley safely and as quickly as those who moved with ox teams.

But bitter tragedy struck two of the handcart companies. The story of these is tersely told in two markers standing in the sage-covered country of Wyoming near South Pass. One of them reads:

"Captain James G. Willie's Handcart Company of Mormon emigrants on their way to Utah, greatly exhausted by the deep snows of an early winter and suffering from lack of food and clothing, had assembled here for reorganization for relief parties from Utah, about the end of October, 1856. Thirteen persons were frozen to death during a single night and were buried here in one grave. Two others died the next day and were buried nearby. Of the company of 404 persons 77 perished before help arrived. The

Monument erected in Salt Lake City in honor of the handcart pioneers

survivors reached Salt Lake City November 9, 1856."

While standing in that lonely, tragic spot one may easily imagine the sorry situation in which these emigrants of 1856 found themselves—a group of hungry men, women, and children huddled together in the midst of a bleak and desolate wilderness, weary from walking more than a thousand miles, many of them sick from exhaustion and insufficient food, the handcarts they had pulled standing beside the makeshift tents they had contrived to erect against the swirling snow.

These two companies had been delayed in

their departure from Iowa City because their carts were not ready as expected. The authorities in Salt Lake City were not notified of their coming and consequently had made no preparations to see them through. When early storms caught them in the western country of Wyoming, they found themselves in desperate circumstances.

Fortunately, they had been passed on the way by returning missionaries traveling in a light wagon. Sensing the situation, these men pushed on to Salt Lake City with all possible speed. They found the Church in general conference, but when Brigham Young heard their story, he dismissed the meeting and immediately organized teams and wagons to go to the aid of the stricken emigrants. After pushing through harrowing experiences themselves, the rescue party reached the Willie Company at Rock Creek Hollow. Leaving aid there, they pressed on to the Martin Company some distance further east. The tragic experiences of these two companies were the most sorrowful in the entire movement of the Mormons.

The Lamanites

If the story of the handcart pioneers is a sorrowful chapter in the history of the Mormons, how much more tragic is the story of the Indians in the history of America. The philosophy that the only good Indian was a dead one was all too often the creed of men of the frontier. In marked contrast with this was Brigham Young's policy that "it was manifestly more economical and less expensive to feed and clothe, than to fight them."[1] His generous treatment of the red men led Senator Chase of Ohio to remark that "no governor had ever done so well by the Indians since William Penn."[2]

125

Respect for the natives arose out of the Book of Mormon. This volume declares that the Indians are descendants of Israel. Their progenitors are known in that volume as the Lamanites, and, in a prophetic vein, the book speaks of a hopeful future for these people.

But though the Mormons were patient and generous, there was occasional trouble. Herds of horses and cattle were a temptation the Indian often could not resist. The natives raided settlements, and two serious outbreaks involved large losses of property. However, in view of the vast territory that they settled, the Mormons had relatively little trouble with the Indians. The history of their relations with the natives demonstrates the wisdom of Brigham Young's policy.

The Utah War

Although the Mormons had little trouble with the Indians, they were to suffer from another source. On July 24, 1857, the inhabitants of Salt Lake City were celebrating both Independence Day and the tenth anniversary of their arrival in the valley. Many of them had gone into one of the mountain canyons adjacent to the city for this purpose.

In the midst of the festivities, a dust-laden and weary horseman hurriedly rode to Brigham Young's tent. He brought ominous news. The United States was sending an army to crush the Mormons! At least that was the story heard from the soldiers, who boasted of what they would do once they reached Salt Lake City.

This had come about largely because two disappointed applicants for government mail contracts had sent to Washington stories that the Mormons were in rebellion against the United States. As was later proved, their stories were absurd. Yet, on only the thin fabric of their tales, the President had ordered twenty-five hundred soldiers to put down a "Mormon rebellion."

Though Brigham Young had properly been installed as governor of the territory, he had been given no notice of the coming of the troops. Not knowing what to expect, the Mormon leaders made preparations. They determined that no other group, armed or otherwise, should again inhabit the homes which they had built. They concluded that if it became necessary they would make Utah the desert it had been before their arrival.

Men were dispatched to do what they could to delay the army and play for time in the hope that something might be done to turn the President from this madness. The prairie was burned and the cattle of the army were stampeded. The bridges which the Mormons had built were destroyed and the fords dredged. But no lives were taken. Because of this carefully executed plan, the army was forced to go into winter quarter in what is now western Wyoming.

But the Mormons were not entirely without friends. Colonel Thomas L. Kane, brother of Elisha Kent Kane, the famed Arctic explorer, had become acquainted with the Saints when they were moving across Iowa and had witnessed the injustices they had suffered. He petitioned the President and received permission to go to Utah to learn the true state of affairs. Largely through his efforts, the President was persuaded to send to Utah a "peace commission" in the spring of 1858.

Brigham Young agreed that the army should be permitted to pass through the city, but should not encamp within it. And lest there should be

any violations of this agreement, he put into effect the plan originally decided upon.

When the soldiers entered the valley they
found the city desolate and deserted except for a

Brigham Young, "the modern Moses"

few watchful men armed with flint and steel and sharp axes. The homes and barns were filled with straw ready to be fired in case of violation, and axes were ready to destroy the orchards.

The people had moved to the south, leaving their homes to be burned, as they had done on more than one occasion previously. Some of the army officers and men were deeply affected as they marched through the silent streets, realizing what their coming had meant. Colonel Philip St. George Cooke, who had led the Mormon Battalion on its long march and knew of the wrongs previously inflicted on these people, bared his head in reverent respect.

Fortunately there was no difficulty. The army camped forty miles southwest of the city, and the people returned to their homes.

A Man at Work

Joseph Smith had been succeeded by a man as peculiarly fitted in his day to lead the Church as the Prophet had been in his own. Brigham Young, called by some of his biographers "the Modern Moses," had led Israel to another Canaan with its Dead Sea. An interesting description of this man is given by Horace Greeley, editor of the *New York Tribune,* who interviewed the Mormon leader in 1859:

"[Brigham Young] spoke readily, . . . with no appearance of hesitation or reserve, and with no apparent desire to conceal anything, nor did he repel any of my questions as impertinent. He was very plainly dressed in thin summer clothing, and with no air of sanctimony or fanaticism. In appearance he is a portly, frank, good-natured, rather thickset man of fifty-five, seeming to enjoy life, and to be in no particular hurry to get to heaven. His associates are plain men, evidently

The Pony Express was a significant chapter in America's pioneer history.

born and reared to a life of labor, and looking as little like crafty hypocrites or swindlers as any body of men I ever met."[3]

In 1860 the famed Pony Express was begun. Mail, which first had been carried from the East in slow, ox-drawn wagons, and later on the overland stage, now reached Salt Lake City in six days from St. Joseph, Missouri. The arrival of each pony was an event.

Not long after riders started delivering mail to the valley, news of tremendous significance reached the West. The Southern States had seceded from the Union. America was torn by Civil War. To the Mormons this tragic news was confirmation of the prophecy issued by Joseph Smith on December 25, 1832. Though Utah was not a state, in loyalty she was tied to the Union. That loyalty was expressed by Brigham Young in the first message sent over the overland telegraph in October 1861: "Utah has not seceded, but is firm for the Constitution and laws of our once happy country."[4]

On May 10, 1869, the Union Pacific Railroad building west from the Missouri River, and the Central Pacific, building east from California, met at Promontory, Utah. For the Mormons it meant the end of isolation and ox-team journeys across the plains. It also meant a better understanding of the Saints and their work, as thousands of curious visitors arrived to witness the miracle they had wrought in the desert. The picture that the cross-country traveler saw in these valleys was truly interesting. Here were scores of neat little cities, surrounded by irrigated fields, and beyond these, range lands well stocked with cattle. And on Temple Square in Salt Lake City was a great tabernacle and a partially completed temple.

Ground had been broken for the temple in 1853 and a stone quarry opened in Little Cottonwood Canyon twenty miles south of the city. Hauling the granite, however, posed a serious problem. During the early years of construction, four yoke of oxen required four days to make a round trip in hauling each of the huge foundation stones.

When the army came to Utah, the excavation was filled and the foundation covered to give the site the appearance of a newly plowed field. Construction was not resumed until the policy of the government had been determined.

The work on the temple was executed with great care. Brigham Young, in directing the construction of the temple, had said, "When the Millennium is over . . . I want that Temple still to stand as a proud monument of the faith, perseverance and industry of the Saints of God in the mountains, in the nineteenth century."[5]

Completion of the transcontinental railroad at Promontory, Utah, May 10, 1869

The Salt Lake Tabernacle as it appeared soon after construction

While the temple in Salt Lake City was under construction, similar structures were being built at St. George, 325 miles south; at Manti, 150 miles south; and at Logan, 80 miles north.

In 1863, while work was going forward on the Salt Lake Temple, construction of the Tabernacle on Temple Square was also begun. It has since become one of the most famous buildings in America.

In dimension, the Tabernacle is 250 feet long by 150 feet wide and 80 feet high. The problem of building a roof over this area was serious

133

because neither steel rods, nails, nor bolts were available. First, the forty-four buttresses of sandstone were laid up. These were to become in effect the walls of the building, with doors between. Each of these pillars is twenty feet high, three feet wide, and nine feet through. On these was constructed the huge roof, formed by building a vast bridgework of timbers in lattice fashion. These were pinned together with wooden pegs and bound with rawhide to prevent splitting. This trusswork occupies a space of ten feet from the inside plastered ceiling to the outside roofing. No interior pillar supports the roof.

As a fitting complement to this vast auditorium, Brigham Young requested a magnificent organ. The assignment was given to Joseph Ridges, an organ builder who had joined the Church in Australia. Wood for the organ was hauled by ox team three hundred miles to Salt Lake City from Pine Valley, near St. George, and was laboriously shaped by skilled artisans.

With the completion of the building and the organ in 1870, a choir was organized. This was the beginning of the famed Tabernacle Choir, which has become known throughout the world for its weekly broadcasts from Temple Square and through its concerts in many nations.

The Death of Brigham Young

In 1875 the President of the United States, Ulysses S. Grant, visited Utah. On his arrival in Salt Lake City he was driven through streets thronged with people. He had accepted as true the falsehoods that were still circulated in the East concerning the Mormons, and while passing long lines of rosy-cheeked children who were waving and cheering, he turned to the governor, who was his host, and asked whose children they were. "Mormon children," the governor replied. To this the President remarked, "I have been deceived."[6]

Brigham Young by this time was a man seventy-four years of age. He was in good health, but the trial of the years was telling on him. Life had been a constant struggle from the time he had joined the Church in 1833. In summing up the results of that struggle, he wrote an article for the editor of a New York paper in response to a request for a summary of his labors:

"I thank you for the privilege of representing facts as they are; I will furnish them gladly at any time you make the request.

* * *

"The result of my labors for the past 26 years, briefly summed up, are: The peopling of this Territory by the Latter-day Saints of about 100,000 souls; the founding of over 200 cities, towns and villages inhabited by our people, . . . and the establishment of schools, factories, mills and other institutions calculated to improve and benefit our communities.

* * *

"My whole life is devoted to the Almighty's service, and while I regret that my mission is not better understood by the world, the time will come when I will be understood, and I leave to futurity the judgment of my labors and their result as they shall become manifest."[7]

The end of his labors came on August 29, 1877. A few days earlier he had fallen seriously ill. His last words as he lay dying were a call to the man he had succeeded — "Joseph . . . Joseph . . . Joseph. . . ."[8]

13 YEARS OF ENDURANCE

THE history of the Mormon Church is so inextricably interwoven with the doctrine of polygamy that no history of the Church can be complete without some discussion of the practice.

The doctrine was first announced by Joseph Smith at Nauvoo in 1842. Many of the men close to him knew of it and accepted it as a principle of divine pronouncement. However, it was not until 1852 that it was publicly taught. It should be said at the outset that the practice among the Mormons was radically different from that of oriental peoples. Each wife, with her children, occupied a separate house, or, if the wives lived in the same house, as was sometimes the case, in separate quarters. No distinction was made between either of the wives or the children. The husband provided for each family, was responsible for the education of the children, and gave both the children and their mothers the same advantages he would have given to his family under a monogamous relationship. If it was thought he could not do this, he was not permitted to enter into plural marriage.

While the practice was extremely limited — only a small minority of the families were involved — it was the kind of thing of which enemies of the Church could easily take advantage.

Reaction against the doctrine developed throughout the country, and it entered into the presidential campaign of 1860. When Lincoln was asked what he proposed to do about the Mormons, he replied, "Let them alone."[1] In 1862 Congress passed an anti-polygamy law, but it was aimed at plural marriages and not polygamous relations. Ten years later the Congress passed a bill prohibiting polygamy. It was considered unconstitutional by many people in the nation, and generally by the Mormons. A test case was brought into the courts of Utah and carried through the Supreme Court of the United States, resulting in a decision adverse to the Mormons. In the midst of this difficulty, John Taylor succeeded to the presidency of the Church. The years that followed were truly years of endurance.

"Champion of Liberty"

Elder Taylor was a native of England, where he had been a lay Methodist preacher. He emigrated to Canada about 1832, and heard Mormonism preached for the first time four years later. When he joined the Church, his bold spirit, educated mind, and ready tongue made of him an outstanding advocate of the cause. He served as a missionary in Canada, in his native England, and in France.

This man selected as his motto, "The kingdom of God or nothing."[2] He once remarked: "I do not believe in a religion that cannot have all my affections, but in a religion for which I can both live and die. I would rather have God for my friend than all other influences and powers."[3] In this spirit he defended Mormonism with such

Joseph Smith

Brigham Young

John Taylor

Wilford Woodruff

Lorenzo Snow

Joseph F. Smith

The Presidents of The Church of Jesus Christ of Latter-day Saints since its organization in 1830 to the present (1979)

Heber J. Grant

George Albert Smith

David O. McKay

Joseph Fielding Smith

Harold B. Lee

Spencer W. Kimball

vigor that his friends in the Church called him "the Champion of Liberty." He it was who was wounded when Joseph and Hyrum Smith were killed in Carthage jail.

As the senior member of the Council of Twelve Apostles, he succeeded Brigham Young as President of the Church. It was during his administration that the Mormons were again made to feel the bitter hand of persecution. In 1882 the Edmunds Act was passed by Congress, making polygamy punishable by fine or imprisonment—usually imprisonment. No man who had more than one wife could act as a juror in any Utah court. In Idaho, those who were members of the Church were disfranchised. No one who admitted belief in polygamy could become a citizen.

President Taylor foresaw these difficulties. In April, 1882, he counseled the Saints: "Let us treat it [the Edmunds Act] the same as we did this morning in coming through the snow-storm—put up our coat collars . . . and wait till the storm subsides . . . There will be a storm in the United States after awhile; and I want our brethren to prepare themselves for it. In the last conference . . . I advised all who were in debt to take advantage of the prosperous times and pay their debts; so that they might not be in bondage to anyone, and when the storm comes they might be prepared to meet it."[4]

The storm broke in full fury five years later. In 1887 the Edmunds-Tucker Act gave added power to the judges who tried polygamy cases. This act also disincorporated The Church of Jesus Christ of Latter-day Saints, which was ordered by the Supreme Court to wind up its affairs and turn its property over to the nation.

The law was administered with extreme harshness. Thousands of Mormons were disfranchised. A thousand men were imprisoned because they had plural families. Homes were broken. The election machinery was taken from the hands of the people.

Under these conditions John Taylor died on July 25, 1887. He was succeeded by Wilford Woodruff.

A Manifesto to the People

To undertake the responsibility of Church leadership under such circumstances was no small task. Colonies of Latter-day Saints were now scattered from Canada to Mexico. Active misionary work was carried on throughout the United States, in the British Isles, in most of the nations of Europe, and in the islands of the Pacific. In spite of determined opposition, however, many converts to the faith were made in all of these missions. And yet the Church in Utah was dispossessed of its property, and most of its leaders were in prison or were facing prosecution. Under these conditions Wilford Woodruff undertook the responsibility of leadership. He was eighty years of age at the time.

Fortunately, he had been well trained to take up the reins of leadership, having joined the Church only three years after its organization. He had marched from Ohio to Missouri to aid his brethren when they were driven from Jackson County, and he had passed through the Missouri persecutions. As we have previously seen, he was a powerful missionary in England, where he had brought more than two thousand converts into the Church.

He had gone west as one of the pioneer company, and Brigham Young was in his wagon when he made the prophetic statement concerning the Salt Lake Valley, "This is the right place." He had participated in most of the significant events connected with the building of the territory since that time.

But now, most progress had ceased under the heavy hand of law enforcement, and President Woodruff was responsible for finding a way out of the difficulty. As he struggled with the problem, he turned to the scriptures for direction.

In a revelation given to the Church in 1841, the Prophet Joseph Smith had declared as the word of the Lord, "Verily, verily, I say unto you, that when I give a commandment to any of the sons of men to do a work unto my name, and those sons of men go with all their might and with all they have to perform that work, and cease not their diligence, and their enemies come upon them and hinder them from performing that work, behold it behooveth me to require that work no more at the hands of those sons of men, but to accept of their offerings."[5] Another fundamental teaching of the Church which also applied is the twelfth article of faith of the organization. It reads, "We believe in being subject to kings, presidents, rulers, and magistrates, in obeying, honoring, and sustaining the law."

What was to be done under the circumstances? The practice had come by revelation.

And it came to an end by the same means. After earnest prayer before the Lord, President Woodruff issued on October 6, 1890, what is known in Church history as the "Manifesto." It declared an end to the practice of plural marriage. Since that time the Church has neither practiced nor sanctioned such marriages.

On April 6, 1893, the great temple in Salt

The Salt Lake Temple nearing completion of construction

Lake City was declared completed, and the building was dedicated to God as his holy house. Prior to its dedication, non-members of the Church were invited to go through the building, and its various facilities were explained to them. Since its dedication, only members of the Church in good standing have been permitted to enter.

It was fitting that Wilford Woodruff should have lived to offer the dedicatory prayer. Forty-six years earlier he had driven the stake to mark the location of the building. For forty years he had watched its construction. Its dedication was one of the great events in the history of the area.

143

Before his death in September 1898, President Woodruff was to participate in another significant event. Although the residents of the territory had applied for statehood in 1849, this boon had been denied because of anti-Mormon agitation throughout the nation. But on January 4, 1896, Utah was admitted to the Union as a state. In ceremonies incident to the occasion, President Woodruff was asked to offer the prayer. The prayer is indicative of the man's vision:

"Almighty God, the Creator of heaven and earth, thou who are the God of nations and the Father of the spirits of all men, we humbly bow before Thee on this great occasion. . . .

"When we gaze upon these fertile valleys with their abundant products of fields and garden, . . . their pleasant homes and prosperous inhabitants . . . and contrast these with the barren and silent wastes which greeted the eyes of the pioneers when first they looked upon these dry sage lands less than half a century ago, our souls are filled with wonder and with praise! . . .

"And now, when the efforts of several decades to secure the priceless boon of perfect political liberty . . . have at length been crowned with glorious success, we feel that to thee, our father and our God, we are indebted for this inestimable blessing. . . .

"We pray Thee to bless the president of the United States and his cabinet, that they may be inspired to conduct the affairs of this great nation in wisdom, justice and equity, that its rights may be maintained at home and abroad and that all its citizens may enjoy the privileges of free men. . . . And may the privileges of free government be extended to every land and clime, until tyranny and oppression shall be broken down to rise no more, until all nations shall unite for the common good, that war may cease, that the voice of strife may be hushed, that universal brotherhood may prevail, and Thou, O God, shall be honored everywhere as the Everlasting Father and the King of peace!"[6]

14 THE SUNSHINE OF GOOD WILL

PRESIDENT Wilford Woodruff died September 2, 1898, and at the age of 84, when most men have laid aside their life's work, Lorenzo Snow succeeded him as President of the Church. As with the men who had gone before him, early in life he had gained extensive experience in the Church, serving on missions both at home and abroad.

When he took over the leadership of the organization, the Church was in a desperate financial condition. The nation had passed through a severe economic depression, which had been felt in the West as elsewhere. Then, too, under the anti-polygamy prosecution, the payment of tithing had seriously decreased. The property of the Church had been confiscated, and much of the incentive for paying tithing had gone. The organization was under a staggering burden of debt.

Under these conditions, President Snow made a trip in the spring of 1899 to the town of St. George in southern Utah. Drought had blighted the land. The preceding winter had been the driest in thirty-five years, and the one preceding that the driest in thirty-four years. The people were discouraged, for it appeared as if a curse had come over what once had been a garden-land.

By inspiration, as President Snow said, he spoke to the assembled Saints on the law of tithing. Had not the Lord said through the prophet Malachi that Israel had robbed Him in tithes and offerings? And had He not also given them a promise that if they would bring their tithes into the storehouse He would open the

The St. George Temple

windows of heaven and pour out a blessing that they would not have room enough to receive it?

The President then went on to promise the Saints that if they would faithfully pay their tithes, they could plant their crops and rain would come. The people heeded the counsel. They paid their tithes, not only in St. George, but throughout the Church as the President continued his appeals for obedience to this commandment of God. But weeks passed in the southern colony, and still the hot winds blew and the crops wilted.

Then one morning in August a telegram was laid on the President's desk: "Rain in St. George." The creeks and rivers filled, and the crops matured.

In 1907 the last of the Church's debt was paid. Since then, the Church has been free of financial stress.

Joseph F. Smith

Lorenzo Snow died October 10, 1901. He was succeeded by Joseph F. Smith, son of Hyrum Smith, who was murdered in Carthage jail. His life reflects the history of Mormonism from a position of ignominy to one of wide respect.

He was born November 13, 1838, at Far West, Missouri. At the time, his father was a prisoner of the mob-militia, whose avowed purpose was to exterminate the Mormons. When he was an infant, his mother carried him in the flight from Far West to Illinois.

One of his earliest recollections was of that historic night of June 27, 1844, when he was five years of age. A knock was heard on his mother's window, and a trembling voice whispered that his father had been killed by the Carthage mob. As a seven-year-old boy he heard the roar of guns incident to the final expulsion of the Mormons from Nauvoo, and before reaching his eighth birthday he drove a team of oxen most of the way across Iowa.

In 1848 the family crossed the plains. It was no small task for a ten-year-old boy to yoke and unyoke oxen as well as drive most of the day. When the boy was thirteen, his mother died, her vitality exhausted by the experiences through which she had passed.

Two years later he was called on a mission to the Hawaiian Islands. Making his way to the Coast, he worked in a shingle mill to earn money to pay his way to the Islands.

Following his missionary experience in Hawaii, he served the Church in the British Isles as well as in other fields of labor. He became President of the Church in 1901.

Shortly after this, Reed Smoot, a member of the Council of the Twelve Apostles, was elected U.S. Senator from Utah. His seat was soon contested by political enemies who played on the old polygamy issue. It was Joseph F. Smith, however, rather than the senator, who became the principal target of attack. He was cartooned and slandered throughout the nation. But he had seen so much of intolerance that he passed over this new outburst, saying, "There are those . . . who will shut their eyes to every virtue and to every good thing connected with this latter day work, and will pour out floods of falsehood and misrepresentation against the people of God. I forgive them for this. I leave them in the hand of the just Judge."[1]

In spite of all such attacks, these were years of progress for the Church. Missionary work was extended. Scores of beautiful buildings were

The LDS temple in Washington, D.C.

erected, including three temples — one in Arizona, one in Canada, and one in the Hawaiian Islands. A bureau of information was established on Temple Square in Salt Lake City to greet the thousands of tourists who came from all parts of the world, usually out of curiosity. They learned the facts concerning the Mormons, and the old hatred, the old bitterness slowly gave way.

On November 19, 1918, Joseph F. Smith died. Newspapers which had slandered his character paid editorial homage to him, and prominent men throughout the nation voiced high tribute to his memory. The years had vindicated him and the cause to which he had dedicated his life.

Heber J. Grant

Four days following the death of President Smith, Heber J. Grant became President of the Church. His father, who had been a counselor to Brigham Young, had died when the boy was nine days old. He was born November 22, 1856, the first of the presidents of the Church to have been born in the West.

Heber J. Grant was by nature a practical man. He had a recognized talent in the field of finance, and as a young man he made an

The LDS Church Administration Building in Salt Lake City, Utah

enviable record in business. But at the same time he was active in Church affairs, and when only twenty-six years of age, he was ordained a member of the Council of the Twelve Apostles. From that time forward he was a zealous worker in the cause of Mormonism.

His financial abilities were shown to marked degree when, during the depression of the Nineties, he was sent east by the President of the Church to borrow money. In spite of business conditions and the popular attitude toward the Mormons, he returned with hundreds of thousands of dollars, which proved a great boon in those difficult times.

Heber J. Grant was also a leading figure in the establishment of the western beet sugar industry. The Church was interested in this because it meant a cash crop for thousands of its members. Accordingly, he materially assisted in the founding of this industry, which has put millions of dollars into the hands of western farmers.

One of President Grant's favorite projects was giving away books. The funds for this purpose he called his "cigarette money" because, he claimed, the money some of his friends wasted on cigarettes he was able to spend on books. During his lifetime he passed out more than a hundred thousand volumes at his own expense.

Unflinching in his loyalty to his church and its teachings, he was nevertheless a great friend-maker. Leaders in business, education, and government were his intimate friends, and his capacity for getting along with people greatly helped in breaking down the wall of prejudice against the Mormons.

His administration was an era of progress.

The Church passed its hundredth anniversary in 1930, commemorating the event with a great celebration. Unhampered by the oppression of religious bigots, freed from the brutality of mobs, strong enough to assert its power for good, it flourished in an era of good will previously unknown in all of its history.

George Albert Smith

President Grant died May 14, 1945, in his eighty-ninth year. He was succeeded by George Albert Smith. President Smith was born April 4, 1870. As a young man he served a mission in the southern states, and, after becoming a member of the Council of the Twelve Apostles, he presided over the affairs of the Church in Europe.

One of his major interests was Scouting. He served as a member of the National Executive Board of Boy Scouts of America and received the highest awards for local and national service to the cause of Scouting. An official citation given him by national officials stated that "to his enthusiasm for its [Scouting's] program must be largely traced the fact that Utah stands above all other states in the percentage of boys who are Scouts."[2]

For many years President Smith took a leading part in preserving the story of America's pioneers. He was the organizer and served as president of the Utah Pioneer Trails and Landmarks Association, under whose sponsorship the Mormon trail from Nauvoo to Salt Lake City was marked with stone and bronze. He likewise served as vice-president of the Oregon Trail Memorial Association, and was one of the organizers of the American Pioneer Trails Association.

David O. McKay

President Smith passed away on April 4,

The New Zealand Temple

1951, his eighty-first birthday. His funeral was held in the Salt Lake Tabernacle on April 7, and two days later, in the same building, members of the Church, "in solemn assembly," sustained David Oman McKay as president of the Church. President McKay was then seventy-seven, having been born at Huntsville, Utah, September 8, 1873.

By training he was an educator, but he devoted most of his life to the Church. He was named a member of the Council of the Twelve Apostles at the age of 32. A man of commanding appearance and dynamic personality, he won friends for the Church wherever he went on his worldwide travels in the interest of the cause to which he had given his heart.

He promoted a greatly expanded building program which created thousands of new houses of worship; temples in Switzerland, England, New Zealand, and the United States; and a dramatic expansion of the Church school system.

Joseph Fielding Smith

President McKay passed away in Salt Lake City, January 18, 1970, at the age of 96, and was succeeded five days later by Joseph Fielding Smith, President of the Council of the Twelve Apostles, of which he had been a member for sixty years. He was the son of Joseph F. Smith, the sixth president of the Church, and a grandson of Hyrum Smith, who was murdered with the Prophet Joseph in 1844.

President Joseph Fielding Smith was a lifelong student of the doctrine and history of the Church. His extensive writings on these subjects made of him a recognized authority in these fields, and for many years he served as Church Historian and Recorder, responsible for maintaining the extensive archives which have become a treasure house of information, not only on the Church and its history, but also on the cultures in which it has developed.

Harold B. Lee

President Smith died in Salt Lake City on July 2, 1972, and was succeeded by Harold B. Lee on July 7th of the same year. In 1936, when the nation and most of the world were paralyzed by a tragic economic depression, officers of the Church, building on principles laid down by Joseph Smith, inaugurated what was termed the Church Security Program, later called the Church Welfare Program. Governments were trying to stem the tide of unemployment with various make-work and dole systems. But the Church taught the principle that in times of stress, responsibility for remedying the problem lay first with the individual, then with his family, and then with the Church, rather than with his government. Elder Lee was given the major task for setting up a system under which "the curse of idleness would be done away with, the evils of a dole abolished, and independence, industry, thrift and self respect be once more established amongst our people."[3] All Church members were expected to work together to help those in distress.

Farms were acquired; processing, production, and distribution facilities were constructed; and other resources were put in motion to provide the unemployed with the opportunity to fulfill their needs and preserve their integrity. This program, which continues to expand as the Church grows, has been commended by social welfare experts from many parts of the world.

The LDS Church Office Building in Salt Lake City, Utah

Spencer W. Kimball

President Lee died in Salt Lake City, December 26, 1973. Four days later, Spencer W. Kimball was given the reins of presidency. Church membership had now passed the three million mark, and within five years, under his dynamic leadership, another million members were added to the rolls. President Kimball was born in Salt Lake City, March 28, 1895, but was reared in Arizona, where he served in many Church capacities while carrying on his private business. He was ordained an Apostle in 1943, and since that time has traveled over much of the earth building and strengthening the kingdom.

Although small of stature, he has been a veritable dynamo in fulfilling the responsibilities of president of an expanding Church. He has repeatedly called to the membership to "lengthen our stride" and "quicken our pace." New missions have been opened in many parts of the earth, and thousands of young men and women are serving in those missions, giving freely of their time and means to teach the restored gospel of Jesus Christ to the nations of the earth.

Of great significance was President Kimball's announcement of June 9, 1978, that the Lord "has heard our prayers, and by revelation has confirmed that the long-promised day has come when every faithful, worthy man in the Church may receive the holy priesthood, with power to exercise its divine authority, and enjoy with his loved ones every blessing that flows therefrom, including the blessings of the temple. Accordingly, all worthy male members of the Church may be ordained to the priesthood without regard for race or color."[4]

News of this change in a policy that had been observed for almost a century and a half was carried in news media across the world, and the response was highly favorable.

President Kimball's grandfather was Heber C. Kimball, who had first opened the work in the British Isles in 1837, and who later served as counselor to Brigham Young in the years of the movement of the Mormons from Nauvoo to the Salt Lake Valley. That pioneer era is gone. Gone are the days of forced marches, of burning homes and desecrated temples, of lonely graves on the prairie.

The Church now experiences an ever-growing measure of respect. Three items indicative of this may be mentioned.

As we have previously noted, the Latter-day Saints were driven from Missouri by an inhumane and illegal extermination order issued by Governor Boggs. On June 25, 1976, his successor-in-office, Governor Christopher S. Bond, issued another executive order which reads in part: "Whereas, Governor Boggs' order clearly contravened the rights of life, liberty, property and religious freedom as guaranteed by the Constitution of the United States, as well as the Constitution of the State of Missouri; . . .

"Now, therefore, I . . . do hereby order as follows: Expressing on behalf of all Missourians our deep regret for the injustice and undue suffering which was caused by this 1838 order, I hereby rescind Executive Order Number 44 dated October 27, 1838, issued by Governor Lilburn W. Boggs."

In 1978 an impressive memorial to the women of the Church was dedicated in Nauvoo, Illinois. It portrays in a variety of bronze figures set in a spacious park, women young and older, mothers and children who lived in Nauvoo and were compelled to leave their homes and flee to the sanctuary they established in the mountains, many of them dying on the way. On the occasion of this dedication, national and state officials and men and women of prominence from Illinois and other parts of the nation paid tribute to the Mormons who once had built a beautiful city from the swamplands they found there.

Also in 1978 the President of the United States signed a bill passed by Congress which repealed the Edmunds-Tucker Act of 1887 — the legislation that had been employed to disincorporate the Church and escheat its property in the harsh persecutions and prosecutions against the Latter-day Saints during the last decades of the nineteenth century.

It is a new era, an era of widespread respect and admiration and ever-accelerating growth. But the present also has its challenges as the work moves over the world. The Church is no longer a Utah Church or an American Church. Not alone in the United States and Canada is the work strong and growing; in other areas of the world, the rate of growth is even greater. In the British Isles and Western Europe, throughout Mexico, Central and South America, in Africa, in the ancient lands of Asia, in Australia, in New Zealand, and in the islands of the South Pacific, are found strong and developing congregations of the Saints. Once converts in the overseas missions "gathered to Zion." Now they remain in their native lands to build Zion there with the identical organization, the identical programs, and the same teachings found wherever the Church has been established.

Today, the same testimony Joseph Smith first bore to his neighbors in upper-state New York may be heard in a score of languages, declaring that God lives, that Jesus is the Christ, that His ancient gospel has been restored to the earth, and that the Church of Jesus Christ is again available to all mankind.

NOTES

Chapter 1

1. In Preston Nibley, *Joseph Smith, the Prophet* (Salt Lake City: Deseret News Press, 1946), pp. 21-22.

2. Joseph Smith-History 1:11-19 (formerly Joseph Smith 2:11-19).

3. Joseph Smith-History 1:24-25.

Chapter 2

1. Joseph Smith-History 1:28-50.

2. Oliver Cowdery's account of the experience as found in a letter from Cowdery to W. W. Phelps dated 28 May 1835. (See *Cowdery's Letters on the Bringing in of the New Dispensation* [Burlington, Wis.: Free Press Print, 1899], pp. 26-27.) The letter was first published in 1854.

3. Joseph Smith-History 1:54, 59.

4. Joseph Smith-History 1:65.

5. John 10:16.

Chapter 3

1. See D&C 13.

2. See Matthew 3:13-15.

3. See D&C 128:20.

4. 2 Nephi 27:12.

5. In Joseph Smith, *History of The Church of Jesus Christ*

of Latter-day Saints, 7 vols., 2nd ed. rev., edited by B. H. Roberts (Salt Lake City: The Church of Jesus Christ of Latter-day Saints, 1932-51), 1:55. Hereafter cited as HC.

6. Moroni 10:5.

Chapter 4

1. D&C 21:1.

2. In B. H. Roberts, *A Comprehensive History of The Church of Jesus Christ of Latter-day Saints, Century One,* 6 vols. (Salt Lake City: The Church of Jesus Christ of Latter-day Saints, 1930), 2:470. Hereafter cited as CHC.

3. *Autobiography of Parley P. Pratt,* ed. Parley P. Pratt, Jr. (Salt Lake City: Deseret Book, 1938), p. 48.

4. *Autobiography of Parley P. Pratt,* p. 52.

5. CHC 1:255.

Chapter 5

1. D&C 76:22-24.

2. John 14:2.

3. 1 Corinthians 15:40-42.

4. D&C 87:2-3.

5. D&C 88:118.

6. D&C 93:36.

7. D&C 130:18-19.

8. In Lucy Mack Smith, *History of Joseph Smith,* ed. Preston Nibley, reprint (Salt Lake City: Bookcraft, 1954), p. 230.

9. *History of Joseph Smith,* pp. 231-32.

10. "Kirtland Temple (Mormon)," *Architecture Forum* 64 (March 1936):179.

11. D&C 110:1-4.

Chapter 6

1. CHC 1:311-12.

2. See HC 1:372.

3. See HC 1:374.

4. D&C 119.

5. HC 3:157.

6. HC 3:175.

7. HC 3:190-91.

Chapter 7

1. HC 3:375.

2. In Matthias F. Cowley, *Wilford Woodruff* (Salt Lake City: Bookcraft, 1964), pp. 104-5.

3. CHC 2:45.

4. HC 4:457.

5. HC 4:80.

6. John 3:5.

7. 1 Corinthians 15:29.

8. In George Q. Cannon, *Life of Joseph Smith the Prophet* (Salt Lake City: Deseret Book, 1964), pp. 354-55.

9. *The Mormons* (Philadelphia: King and Baird, 1850), pp. 3-4.

10. In Cannon, *Life of Joseph Smith the Prophet,* p. 353.

11. *Figures of the Past from the Leaves of Old Journals* (Boston: Roberts Brothers, 1883), p. 376.

Chapter 8

1. Dallin H. Oaks, "The Suppression of the *Nauvoo Expositor,*" *Utah Law Review* 9(1965): 875.

2. HC 6:448.

3. *Utah Law Review* 9(1965):903.

4. HC 6:537.

5. HC 6:540.

6. HC 6:546.

7. HC 6:549-50.

8. HC 6:554.

9. D&C 135:4.

10. See HC 6:570.

11. HC 6:605.

12. See HC 6:612-21.

13. HC 5:85.

Chapter 9

1. In Edward W. Tullidge, *The Women of Mormondom* (New York: Tullidge and Crandall, 1877), pp. 307-8.

2. CHC 3:52.

3. Journal History, 13 and 18 July 1846.

4. CHC 3:119-20.

5. *The Mormons,* pp. 9-10.

Chapter 10

1. D&C 136:1-4, 19-21, 23-30.

2. *Millennial Star* 12(15 Mar. 1850):82-83.

3. *Millennial Star* 12(15 Mar. 1850):146.

Chapter 11

1. See Journal History, 25 July 1847.

2. Diary of Wilford Woodruff, 28 July 1847.

3. CHC 3:319.

4. CHC 3:362.

5. In Preston Nibley, *Brigham Young: the Man and His Work* (Salt Lake City: Deseret News Press, 1936), pp. 127-28.

6. CHC 3:349-50.

7. *Mormon Settlement in Arizona* (Phoenix: James H. McClintock, 1921), pp. 4-6.

8. Ibid., p. 6.

Chapter 12

1. CHC 4:51.

2. *History of Brigham Young 1847-1867* (Berkeley, Cal.: MassCal Associates, 1964), pp. 159-60.

3. *An Overland Journey* (New York: Alfred A. Knopf, 1963), pp. 183-84.

4. *Deseret News,* 23 Oct. 1861, p. 189.

5. *Journal of Discourses,* 26 vols. (London: Latter-day Saints' Book Depot, 1854-86), 10:254.

6. CHC 5:504-5.

7. In Preston Nibley, *Brigham Young: the Man and His Work,* p. 492.

8. See Susa Young Gates and Leah D. Widtsoe, *The Life Story of Brigham Young* (New York: the Macmillan Company, 1930), p. 362.

Chapter 13

1. CHC 5:70.

2. See *Journal of Discourses* 6:18-27. The phrase was first used by Brigham Young in a letter to a Colonel Alexander, dated 16 October 1857. The text of the letter can be found in *The Millennial Star* 20 (30 Jan. 1858):75-76.

3. In B. H. Roberts, *The Life of John Taylor* (Salt Lake City: George Q. Cannon and Sons, 1892), p. 423.

4. Ibid., pp. 360-61.

5. D&C 124:49.

6. *The Salt Lake Herald,* 7 Jan. 1896, p. 1.

Chapter 14

1. In Joseph Fielding Smith, *Life of Joseph F. Smith,*

2nd ed. (Salt Lake City: Deseret Book, 1969), p. 351.

2. In Preston Nibley, *The Presidents of the Church* (Salt Lake City: Deseret Book, 1941), p. 366.

3. Message of the First Presidency, in Conference Report, Oct. 1936, p. 3.

4. In *Ensign,* July 1978, p. 75.

GOSPEL PRINCIPLES

Published by
The Church of Jesus Christ of Latter-day Saints
Salt Lake City, Utah 1978
Revised 1979

©1978 Corporation of the President, The Church
of Jesus Christ of Latter-day Saints

First printed in Missionary Reference Set edition, September 1988

ISBN 0-87579-169-7

All rights reserved

Printed in the United States of America

CONTENTS

MUSIC

Hymns

(The hymns are listed by suggested use, but many of them could be used for more than one purpose. For instance, most of the opening and closing hymns could be used for either purpose. Musical accompaniments for all of these hymns and songs are recorded on *Music for Worship Services* cassettes [VVOT052A] available through the Church distribution centers.)

INTRODUCTION

Our Savior Jesus Christ said that before his second coming "this gospel of the kingdom shall be preached in all the world for a witness unto all nations" (Matthew 24:14). One of his last instructions to his original apostles was: "Go ye . . . and teach all nations, baptizing them in the name of the Father, and of the Son, and of the Holy Ghost: Teaching them to observe all things whatsoever I have commanded you. . . ." (Matthew 28:19–20). In obedience to that commandment, the work of teaching and baptizing in all nations continues.

Throughout the world, many persons are accepting the gospel. This manual has been prepared for new members of the Church. Through studying it, you can learn the basic principles of the gospel and become better prepared to live them.

PURPOSES FOR USING THE MANUAL

The manual is divided into ten units. You should carefully study the table of contents to get an overview of the subjects covered. The manual has been prepared to be used in a variety of ways. You may want to use it for any of the following reasons:

1. To build your own knowledge and testimony of the gospel.

2. To prepare lessons for family home evening.

3. To prepare lessons for Church meetings.

4. To prepare talks.

5. To answer questions about the gospel.

6. To help you study those scriptures which deal with a certain topic.

HOW TO STUDY THE MANUAL

Before you begin to study the principles of the gospel in depth, you may want to read the manual from beginning to end without looking up references or answering questions. This will give you a clear idea of how all of the parts of our Heavenly Father's plan fit together. As you study, if you should forget the meaning of a new term, you may want to look up its definition in the glossary at the end of the manual.

You may want to prepare to present family home evening lessons or talks on certain principles or study the gospel for yourself in more depth. If copies of the standard works are available, you will want to look up the references as you come to them in each chapter. These scriptural references will deepen your understanding of the gospel and draw you nearer to the Lord. A list of additional scriptures at the end of each chapter gives you further information.

Whether you use the manual alone or for teaching a class, you may want to stop when you come to the questions at the end of each section. Ask yourself or the class members to answer the questions before going on to the next section. The manual also has many pictures. If you are teaching a class, you may want to display these pictures as you come to the part of the lesson that tells about them.

The hymns may be learned, taught, and sung by members of the family and in meetings where sacred music is appropriate. Hymns may be sung to open or to close meetings or as a special presentation during the lesson.

If you will study this manual diligently and pray with faith, the Holy Ghost will open your minds and bless you with inspiration so that you can understand. He will bless you with a testimony of the gospel of Jesus Christ (see Moroni 10:4–5).

2

OUR FATHER IN HEAVEN

THERE IS A GOD

Alma, a Book of Mormon prophet wrote: "All things denote there is a God; yea, even the earth, and all things that are upon the face of it, yea, and its motion, yea, and also all the planets which move in their regular form do witness that there is a Supreme Creator" (Alma 30:44). We can look up at the sky at night and have an idea of what Alma meant. There are millions of stars and planets all in perfect order! They did not get there by chance. We can see the work of God in the heavens and on the earth. The many beautiful plants, the many kinds of animals, the mountains, the rivers, the clouds that bring us rain and snow—all these testify to us that there is a God!

Have someone read the first Article of Faith.
What are some of the things around us that show us there is a God?

GOD IS THE RULER OF HEAVEN AND EARTH

The prophets have taught us that God is the almighty ruler of the universe. God dwells in heaven (see D&C 20:17). Through his Son, Jesus Christ, he created heaven and earth and all things that are in them (see Moses 2:1). He made the moon, the stars, and the sun. He organized this world, gave it form, motion, and life. He filled the air and the water with living things. He covered the hills and plains with all kinds of animal life. He gave us day and night, summer and winter, seedtime and harvest. He made man in his own image to be a ruler over his other creations (see Genesis 1:26-27).

Read Mosiah 4:9.
What things did God create?

God is the one supreme and absolute being in whom we believe and whom we worship. He is the Creator, Ruler, and Preserver of all things. (See John A. Widtsoe, ed., *Discourses of Brigham Young*, p. 18–23.)

WHAT KIND OF BEING IS GOD?

The Prophet Joseph Smith said: "If the veil were rent today, and the great God who holds this world in its orbit, and who upholds all worlds and all things by his power, was to make himself visible—I say, if you were to see him today, you would see him like a man in form . . ." (*Teachings of the Prophet Joseph Smith*, p. 345). God is a glorified and perfected man, a personage of flesh and bones. Inside his tangible body is an eternal spirit (see D&C 130:22).

God is perfect. He is a God of love, mercy, charity, truth, power, faith, knowledge, and judgment. He has all power. He knows all things. He is full of goodness.

All good things come from God. Everything that he does is to help his children become like him—a god. He has said, ". . . Behold, this is my work and my glory—to bring to pass the immortality and eternal life of man" (Moses 1:39).

Assign scriptural references: Abraham 3:18–19; John 3:16; Mormon 9:9; 2 Nephi 9:17; Alma 26:35; D&C 109:77; D&C 130:22.
Ask each person to read a scripture verse aloud and tell one fact that helps us know our Heavenly Father.

WHY SHOULD WE TRY TO KNOW GOD?

Knowing God is so important that the Savior said: "This is life eternal, that they might know thee the only true God, and Jesus Christ, whom thou hast sent" (John 17:3).

The first and greatest commandment tells us: "Thou shalt love the Lord thy God with all thy heart . . ." (Matthew 22:37).

The more we know God, the more we love him. If we love him we will keep his commandments. By keeping his commandments we can become like him. (See 1 John 2:3.)

Why is it important to know God?

HOW CAN WE KNOW GOD?

We can know and understand God if we will do the following:

Believe in God. Believe that he exists and that he loves us. (Mosiah 4:9.)

Study the scriptures (see 2 Timothy 3:14–17).

Pray to God (see James 1:5).

Live all God's commandments as best we can (see John 14:21–23).

As we do all of these things, we will come to know God and we will eventually have eternal life.

What are some of the ways we can come to know God?
How can each of us do these things in our lives?
Sing "I Know My Father Lives" or "O My Father."

ADDITIONAL SCRIPTURES
Acts 7:55-56 (Son at right hand of Father)
D&C 88:41-44 (qualities of God)
Psalms 24:1 (earth is the Lord's)
Moses 1:30-39 (creation)
Alma 7:20 (God cannot do wrong)
Joseph Smith 2:17 (Father and Son separate)
Alma 5:40 (good comes from God)
John 14:6-7 (Son and Father alike)
Mormon 9:15-20 (God of miracles)
Abraham 3:19 (Lord most intelligent)
1 John 2:3 (obey to know God)

OUR HEAVENLY FAMILY

WE ARE CHILDREN OF OUR HEAVENLY FATHER .

God is not only our ruler and our creator; he is also our Heavenly Father. "All men and women are . . . literally the sons and daughters of Diety. . . . Man, as a spirit, was begotten and born of heavenly parents, and reared to maturity in the eternal mansions of the Father, prior to coming upon the earth in a temporal [physical] body" (Joseph F. Smith, "The Origin of Man," *Improvement Era,* Nov. 1909, pp. 78, 80).

Every person who was ever born on earth was our spirit brother or sister in heaven. The first spirit born to our heavenly parents was Jesus Christ (see D&C 93:21). He is thus our elder brother (see *Discourses of Brigham Young,* p. 26). Our spirits resemble our heavenly parents although they have resurrected bodies. We have inherited the potential to develop their divine qualities. If we choose to do so, we can become perfect, just as they are.

Who is the father of our spirits?
Where did we live before we were born on earth?
What is our relationship to God, and to each other? Read Hebrews 12:9.
Who was the first spirit born to our heavenly parents?
How are we like our heavenly parents?

WE DEVELOPED OUR PERSONALITIES AND TALENTS WHILE WE LIVED IN HEAVEN

The scriptures teach us that all of our prophets prepared themselves to become leaders on earth while they were still spirits in heaven (see Alma 13:1–3). God foreordained (chose) them to be his leaders on earth before they were

Our Father provided us a heavenly home more glorious and beautiful than any place on earth.

born into mortal bodies. Jesus, Adam, and Abraham were some of these leaders. (See Abraham 3:22–23.) Joseph Smith taught that everyone who has a calling to lead people on earth in the Church was foreordained to do so (see *Teachings of the Prophet Joseph Smith*, p. 365). However, everyone is free on earth to accept or reject his calling.

We were not all alike in heaven. We were given different talents and abilities, and we were called to do different things on earth. (See *Discourses of Brigham Young*, p. 51.) We can learn more about our talents and callings when we receive our patriarchal blessings (see Harold B. Lee, *Stand Ye in Holy Places*, p. 117). Our Father in Heaven remembers who we were and what we did before we came here even though we have forgotten (see *Discourses of Brigham Young*, p. 50). He has chosen the time and the place for each of us to be born so that we can learn the lessons that we personally need. Thus, we can do the most good with our individual talents and personalities. However, he will never force us to do anything. We must learn to obey him because we want to, or we will lose our opportunities to be what we could have been.

What was our pre-earth life like?

OUR HEAVENLY PARENTS DESIRED TO SHARE THEIR JOY WITH US

Our heavenly parents provided us with a celestial home more glorious and beautiful than any place on earth. We were happy there. Yet they knew that we could not progress beyond a certain point unless we left them for a time. They wanted us to develop every godlike quality that they have. To do this, we needed to leave our celestial home to be tested and to gain experience. We needed to choose good over evil. Our spirits needed to be clothed with a physical body. We would need to leave our physical bodies at death and reunite with them in the resurrection. Then we would receive immortal bodies like those of our heavenly parents. If we passed all our tests, we could receive the fulness of joy that our heavenly parents have received. (D&C 93:33.)

How does earth life help to prepare us to become like our heavenly parents?

OUR HEAVENLY FATHER PRESENTED A PLAN FOR US TO BECOME LIKE HIM

Since we could not progress further in heaven, our Heavenly Father called a Grand Council (see *Teachings of the Prophet Joseph Smith,* pp. 348, 349, 365) to present us his plan for our progression. We learned that if we followed his plan, we would become like him. We would have a resurrected body; we would have all power in heaven and on earth; we would become heavenly parents and have spirit children just as he does. (D&C 132:19–20.)

We learned that he would provide an earth for us where we would be tested. (Abraham 3:24–26.) A veil would cover our memories, and we would forget our heavenly home. This would be necessary so that we could choose good or evil because of our natural desire for good or evil. We would not be influenced by the memory of living with our Heavenly Father. Thus we could obey him because of our faith in him, not because of our knowledge, or memory of him. He would help us recognize the truth when we heard it again on earth (see John 18:37).

At the Grand Council we also learned the purpose for our progression. We learned that we might have a fulness of joy. However, we also learned that not all of our Father's children would want to receive a fulness of joy. Some of us would be deceived, choose other paths, and lose our way. We learned that all of us would have trials in our lives: sickness, disappointment, pain, sorrow, and death. But we understood that these would be given to us for our experience and our good (see D&C 122:7). If we allowed them to, these trials would purify us rather than defeat us. They would teach us to have endurance, patience, and charity (see Spencer W. Kimball, *Tragedy or Destiny?* p. 4).

At this council we also learned that because of our weakness, all of us would sin. We learned that a Savior would be provided for us so that we could overcome our sins and overcome death with resurrection. We learned that if we obeyed his word and followed his example we would be exalted and become like our heavenly parents. We would receive a fulness of joy.

What plan did our Heavenly Father present to us?
What did we learn would happen to us on earth?
Why would our Father in Heaven permit us to experience suffering and death on earth?
Sing "I Am a Child of God," "O My Father."

ADDITIONAL SCRIPTURES
Hebrews 12:9 (God the father of spirits)
Job 38:4-7 (premortal life implied)
Abraham 3:22-28 (vision of premortal life)
Jeremiah 1:5 (vision of premortal life)
D&C 29:31-38 (vision of premortal life)
Moses 3:4-7 (spiritual then temporal creations)
1 Corinthians 15:44 (spiritual and temporal creations)
D&C 76:23-24 (begotten sons and daughters)
D&C 132:11-26 (plan for progression)

In our heavenly home, we walked and talked with our spirit brothers and sisters.

JESUS CHRIST, OUR CHOSEN LEADER AND SAVIOR

When the plan for our salvation was presented to us in the spirit world, we were so happy that we shouted for joy (see Job 38:7).

A SAVIOR AND LEADER WAS NEEDED

We understood that we would have to leave our heavenly home for a time. We would not live in the presence of our heavenly parents. While we were away from them, all of us would sin and some of us would lose our way. Our Heavenly Father knew and loved each one of us. He knew that we would need help, so he planned a way to help us.

We needed a Savior to pay for our sins and to teach us how to return to our Heavenly Father. Our Father said, "Whom shall I send?" (Abraham 3:27). Two of our brothers offered to help. Our oldest brother, Jesus Christ, who was then called Jehovah, said, "Here am I, send me" (Abraham 3:27).

Jesus was willing to come to the earth, to give his life for us, and to take upon himself our sins. He, like our Heavenly Father, wanted us to choose whether we would obey Heavenly Father's commandments. He knew that we must be free to choose in order to prove ourselves worthy of exaltation. Jesus said: "Father, thy will be done, and the glory be thine forever" (Moses 4:2). Satan, who was called Lucifer, also came, saying: "Behold, here am I, send me, I will be thy son, and I will redeem all mankind, that one soul shall not be lost, and surely I will do it; wherefore give me thine honor" (Moses 4:1).

Jehovah, the firstborn of our Heavenly Father's spirit children, created the earth under Heavenly Father's direction.

Satan wanted to force us all to do his will. Under his plan, we would not be allowed to choose. He would take away from us the freedom of choice that our Father had given to us. Satan wanted to have all the honor for our salvation. He wanted to be our God.

Who is our leader and savior?
Who besides Jesus wanted to be our leader?

JESUS CHRIST BECAME OUR CHOSEN LEADER AND SAVIOR

After hearing both sons speak, our Heavenly Father said, "I will send the first" (Abraham 3:27).

Jesus Christ was chosen and ordained to be our savior. Many scriptures tell about this. One scripture tells us that the Lord Jesus Christ said to the brother of Jared, a Book of Mormon prophet: "Behold, I am he who was prepared from the foundation of the world to redeem my people. Behold, I am Jesus Christ. . . . In me shall all mankind have light, and that eternally, even they who shall believe on my name" (Ether 3:14).

When Jesus lived on the earth he said to his followers, "I came down from heaven, not to do mine own will, but the will of him that sent me. . . . And this is the will of him that sent me, that everyone which seeth the Son, and believeth on him, may have everlasting life: and I will raise him up at the last day" (John 6:38, 40).

Have each person tell something that he knows about Jesus.

THE WAR IN HEAVEN

Because our Heavenly Father chose Jesus Christ to be our Savior, Satan became angry and rebelled. There was war in heaven. Satan and his followers fought against Jesus and his followers.

In this great rebellion, Satan and all the spirits that followed him were sent away from the presence of God. One third of the spirits in heaven followed Satan. They were cast down from heaven. Satan and those who followed him were punished. They were denied the right to receive mortal bodies.

We are here on the earth and have mortal bodies of flesh and bone. Because we are here on earth and have mortal bodies, we know that we chose to follow Jesus Christ and our Heavenly Father. Satan and his followers are also on the earth, but as spirits. They have not forgotten who we are and that we fought against them. They are around us daily tempting us and enticing us to do things that are not pleasing to our Heavenly Father. In our pre-earth life, we chose the right. We must continue to choose the right here on earth. It is only by following Jesus that we can return to our heavenly home.

How do we know that we chose to follow Jesus?

WE HAVE THE SAVIOR'S TEACHINGS TO FOLLOW

From the beginning, Jesus Christ has revealed the gospel, which tells us what we must do to return to our Heavenly Father. At the appointed time, he came to earth himself. He taught us the plan of salvation and exaltation by his word and by the way he lived. He established his Church and his priesthood on the earth. His teachings are written in the scriptures. He took our sins upon himself. If we follow his teachings, we can return to live with him and our heavenly parents in the celestial kingdom. He was chosen to be our savior when we all attended the great council with our heavenly parents. He became our savior and has done his part to help us return to our heavenly home. It is now up to each of us to do our part and to prove ourselves worthy of exaltation.

What are some of the things we must do to follow Jesus?
Bear testimony of the Savior.
Sing "I Stand All Amazed."

ADDITIONAL SCRIPTURES
Moses 4:1-4 (Council in Heaven)
Abraham 3:22-28 (Council in Heaven)
Doctrine & Covenants 76:24-29 (war in heaven)
Revelation 12:7-9 (war in heaven)
Isaiah 14:12-15 (why Lucifer was cast out)
2 Nephi 9:6-26; 3 Nephi 27:13-20 (purpose of the Atonement)

FREEDOM TO CHOOSE

"Thou mayest choose for thyself, for it is given unto thee" (Moses 3:17).

God has told us through his prophets that we are free to choose between good and evil. We may choose liberty and eternal life by following Jesus Christ. We are also free to choose captivity and death by following Satan. (See 2 Nephi 2:27). The right to choose between good and evil is called *agency.*

Sing "Do What Is Right" or "Dare to Do Right."

AGENCY IS AN ETERNAL PRINCIPLE

Agency is an eternal principle. In the pre-earth life, we were free agents. That means that we had power to act for ourselves (see D&C 93:29-30). One purpose of our earth life is to show what choices we will make (see 2 Nephi 2:15-16). If we were forced to choose the right, we would not be able to show what we would choose for ourselves. Also, we are happier doing things when we have made our own choice. Even unpleasant tasks seem easier if we are persuaded rather than forced to do them.

Agency may have been one of the first issues to arise in the premortal council in heaven. It was one of the main causes of the conflict between the followers of Christ and the followers of Satan. Satan said that he would bring all of us back to our Father's presence, but he would have taken away our agency. When his offer was rejected, he rebelled and was cast out of heaven with his followers (see D&C 29:36–37).

Ask the members to compare and discuss the feelings the words force *and* choice *call to mind.*

AGENCY IS A NECESSARY PART OF THE PLAN OF SALVATION

Agency makes our life on earth a period of testing to see whether we are worthy to become like our Heavenly Father. When planning the creation of man in his mortal state, God said, "We will prove [test] them herewith, to see if they will do all things whatsoever the Lord their God shall command them" (Abraham 3:25). Without the gift of agency, we would have been unable to show our Heavenly Father whether we would do all that he commanded us. Because we are able to choose, we are responsible for our actions (see Helaman 14:30–31).

When we choose to live according to God's plan for us, our agency is strengthened. Right choices increase our power to make more right choices.

As we obey each of our Father's commandments, we become free to learn and obey other commandments. We grow in wisdom and in strength of character. Our faith increases. We find it easier to make right choices (see D&C 50:24).

We began to make choices as spirit children in our Heavenly Father's presence. Our choices there made us worthy to come to earth. Our Heavenly Father wants us to grow in faith, power, knowledge, wisdom, and all other good things. If we keep his commandments and make right choices, we will learn and understand. We will become like him. (See D&C 93:28.)

Read Moses 3:17 and Joshua 24:14–15.
What choices have you made this week?
Did these choices bring you closer to the Lord?
Why is agency necessary?
Read 2 Nephi 28:30.
How does making right choices help us make more right choices?

Chapter 4

AGENCY REQUIRES THAT THERE BE A CHOICE

We cannot choose unless the opposites of good and evil are placed before us. Lehi, a great Book of Mormon prophet, told his son that in order to bring about the eternal purposes of God there must be "an opposition in all things. If not so, . . . righteousness could not be brought to pass, neither wickedness, neither holiness nor misery, neither good or bad" (2 Nephi 2:11).

God allows Satan to oppose the good. God said of Satan: "I caused that he should be cast down. And he became Satan, yea, even the devil, the father of all lies, to deceive and to blind men, and to lead them captive at his will, even as many as would not hearken unto my voice" (Moses 4:3–4).

Satan continues to oppose God. He does all that he can to destroy God's work. He seeks "the misery of all mankind . . . for he seeketh that all men might be miserable like unto himself" (2 Nephi 2:18, 27). He does not love us. He does not want any good thing for us. He does not want us to be happy. He wants to make us his slaves. He uses many disguises to lead us captive.

When we follow the temptations of Satan we limit our choices. The following example shows this. Imagine seeing a sign on the seashore that reads: "Danger—whirlpool. No swimming allowed here." We might think that that is a restriction. But is it? We still have many choices. We are free to swim somewhere else. We are free to walk along the beach and pick up seashells. We are free to watch the sunset. We are free to go home. We are also free to ignore the sign and swim in the dangerous spot. But once the whirlpool has us in its grasp and we are pulled under, we have very few choices. We can try to escape, or we can call for help, but we may drown.

We must understand that even though we are free to choose our course of action, we are not free to choose the consequences of our actions. The consequences, whether good or bad, follow as a natural result of any choice we make (see

20

Revelation 22:12). If we touch a hot flame, for example, we are burned.

Heavenly Father has told us how to escape the captivity of Satan. We must watch and pray always, asking God to help us withstand the temptations of Satan (see 3 Nephi 18:15). Our Heavenly Father will not allow us to be tempted beyond our power to resist (see 1 Corinthians 10:13).

God's commandments direct us away from danger and toward eternal life. By choosing wisely, we will gain exaltation, progress eternally, and enjoy perfect happiness (see 2 Nephi 2:27-28).

Place a treat within the reach of some person. Loosely wrap a cord around him, binding his arms to his body. Ask him if he can reach the treat. Tighten the cord so that the person is bound. Explain that sin and ignorance also interfere with agency and prevent us from receiving blessings from God. Point out that repentance and righteous living free us from the bondage of sin.

List several things and have the class members tell the opposite, such as the following: black _____, up _____, hot _____, love _____, fear _____.

Why is opposition necessary? (See 2 Nephi 2:15-16.)

Read 2 Nephi 2:28.

How can you choose eternal life?

ADDITIONAL SCRIPTURES
Moses 7:32 (freedom of choice)
D&C 29:36-37 (agency in pre-existence)
Abraham 3:24-25 (earth life—a test)
Moroni 7:5-6 (works judged)
2 Nephi 2:11-16 (opposition is necessary)
Moroni 7:12-17 (choosing good and evil)
2 Peter 2:19; John 8:34 (sin is bondage)
Revelation 22:12; 2 Nephi 2:28-29; Alma 40:12-13 (reward according to works)

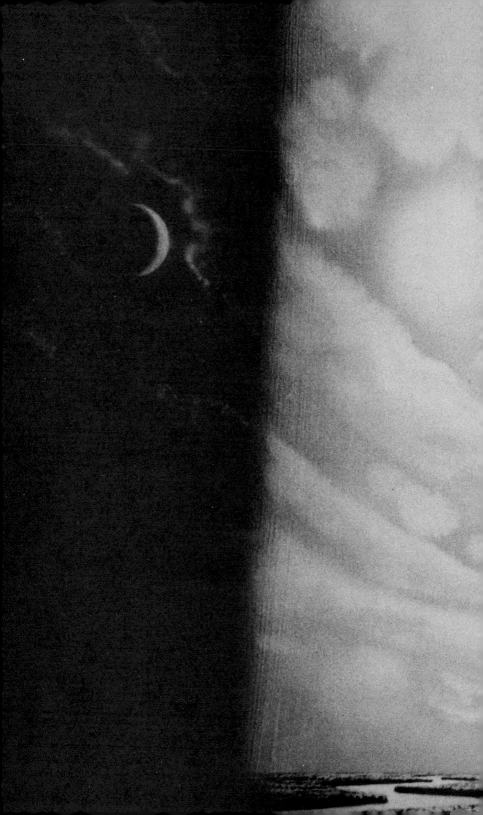

Chapter 5

THE CREATION

When we lived as spirit children with our heavenly parents, our Heavenly Father told us about his plan for us to become more like him. We shouted for joy when we heard his plan. We were eager for new experiences. In order for these things to happen, we needed to leave his presence and receive mortal bodies. We needed another place to live where we could prepare to become like him. Our new home was called *earth.*

WHO CREATED THE EARTH FOR US?

Jesus Christ created this world and everything in it. He also created many other worlds. He did so through the power of the priesthood, under the direction of our Heavenly Father. God the Father said, ". . . Worlds without number have I created; . . . and by the Son I created them, which is mine Only Begotten" (Moses 1:33). We have other testimonies of this truth. Joseph Smith and Sidney Rigdon saw Jesus Christ in a vision. They testified that "by him, and through him, and of him, the worlds are and were created, and the inhabitants thereof are begotten sons and daughters unto God" (D&C 76:24).

Who created our earth?
Read together Hebrews 1:1–2 and Moses 1:33.

CARRYING OUT THE CREATION

The earth and everything on it were created spiritually before they were created physically (see Moses 3:5). In planning to create the physical earth, Christ said to those who were with

Jehovah divided the light from the darkness to make the day and the night. He formed the sun, moon, and stars.

23

him: "We will go down, for there is space there, . . . and we will make an earth whereon these [the spirit children of our Father in Heaven] may dwell" (Abraham 3:24).

Under the direction of the Father, Christ formed and organized the earth. He divided light from darkness to make the day and the night. He formed the sun, the moon, and the stars. He divided the waters from the dry land to make seas, rivers, and lakes. Christ made the earth beautiful and productive. He made grass, trees, flowers, and other plants of all kinds. These plants contained seeds from which new plants could grow, so that there could always be plant life on the earth. Then he created the animals—fish, cattle, insects, birds of all kinds. These animals had the ability to reproduce their own kind.

Now the earth was ready for the greatest creation of all—mankind. The spirits of men would be given bodies of flesh and bone so that they could live on this beautiful earth. "And I, God, said unto mine Only Begotten, which was with me from the beginning: Let us make man in our own image, after our likeness; and it was so" (Moses 2:26). And so the first man, Adam, and the first woman, Eve, were formed and given bodies which resembled those of our heavenly parents. ". . . In the image of God created he him; male and female created he them" (Genesis 1:27). When the Lord had finished his creations, he was pleased and knew that his work was good, and he rested for a time.

Show a food recipe and a dress pattern.
What is another word for *recipe* and *pattern*? (*Plan.*)
Read Abraham 3:24 to show that God also plans for all of his creations.

THE CREATIONS SHOW GOD'S LOVE

We are now living in this marvelous and beautiful world. Think of the sun, which gives us warmth and light. Think of the rain, which makes plants grow and which makes the world feel clean and fresh. Think of how good it is to hear a bird singing or a friend laughing. Think of how wonderful our own bodies are—how we can work and play and rest. When we consider all of these creations, we begin to understand

Jehovah planted a beautiful garden on the earth, called "the Garden of Eden."

what wise, powerful, and loving beings Jesus Christ and our Heavenly Father are. They have shown great love for us by providing for all of our needs.

Plant life and animal life were also made to give us joy. The Lord said, "Yea all things which come of the earth, in the season thereof, are made for the benefit and the use of man, both to please the eye and to gladden the heart; Yea, for food and for raiment, for taste and for smell, to strengthen the body and to enliven the soul" (D&C 59:18-19). Even though God's creations are many, he knows and loves them all. He said, ". . . All things are numbered unto me, for they are mine and I know them" (Moses 1:35).

Discuss how we can show reverence for plants and animals.
Discuss the purpose, mentioned in D&C 59:18-19, of God's creations.
How do God's creations show that he loves us?
To help develop an appreciation for the beauty of God's creations, you might wish to do the following for home evenings: plan a picnic, plant a garden, take a nature walk, enjoy a sunrise or sunset.
Sing "I Thank Thee, Dear Father."

ADDITIONAL SCRIPTURES
Genesis 1-2:7; Abraham 3:22-23 and chapters 4-5; Moses 1:27-42 and chapters 2-3 (accounts of the creation)
Hebrews 1:1-3; Colossians 1:13-17; D&C 38:1-3 (Jesus the creator)
D&C 59:18-20; Moses 2:26-31; D&C 104:13-17; Matthew 6:25-26 (creation shows God's love)

Jehovah placed animals upon the earth and fish in the seas.

Chapter 6

THE FALL OF
ADAM AND EVE

ADAM AND EVE WERE THE FIRST TO COME TO EARTH

God prepared this beautiful earth with all its plant and animal life as a home for man. Adam and Eve were chosen to be the first people to live on the earth (see Moses 1:34). Their part in the Father's plan was to bring mortality into the world. They were to be the first parents (D&C 107:54–56).

Read D&C 107:54–56.
Who was Adam?
What was he chosen to do?

ADAM AND EVE WERE VALIANT SPIRITS

Adam and Eve were among our Father's noblest children. In the spirit world Adam was called Michael the Archangel (see D&C 27:11; Jude 9). He was chosen by our Heavenly Father to lead the righteous in the battle against Satan (see Revelation 12:7–9). Adam and Eve were foreordained to become the parents of the human race. The Lord promised Adam great blessings: "I have set thee to be at the head; a multitude of nations shall come of thee, and thou art a prince over them forever" (D&C 107:55).

Although the scriptures do not tell us anything about Eve before she came to this earth, she must have been a choice daughter of God. She was called Eve because she was the mother of all living (see Moses 4:26). She was given to Adam because God said "that it was not good that man should be alone" (Moses 3:18). She shared Adam's responsibility and will also share his eternal blessings.

Adam and Eve were cast out of the Garden of Eden.

Read Revelation 12:7-9.
How did Adam (Michael) prove that he was a valiant spirit?
Why was Eve given to Adam?

THE GARDEN OF EDEN

When Adam and Eve were placed in the Garden of Eden they were not yet mortal. They were not able to have children. There was no death. They had *physical* life because their spirits were housed in physical bodies made from the dust of the earth (see Abraham 5:7). They had *spiritual* life because they were in the presence of God (see Bruce R. McConkie, *Mormon Doctrine,* p. 268). They had not yet made a choice between good and evil.

God commanded them to have children and to learn to control the earth. He said, "Be fruitful, and multiply, and replenish the earth, and subdue it, and have dominion over . . . every living thing that moveth upon the earth" (Moses 2:28). God told them that they could freely eat of every tree in the garden except one, the tree of knowledge of good and evil. Of that tree God said: "In the day thou eatest thereof thou shalt surely die" (Moses 3:17).

Satan, not knowing the mind of God but seeking to destroy God's plan, came to Eve in the Garden of Eden. He tempted her to eat of the fruit of the tree of knowledge of good and evil. He assured her that she would not die, but that she would "be as gods, knowing good and evil" (Moses 4:11). Eve yielded to the temptation and ate the fruit. When Adam learned what had happened he chose to partake also. The changes that came upon Adam and Eve because they ate the fruit are called the *fall of Adam.*

Read Moses 4:6-32.
How was the Garden of Eden different from the world as we know it?
Discuss the conditions of Adam and Eve in the Garden of Eden.

ADAM AND EVE'S SEPARATION FROM GOD

Because Adam and Eve had eaten the fruit of the tree of knowledge of good and evil, the Lord sent them out of the Garden of Eden into the world as we now know it. Their physical condition changed as a result of their eating the forbidden fruit. As God had promised, they became mortal. They were able to have children. They and their children could experience sickness, pain, and physical death.

Because of their transgression, they also suffered spiritual death. This meant that they and their children could not walk and talk face to face with God. Satan had introduced evil into the world. Thus Adam and Eve and the rest of mankind were separated from God both physically and spiritually.

As a result of their transgression, what physical change occurred in Adam and Eve? What spiritual change occurred?
Read Moses 5:1–5. How did Adam and Eve live outside the Garden of Eden?

GREAT BLESSINGS RESULTED FROM THE TRANSGRESSION

Some people believe that Adam and Eve committed a serious sin when they ate of the tree of knowledge of good and evil. However, latter-day scriptures help us understand that their fall was a necessary step in the plan of life and a great blessing to all mankind. Because of the fall, we are blessed with physical bodies, the right to choose between good and evil, and the opportunity to gain eternal life. None of these privileges would have been ours had Adam and Eve remained in the garden. After her transgression, Eve said, "Were it not for our transgression we never should have had seed [children], and never should have known good and evil, and the joy of our redemption, and the eternal life which God giveth unto all the obedient" (Moses 5:11).

The prophet Lehi explained: "And now, behold, if Adam had not transgressed he would not have fallen [been cut off from the presence of God], but he would have remained in the Garden of Eden. And all things which were created must have remained in the same state in which they were after they were created; . . . And they would have had no children; wherefore they would have remained in a state of innocence, having no joy, for they knew no misery; doing no good, for they knew no sin. But behold, all things have been done in the wisdom of him who knoweth all things. Adam fell that

31

men might be; and men are, that they might have joy'' (2 Nephi 2:22-25).

Read Moses 5:6-12.
After the Fall, how did Adam and Eve feel about their transgression and the Lord's promise to redeem them?

ADDITIONAL SCRIPTURES
D&C 107:54; Moses 1:34 (Adam identified)
1 Nephi 5:11; 2 Nephi 2:20 (Adam and Eve first parents, family)
2 Nephi 2:14-21 (opposition and the Fall; life a probation)
2 Nephi 2:22-26 (Adam and Eve fell that man might be)

SUGGESTED SONG
''How Great the Wisdom and the Love''

Chapter 7

THE HOLY GHOST

After Adam and Eve left the Garden of Eden, they began to till the earth and work at other tasks for their living. They began to have children, and many sons and daughters were born to them. Their sons and daughters also married and had children (see Moses 5:1–3). Thus, spirit children of our Heavenly Father began leaving his presence to come to the earth as they had been promised. As they came to this earth, the memory of their heavenly home was taken from them. But our Father did not shut them away from his influence. He sent the Holy Ghost to comfort and help and guide all of his spirit children.

Sing "O My Father."
Read the second verse of the hymn.
Who is the "secret something" that whispers to us?

WHY DID THE HOLY GHOST COME TO ADAM?

Adam and Eve called upon Heavenly Father in prayer. He spoke to them and gave them commandments (see Moses 5:4–5). Adam was obedient to these commandments. An angel of the Lord came and taught Adam and Eve the plan of salvation. The Lord sent the Holy Ghost to testify of the Father and of the Son and to teach Adam and Eve the gospel (see Moses 5:9). Through the power of the Holy Ghost, Adam "began to prophesy concerning all the families of the earth, saying: Blessed be the name of God, for because of my transgression my eyes are opened, and in this life I shall have joy, and again in the flesh I shall see God" (Moses

5:10). Because of the witness of the Holy Ghost to Eve, she said: "Were it not for our transgression we never should have had seed, and never should have known good and evil, and the joy of our redemption, and the eternal life which God giveth unto all the obedient" (Moses 5:11).

Read the account of the Holy Ghost being sent to Adam and Eve (see Moses 5:4–11). Discuss why the Holy Ghost was sent to them.

WHO IS THE HOLY GHOST?

The Holy Ghost is a member of the Godhead (see 1 John 5:7; D&C 20:28). He has a body of spirit. His body of spirit is in the form and likeness of a man (see D&C 130:22). He can be only in one place at a time, but his influence can be every place at the same time.

Heavenly Father, Jesus Christ, and the Holy Ghost are called the *Godhead.* They are unified in purpose. Each has an important assignment in the plan of salvation. Our Heavenly Father is our father and ruler. Jesus Christ is our savior. The Holy Ghost is the revealer and testifier of all truth.

The Holy Ghost is our Heavenly Father's messenger and is a special gift to us. How we can receive the Holy Ghost will be discussed in chapter 21.

Read D&C 130:22. Discuss how the Holy Ghost differs from the Father and the Son. Why is the Holy Ghost a personage of spirit only?
How are the Father, Son, and Holy Ghost one? To answer, use the example of a father, mother, and children working for one same purpose. Relate examples.
How can the influence of the Holy Ghost be in many places at one time? To answer, compare the Holy Ghost to the sun. There is just one sun, but its light and warmth are felt by everyone on earth.

WHY IS THE HOLY GHOST NECESSARY?

The mission of the Holy Ghost is to bear witness of the Father and the Son and of the truth of all things.

The Holy Ghost will witness to us that Jesus is our savior and redeemer (see 3 Nephi 28:11; D&C 20:27; Hebrews 10:15). He will reveal to us that our Heavenly Father is, without doubt, the father of our spirits. He will help us to understand that we can become exalted like our Heavenly Father (see Romans 8:16–17). The prophets of the Lord have promised:

"By the power of the Holy Ghost ye may know the truth of all things" (see Moroni 10:5–7).

Without the Holy Ghost, we can never know that Jesus is the Christ. The Savior himself said: ". . . No man can say that Jesus is the Lord, but by the Holy Ghost" (1 Corinthians 12:3). "And this is life eternal, that they might know thee the only true God, and Jesus Christ, whom thou has sent" (John 17:3). It is by the power of the Holy Ghost that we are led to understand and live the gospel of Jesus Christ.

The convincing power of the Holy Ghost is so great that there can be no doubt that what it reveals to us is true. President Joseph Fielding Smith said: "When a man has the manifestation from the Holy Ghost, it leaves an indelible impression on his soul, one that is not easily erased. It is Spirit speaking to spirit, and it comes with convincing force. A manifestation of an angel, or even the Son of God himself, would impress the eye and mind, and eventually become dimmed, but the impressions of the Holy Ghost sink deeper into the soul and are more difficult to erase" (*Answers to Gospel Questions*, II:151). President Smith also said: "Through the Holy Ghost the truth is woven into the very fibre and sinews of the body so that it cannot be forgotten" (*Doctrines of Salvation*, 1:48).

As members of The Church of Jesus Christ of Latter-day Saints, we are able to receive testimony and guidance from the Holy Ghost. We should make ourselves worthy to receive this special messenger and witness of our Heavenly Father and Jesus Christ.

Why is the Holy Ghost necessary? Read again the statement by President Joseph Fielding Smith.

Encourage the members to tell how they felt when the Holy Ghost bore witness to them of the truthfulness of the gospel.

Sing "The Spirit of God like a Fire."

ADDITIONAL SCRIPTURES
Moses 5 (story of Adam's family)
2 Nephi 31:21 (Holy Ghost identified)
John 14:26; John 15:26; John 16:13; Luke 12:12; D&C 8:2–3; D&C 11:12–13; D&C 20:26 (Holy Ghost as comforter, teacher, testator of Christ, guide to all truth, revelator, companion, leader and guide, source of inspiration.)

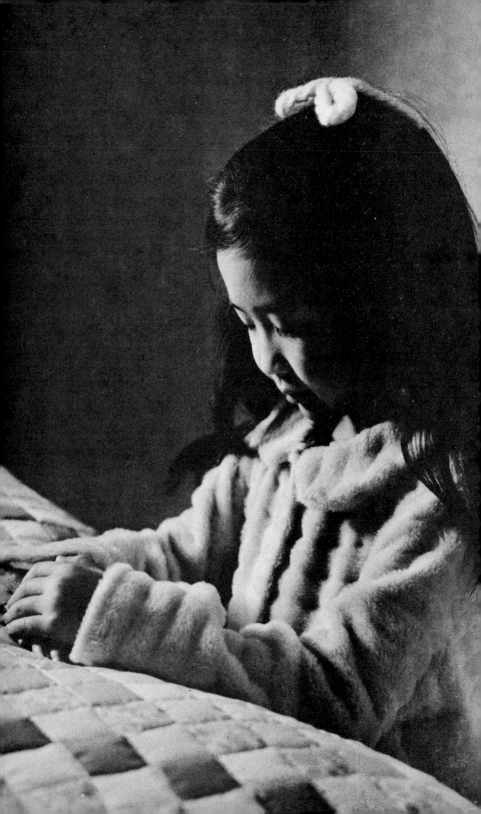

PRAYING TO OUR HEAVENLY FATHER

Jesus taught: "Ye must always pray unto the Father in my name" (3 Nephi 18:19).

Prayer is one of the greatest blessings that we have while we are here on this earth. Through prayer, we can communicate with our Heavenly Father and seek his guidance daily.

Sing "Ere You Left Your Room This Morning," "Family Prayer."

WHAT IS PRAYER?

Prayer is a sincere, heartfelt talk with our Heavenly Father. We should pray to God and to no one else. We do not pray to any other being or to anything made by man or God (see Exodus 20:3–5).

WHY DO WE PRAY?

Prayer has been an important part of the gospel from the beginning of the world. An angel of the Lord commanded Adam and Eve to repent and call upon God in the name of the Son (see Moses 5:8). This commandment has never been taken away. Nothing will help us keep our attention on God and on our duties in the Church more than prayer. All of our thoughts, our words, and our actions are influenced by our prayers.

We should pray for strength to resist the temptations of Satan and his followers (see 3 Nephi 18:15; D&C 10:5). We should pray to confess our sins to God and to ask him to forgive us (see Alma 38:14).

We should pray to ask the Lord's guidance and help in our daily lives. We need to pray for our families and friends, our neighbors, our crops, and our animals, our daily work, and our other activities. We should pray for protection from our enemies (see Alma 34:17–25).

We should pray to express our love to our Heavenly Father and to feel closer to him. We should pray to our Father to thank him for our welfare and comfort and for all things he gives us each day (see 1 Thessalonians 5:18). We need to pray to ask our Heavenly Father for all those things that will help us to live the gospel here on the earth.

We should pray so that we can keep on the straight and narrow path that leads to eternal life. We must remember that we pray to God, the author of all righteousness, so that we may be righteous in our thoughts, our words, and our actions.

How can prayer help us grow closer to our Heavenly Father?
Tell the story of Daniel (see Daniel 6:1–23) to the class.
How did Daniel pray?
How important was prayer to Daniel?

WHEN SHOULD WE PRAY?

We can pray whenever we feel the need to communicate with our Heavenly Father, whether silently or vocally. At times we need to be alone where we can pour out our souls to our Heavenly Father (see Matthew 6:6). In addition, we can pray during our daily activities. We can pray while we are in a Church meeting, in our house, walking down a path or street, working, preparing a meal, or wherever we may be and whatever we may be doing. We may pray at anytime of the day or night. We can pray when we are alone or when we are with other people. We can keep our Heavenly Father in our thoughts at all times (see Alma 34:27).

At times we may not feel like praying. We may be angry or discouraged or upset. At these times we should make a special effort to pray.

We should each pray privately at least every night and every morning. The scriptures speak of praying morning, midday, and evening (Alma 34:21).

We are commanded to have family prayers so that our families may be blessed (3 Nephi 18:21). Our Church leaders have counseled us to pray as families each morning and night.

We also have the privilege of praying to give thanks and ask a blessing on the food before each meal.

We open and close all of our Church meetings with prayer. We thank the Lord for his blessings and ask for his help so that we may worship in a manner that is pleasing to him.

Ask someone to read with you the story of Enos (see Enos 1–12). What words did Enos use to describe how he prayed?

HOW SHOULD WE PRAY?

No matter where we are, whether we stand or kneel, whether we pray vocally or silently, whether we pray privately or in behalf of a group, we should always pray in faith, "with a sincere heart, with real intent" (Moroni 10:4).

As we pray to our Heavenly Father we should tell him what we really feel in our hearts, confide in him, ask him for forgiveness, plead with him, thank him, express our love for him. We should not repeat meaningless words and phrases (see Matthew 6:7–8). We should always ask that his will be done. Remember that what we desire may not be best for us (see 3 Nephi 18:20). At the end of our prayer, we close in the name of Jesus Christ (see 3 Nephi 18:19).

HOW ARE PRAYERS ANSWERED?

Our sincere prayers are always answered. Sometimes the answer may be no, because what we have asked for would not be best for us. Sometimes the answer is yes, and we have a warm, comfortable feeling about what we should do (see D&C 9:8–9). Sometimes the answer is "wait awhile." Our prayers are always answered at the time and in a way that the Lord knows will help us the most.

Sometimes the Lord answers our prayers through other people. A good friend, a husband or wife, a parent, or other family member, a Church leader, a missionary—any of these individuals may be inspired to perform acts that will answer our prayers. An example of this is the experience of a young mother whose baby was injured in an accident at home. She had no way to get the baby to a doctor. She was new in the neighborhood and did not know her neighbors. The young mother prayed for help. In a few minutes, a neighbor lady came to the door saying, "I had a feeling I should come and see if you needed any help." The neighbor helped the young mother get the baby to a doctor where she was given medical help.

Often God gives us the power to help answer our own prayers. As we pray for help, we should be doing all we can to bring about the things we desire.

As we live the gospel of Jesus Christ and pray always, we will have much joy and happiness. "Be thou humble; and the Lord thy God shall lead thee by the hand, and give thee answer to thy prayers" (D&C 112:10).

Are we always given what we ask for? Why not?
Read D&C 46:30.
Why is it important to pray "if it be thy will"?
Ask members to share experiences of when and how the Lord has answered their prayers.
Close with your own testimony of prayer.
Encourage prayers in the family, blessings on the food, and individual prayer.
Sing "I Need Thee Every Hour."

ADDITIONAL SCRIPTURES
James 1:5 (what to pray for)
1 Thessalonians 5:17; Psalms 55:17; 2 Nephi 32:9 (when to pray)
Matthew 6:6; Alma 34:26 (where to pray)
3 Nephi 19:6; 1 Timothy 4:15; 3 Nephi 19:24; D&C 46:30 (how to pray)
D&C 88:63–65 (how prayers are answered)
Moroni 10:3–5; Alma 37:37 (promises for prayer)

We should pray with our families morning and night.

Joseph Smith

Brigham Young

John Taylor

Wilford Woodruff

Lorenzo Snow

Joseph F. Smith

Heber J. Grant

George Albert Smith

David O. McKay

Joseph Fielding Smith

Harold B. Lee

Spencer W. Kimball

PROPHETS OF GOD

"Surely the Lord God will do nothing, but he revealeth his secret unto his servants the prophets" (Amos 3:7).

Many people live in darkness, unsure of God's will. They believe that the heavens are closed and that people must face the world's perils alone. How fortunate are the Latter-day Saints! We know that God communicates to the Church through his prophet. With grateful hearts, Saints the world over sing the hymn, "We thank thee, O God, for a prophet to guide us in these latter days."

Who is this prophet who guides us? What are his powers and gifts? How can we sustain him?

Sing "We Thank Thee, O God, for a prophet."

Ask someone to tell the class who the prophet, seer, and revelator of the Church is today.

WHAT IS A PROPHET?

A prophet is a man called by God to be his representative on earth. When a prophet speaks for God, it is as if God were speaking. A prophet has responsibilities. He is a special witness for Christ, testifying of his divinity and teaching his gospel. He teaches truth and interprets the word of God. He calls the unrighteous to repentance. He receives revelations and directions from the Lord for our benefit. He may see into the future and foretell coming events so that the world may be warned.

A prophet may come from various stations in life. He may be young or old, highly educated or unschooled. He may be a farmer, a lawyer, or a teacher, or come from any other hon-

The Lord has sent prophets in our own day.

orable walk of life. Ancient prophets wore tunics and carried staffs. Modern prophets wear business suits and carry brief-cases. What, then, identifies a true prophet? A true prophet is always chosen by God and called through proper priest-hood authority.

Latter-day Saints sustain the first presidency, the twelve apostles, and the patriarch, as prophets. However, when we speak of "the prophet of the Church," we mean the President of the Church who is President of the High Priesthood.

THROUGH THE AGES GOD HAS CALLED PROPHETS TO LEAD MANKIND

There have been prophets on the earth since the days of Adam. Experiences of these great men excite and inspire us. Moses, an Old Testament prophet, led thousands of his people out of Egypt and slavery into the promised land. He wrote the first five books of the Old Testament and recorded the Ten Commandments. Nephi, a Book of Mormon prophet, sailed from Jerusalem to the American continent about 600 years before the birth of Christ. This great leader and colo-nizer gave to us many important writings in the Book of Mor-mon. John the Baptist was chosen to prepare the world for the coming of the Lord Jesus Christ. A modern prophet, Jo-seph Smith, restored the Church and translated the Book of Mormon while still a boy.

What is a prophet?
What power does he have?
What does he do?
What office does he hold in the Church?

WE HAVE A LIVING PROPHET ON THE EARTH TODAY

We have a prophet living on the earth today. This prophet is the president of The Church of Jesus Christ of Latter-day Saints. He has the right to revelation for the entire Church. He holds the "keys of the kingdom," meaning that he has the right to control the administration of the ordinances (see Matthew 16:19). No person except the chosen prophet and president can receive God's will for the membership of the Church.

We should do those things the prophets tell us to do. President Wilford Woodruff said that a prophet will never be allowed to lead the Church astray:

"I say to Israel, the Lord will never permit me or any other man who stands as president of this Church to lead you astray. It is not in the program. It is not in the mind of God. If I were to attempt that the Lord would remove me out of my place, and so he will any other man who attempts to lead the children of men astray from the oracles of God and from their duty. God bless you." (Wilford Woodruff, *The Discourses of Wilford Woodruff*, pp. 212–13.)

Ask the class to name as many prophets as they can.
Have a class member tell about the living prophet of the Church.

WE SHOULD SUSTAIN THE LORD'S PROPHET

Many people find it easy to believe in the prophets of the past. But it is much greater to believe in and follow the living prophet. We raise our hands to sustain the president of the Church as prophet, seer, and revelator. How can we sustain the prophet?

We should pray for him. His burdens are heavy, and he needs to be uplifted and strengthened by the prayers of the Saints.

We should study his words. We can listen to his conference addresses on the radio or read them in Church publications. We can attend area conferences.

We should follow his teachings completely. We should not choose to follow part of his counsel and discard that which is unpleasant or difficult. The Lord commanded us to follow the teachings of his prophet:

"Thou shalt give heed unto all his [the prophet's] words and commandments which he shall give unto you as he receiveth them, walking in all holiness before me;

"For his word ye shall receive, as if from mine own mouth, in all patience and faith" (D&C 21:4-5).

The Lord will never allow the president of the Church to teach us false doctrine.

Discuss what we can do to show that we believe the prophet.
Where can we learn of his counsel today?

GREAT BLESSINGS FOLLOW OBEDIENCE TO THE PROPHET

If we obey, the Lord promises these things: "The gates of hell shall not prevail against you; yea, and the Lord God will disperse the powers of darkness from before you; and cause the heavens to shake for your good, and his names's glory" (D&C 21:6).

When we do as our prophet directs, blessings pour down from heaven. A story from the life of Lorenzo Snow, the fifth president of the restored Church, shows how God rewards his people for their obedience. In those days, the Church was suffering great financial trouble. The Church had little money to pay its debts. Then more trouble came. A great drought afflicted many of the Saints. President Snow went to the Lord and begged for relief. One day as the prophet was speaking in the St. George Tabernacle in Utah, he was moved upon by the Holy Ghost. He promised the Saints that they would receive rain if they would pay a full tithe. He quoted Malachi: "Bring ye all the tithes into the storehouse . . . and prove me herewith, saith the Lord of Hosts, if I will not open you the windows of heaven, and pour you out a blessing, that there shall not be room enough to receive it" (Malachi 3:10). The people obeyed their prophet, and the rains fell on the parched crops.

In order to stand, the true church must be built upon the foundation of prophets (Ephesians 2:20). We are blessed in this insecure world to have at our head a prophet through whom the Lord reveals his will.

Have someone share an experience in which obedience to the counsel of the prophet was a blessing (such as tithing, Word of Wisdom, Sabbath day, prayer, fasting).

Chapter 9

ADDITIONAL SCRIPTURES
Numbers 12:6 (God speaks through prophets)
1 Samuel 9:9 (prophet called a seer)
Luke 1:70 (God speaks through prophets)
D&C 45:10, 15 (God speaks today as in days of old)
1 Nephi 22:2 (by the Spirit, things are made known to prophets)
D&C 68:3-5 (when the Lord's servants speak as moved by the Holy Ghost, it is the mind, will, and voice of the Lord)
D&C 107:65-67, 91-92 (duties of the president of the Church)
D&C 43:1-7 (only the prophet authorized to receive revelations for the Church)

Chapter 10

SCRIPTURES

When the Lord's servants speak or write under the influence of the Holy Ghost, their words become scripture (see D&C 68:4). From the beginning, the Lord has commanded his prophets to keep a record of his revelations and his dealings with his children. He said, "I command all men, both in the east and in the west, and in the north, and in the south, and in the islands of the sea, that they shall write the words which I speak unto them; for out of the books which shall be written I will judge the world, every man according to their works, according to that which is written" (2 Nephi 29:11).

WHAT SCRIPTURES DO WE HAVE TODAY?

The Church of Jesus Christ of Latter-day Saints accepts four books as scripture: the Bible, the Book of Mormon, the Doctrine and Covenants, and the Pearl of Great Price. These books are called the standard works of the Church. The words of our living prophets are also accepted as scripture.

The Bible is a collection of sacred writings containing God's revelations to man. These writings cover many centuries, from the time of Adam through the time when the Apostles of Jesus Christ lived. They were written by many prophets who lived at various times in the history of the world.

The Bible is divided into two sections, the Old Testament and the New Testament. Many prophecies in the Old Testament foretell the coming of a Savior and Redeemer. The New Testament tells of the life of that Savior and Redeemer, who is

Four books of scripture are the standard works of the Church of Jesus Christ.
Photograph by Eldon K. Linschoten

Jesus Christ. It also tells of the establishing of his church in that day. "We believe the Bible to be the word of God as far as it is translated correctly" (eighth article of faith).

The Book of Mormon is a sacred record of some of the people who lived on the American continents between about 2,000 B.C. and A.D. 400. It contains the fullness of the gospel of Jesus Christ (see D&C 20:9, 42:12; and 135:3). Its main purpose is to convince all the people that Jesus is the Savior and Redeemer of the world. Both the Book of Mormon and the Bible testify of Jesus Christ (see Ezekiel 37:16–19). The Book of Mormon tells of the visit Jesus Christ made to the people on the American continent soon after his resurrection.

Joseph Smith translated the Book of Mormon into English through the gift and power of God. He said that it is "the most correct of any book on earth, and the keystone of our religion, and a man would get nearer to God by abiding by its precepts, than by any other book" (*History of the Church of Jesus Christ of Latter-day Saints,* 4:461).

Many of the Book of Mormon prophets saw into the future and knew that they were writing for our benefit as well as for the benefit of their own people. The prophet Moroni said to us: "Behold, I speak unto you as if ye were present, and yet ye are not. But behold, Jesus Christ hath shown you unto me, and I know your doing" (Mormon 8:35).

The Doctrine and Covenants is a collection of modern revelations. In section 1 of the Doctrine and Covenants, the Lord tells us that the book is published to the inhabitants of the earth to prepare them for the coming of the Lord:

"Wherefore the voice of the Lord is unto the ends of the earth, that all that will hear may hear:

"Prepare ye, prepare ye for that which is to come, for the Lord is nigh" (D&C 1:11–12).

This book contains the revelations regarding the Church of Jesus Christ as it has been restored in these last days. Several sections of the book explain the organization of the Church and define the offices of the priesthood and their functions. Other sections, such as sections 76 and 88, contain glorious truths which were lost to the world for hundreds of years. Still others, such as sections 29 and 93, shed light on teachings in the Bible. In addition, some sections, such as section 133, contain prophecies of events to come. God has commanded us to study his revelations in this book: "Search these commandments, for they are true and faithful, and the prophecies and promises which are in them shall all be fulfilled" (D&C 1:37).

The Pearl of Great Price contains the Book of Moses, the Book of Abraham, the Writings of Joseph Smith, and President Joseph F. Smith's Vision of the Redemption of the Dead. The Book of Moses contains an account of some of the visions and writings of Moses, revealed to the Prophet Joseph Smith in June and December 1830. It clarifies doctrines and teachings that were lost from the Bible and gives added information concerning the creation of the earth.

The Book of Abraham was translated by the Prophet Joseph Smith from a papyrus scroll taken from the Egyptian catacombs. This book contains valuable information about the creation, the gospel, the nature of God, and the priesthood.

The Writings of Joseph Smith include part of Joseph Smith's inspired translation of the Bible, selections from his *History of the Church of Jesus Christ of Latter-day Saints,* the Articles of Faith, and Vision of the Celestial Kingdom.

Vision of the Redemption of the Dead is a vision given to President Joseph F. Smith, 3 October 1918, showing the visit of the Lord Jesus Christ in the spirit world. It also sets forth the doctrine of the redemption of the dead.

WORDS OF OUR LIVING PROPHETS

In addition to these four books of scripture, the inspired words of our living prophets become scripture to us. Their words come to us through conferences, Church publications, and instructions to local priesthood leaders. "We believe all that God has revealed, all that he does now reveal, and we believe that he will yet reveal many great and important things pertaining to the kingdom of God" (ninth article of faith).

Read D&C 68:4.
What is scripture?
Name the standard works of the Church.
Have four people each tell about what is in one of the standard works and how we received it.
Ask a class member to read or quote the ninth article of faith.
Show a copy of a Church publication.
Have someone read some inspired words of the prophet found there.

STUDYING THE SCRIPTURES

We should each study the scriptures every day. We should share these truths with our children. Our standard works should be placed where our children will see them and learn to love them and use them for the truths they contain.

If we desire to avoid the evils of this world, we must feed our minds with the truth and righteousness found in the scriptures. We will grow closer to God and to each other as we read and ponder the scriptures together.

As we read, ponder, and pray about the scriptures and ask God for understanding, the Holy Ghost will bear witness to us of the truth of these things. We will each know of ourselves that these things are true. We will not be deceived (see Joseph Smith 1:37). We can receive the same feelings Nephi expressed when he said, "My soul delighteth in the things of the Lord; and my heart pondereth continually upon the things which I have seen and heard" (2 Nephi 4:16).

As a group or individually, plan for daily scripture study. Plan the time, place, scripture to study, and set a goal.
Sing "The Golden Plates."

ADDITIONAL SCRIPTURES
1 Nephi 19:1–3; 1 Nephi 14:20–26 (prophets commanded to write)
1 Nephi 19:1–3, 6–7; Alma 37:1–8 (great worth of scriptures)
2 Nephi 33:10 (scriptures testify of Christ)
Alma 29:8 (Lord speaks to all nations through scriptures)
2 Timothy 3:16–17; 1 Nephi 19:21–24 (why and how scriptures are given)
2 Peter 1:20; Alma 13:20; D&C 10:62 (scriptures clear, do not distort)
D&C 128:18; 1 Nephi 14:25–26 (scriptures yet to come)
2 Nephi 29:3–10 (scriptures to Jews and to Gentiles)

THE LIFE OF CHRIST

Every person who comes to earth depends on Jesus Christ to fulfill the promise he made in heaven to be our savior. Without him, the whole plan of salvation would have failed. Because his mission was necessary, all of the prophets from Adam to Christ testified that he would come (see Acts 10:43). All of the prophets since Christ have testified that he did come. Each of us needs to study the life of the Savior and strive to keep his commandments throughout our lives in order to develop a personal relationship with him.

Sing or read the words to the song "Come Follow Me."

THE LIFE OF CHRIST WAS PREDICTED LONG BEFORE HIS BIRTH

Adam was told by an angel that the Savior's name would be Jesus Christ (see Moses 6:51–52). Enoch saw that Jesus would die upon the cross and take up his body again (see Moses 7:55–56). Noah and Moses also testified of him (see Moses 8:23–24). About 800 years before the Savior was born on the earth, Isaiah foresaw his life. When he saw the grief and sorrow that the Savior would suffer in order to pay the price for our sins he exclaimed: "He is despised and rejected of men; a man of sorrows, and acquainted with grief. . . . Surely he hath borne our griefs, and carried our sorrows. . . . he was wounded for our transgressions, he was bruised for our iniquities. . . . he was oppressed, and he was afflicted, yet he opened not his mouth: he is brought as a lamb to the slaughter" (Isaiah 53:3–7).

Nephi also saw a vision of the Savior's future birth and mission. He saw a beautiful virgin, and an angel explained: "Behold, the virgin whom thou seest is the mother of the Son of God, after the manner of the flesh" (1 Nephi 11:18). Then he saw the virgin holding a child in her arms. The angel declared: "Behold the lamb of God, yea, even the Son of the Eternal Father!" (1 Nephi 11:21). About 124 years before Jesus was born, King Benjamin, another Nephite prophet and king, also foresaw the Savior's life:

"For behold, the time cometh, and is not far distant, that with power, the Lord Omnipotent who reigneth, who was, and is from all eternity to all eternity, shall come down from heaven among the children of men, and shall dwell in a tabernacle of clay, and shall go forth amongst men, working mighty miracles, such as healing the sick, raising the dead, causing the lame to walk, the blind to receive their sight, and the deaf to hear, and curing all manner of diseases.

"And he shall cast out devils, or the evil spirits which dwell in the hearts of the children of men.

"And lo, he shall suffer temptations, and pain of body, hunger, thirst, and fatigue, even more than man can suffer, except it be unto death; for behold, blood cometh from every pore, so great shall be his anguish for the wickedness and the abominations of his people.

"And he shall be called Jesus Christ, the Son of God, the Father of heaven and earth, the Creator of all things from the beginning; and his mother shall be called Mary" (Mosiah 3:5–8).

Read Timothy 2:6.
Why was it important for people who lived before Jesus was born to know about him?

HE WAS THE ONLY BEGOTTEN OF THE FATHER

The story of the birth and life of the Savior is found in the New Testament in the books of Matthew, Mark, Luke, and John. From their accounts, we learn that Jesus was born of a virgin named Mary. She was engaged to marry Joseph when an angel of the Lord appeared to her. The angel told her that

The Savior Jesus Christ, known as Jehovah in the premortal existence, was born in a humble stable.

she was to be the mother of the Son of God. She asked him how this was possible (see Luke 1:34). He told her: "The Holy Ghost shall come upon thee, and the power of the Highest shall overshadow thee: therefore also that holy thing which shall be born of thee shall be called the Son of God" (Luke 1:35). Thus, God the Father became the literal father of Jesus Christ. Jesus was born of a mortal mother and an immortal father. He is the only one to be born in this way on the earth. That is why he is called the Only Begotten Son. He inherited divine powers from his Father. No man could take the Savior's life from him unless he willed it. He had power to lay it down and the power to take up his body again after dying (see John 10:17–18). From his mother, he inherited mortality and was subject to hunger, thirst, fatigue, pain, and death.

Read Luke 1:34–35.
Why was Jesus Christ known as the Only Begotten of the Father?
What did he inherit from his Father?
What did he inherit from his mother?

HE LED A PERFECT LIFE

From his youth, Jesus obeyed all that was required of him by our Heavenly Father. Under the guidance of Mary and Joseph, Jesus grew much as other children grow. He loved and obeyed the truth. Luke tells us: "And the child grew, and waxed strong in spirit, filled with wisdom: and the grace of God was upon him" (Luke 2:40).

By the time he was twelve years old, he knew that he had been sent to do the will of his father. He went with his parents to Jerusalem. When his parents were returning home, they discovered that he was not with their group. They went back to Jerusalem to look for him. "After three days they found him in the temple, sitting in the midst of the doctors, both hearing them, and asking them questions. And all that heard him were astonished at his understanding and answers" (Luke 2:46–47). Joseph and Mary were relieved to find him but unhappy that he had treated them so. Mary said: "Son, why hast thou thus dealt with us? Behold, thy father

The Savior as a boy taught the learned men in the temple.

KEY TO ILLUSTRATIONS 1–16

1. Isaiah, one of the prophets of the Old Testament, foretold the coming of Jesus Christ.

2. John the Baptist baptized Jesus in the Jordan River.

3. Jesus called Peter and others to follow him.

4. Jesus ordained twelve apostles.

5. Jesus loved and blessed the children.

6. Jesus taught the people the gospel.

7. In the Garden of Gethsemane, Christ atoned for the sins of all mankind.

8. Christ died on the cross at Calvary.

9. On the third day, Christ rose from the grave.

10. The resurrected Christ showed his wounds to his apostles.

11. The resurrected Christ visited his people in the Americas.

12. Joseph Smith was inspired by James 1:5–6 to ask God which was the true church of Jesus Christ.

13. In answer to his prayer, Heavenly Father and Jesus Christ visited Joseph Smith.

14. The angel Moroni delivered to Joseph Smith the golden plates which contained the Book of Mormon.

15. John the Baptist visited Joseph Smith and Oliver Cowdery and conferred upon them the Aaronic Priesthood.

16. Peter, James, and John conferred the Melchizedek Priesthood upon Joseph Smith and Oliver Cowdery.

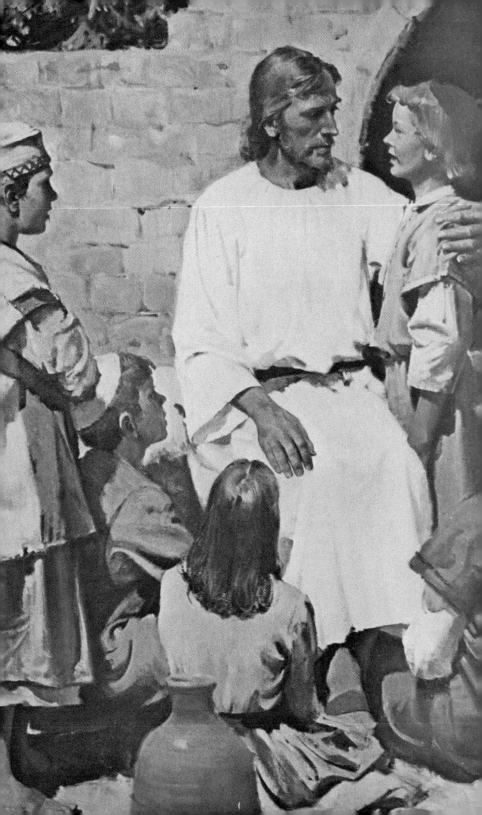

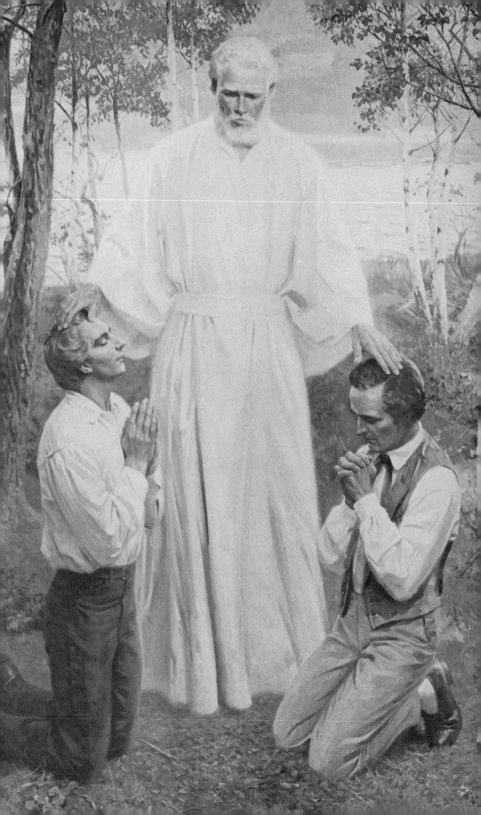

[Joseph] and I have sought thee sorrowing.'' Jesus answered her gently, reminding her that Joseph was only a stepfather: "Wist ye not that I must be about my [Heavenly] Father's business?'' (Luke 2:48–49). In order to fulfill his mission, he was to do the will of his father in heaven. Later he declared; "I do nothing of myself; but as my Father hath taught me, I speak these things. . . . I do always those things that please him'' (John 8:28–29).

When Jesus was thirty years old, he came to his cousin, John, to be baptized in the Jordan River (see Matthew 3:13–17). John was reluctant to baptize Jesus because he knew that Jesus had never sinned. Jesus asked John to baptize him in order "to fulfil all righteousness.'' John did baptize the Savior, immersing him completely in the water. When Jesus was baptized, his Father spoke from heaven saying, "This is my beloved Son, in whom I am well pleased.'' The Holy Ghost descended, as shown by the sign of the dove.

Soon after Jesus' baptism, Satan came to him to tempt him. He wanted Jesus to fail his mission. If he could just get him to commit one sin, then Jesus would not be worthy to be our Savior, and the plan would fail. In this way, Satan could make us just as miserable as he is. We would never be able to return to our Heavenly Father. The temptations of Satan came after Jesus had been fasting for forty days. Jesus firmly resisted all of Satan's temptations, then commanded Satan to leave. When Satan was gone, angels came and ministered to Jesus (see Matthew 4:1–11).

HE TAUGHT US HOW TO LOVE AND SERVE ONE ANOTHER

After being tempted by Satan, Jesus began his public ministry. He had not only come to earth to die for us, but he also came to teach us how to live. He taught that there were two great commandments—first, to love God with all our heart, mind, and strength; and second, to love our fellowmen as we love ourselves (Matthew 22:36–39). His life is an example of how we should obey these two commandments. If we love

God, we will trust and obey him. Jesus was obedient in all things. If we love our fellowmen, we will help them to meet their physical and spiritual needs.

Jesus spent his life in service to others. He cured them of diseases. He made the blind to see, the deaf to hear, and the lame to walk. Once, when he was healing the sick, it became late and the people were hungry. Instead of sending them away, he took five loaves of bread and two fish and blessed them. A miracle happened. From these loaves and fish, he was able to feed a multitude of five thousand people (see Matthew 14:14–21). He taught that whenever we find someone hungry, cold, naked, or lonely, we should help them all we can. When we help others, we are serving him (see Matthew 25:35–46).

Jesus loved his fellowmen with all his heart. Often his heart was so full of compassion that he wept. He loved little children, the elderly, and the humble, simple people who had faith in him. He loved those who had sinned, and with great compassion he taught them to repent and be baptized. He taught: "I am the way, the truth, and the life" (John 14:6). He even loved those who sinned against him and were unrepentant. At the very end of his life, as he hung on the cross, he prayed to the Father for the soldiers who had crucified him, saying: "Father, forgive them; for they know not what they do" (Luke 23:34). He taught: "This is my commandment, that ye love one another as I have loved you" (John 15:12).

Read Matthew 22:36–40.
What are some ways in which we can show we love and serve the Lord?
Read Matthew 5:48.
Is it possible to become perfect in aspects of our own daily lives (such as paying debts, keeping the Sabbath day, fasting, keeping the Word of Wisdom)?

HE ORGANIZED THE ONLY TRUE CHURCH

Jesus wanted his gospel taught to people all over the earth, so he chose twelve apostles to testify of him. They were the original leaders of his church. They received the authority to act in his name and do the works that they had seen him do. Those who received authority from them were also able to teach, baptize, and perform other ordinances in his name. After his death, they continued to do his work until the people became so wicked that they killed the apostles.

Why did Jesus choose the Twelve Apostles?
Read Mark 3:14–15.
For what purpose were they ordained?

HE REDEEMED US FROM OUR SINS AND SAVED US FROM DEATH

When his work of teaching and blessing the people was finished, Jesus prepared to make the ultimate sacrifice for all the sins of mankind. He had been condemned to die because he had revealed to the people that he was the Son of God.

The night before his crucifixion, he went to a garden called Gethsemane. There he knelt and prayed. Soon he was weighted down by deep sorrow. As he prayed, he wept. Apostle Orson F. Whitney was permitted to see the Savior's suffering in a vision. He saw the Savior weep, and he said, "I was so moved at the sight that I also wept, out of pure sympathy. My whole heart went out to Him; I loved Him with all my soul, and longed to be with Him as I longed for nothing else" (Bryant Hinckley, *The Faith of Our Pioneer Fathers,* p. 211). Jesus "went a little further, and fell on his face, and prayed, saying, O my Father, if it be possible, let this cup pass from me: nevertheless not as I will, but as thou wilt" (Matthew 26:39).

In a modern revelation the Savior described how great his suffering really was: "Which suffering caused myself, even God, the greatest of all, to tremble because of pain, and to bleed at every pore, and to suffer both body and spirit" (D&C 19:18). The awful anguish of punishment for every sin that any human being has ever committed went through his body. No mortal person can comprehend just how great this burden was. No other person could have endured such agony of body and spirit. In that hour Christ overcame all the horrors that Satan could inflict. Even his crucifixion would not surpass the bitter anguish that he suffered in Gethsemane. "He descended below all things, that he might be in all things and through all things, the light of truth" (see D&C 88:6).

But his suffering was not yet complete. The following day, Jesus was beaten, humiliated, and spit upon. He was required to carry his own cross up the hill; then he was lifted up and nailed to it. He was tortured in one of the cruelest ways men have ever devised. After nine hours on the cross, he cried out in agony: "My God, my God, why hast thou forsaken me?" (Mark 15:34). In Jesus' bitterest hour, the Father had withdrawn his spirit from him so that Jesus could have all the glory of his victory over sin and death.

When the Savior knew that his sacrifice had been accepted by the Father, he exclaimed in a loud voice, "It is finished" (John 19:30). "Father, into thy hands I commend my spirit" (Luke 23:46). He bowed his head and voluntarily gave up his spirit. The Savior was dead. A violent earthquake shook the earth.

For three days his body lay in the tomb. During this time his spirit went and preached to other spirits who needed to receive his gospel (see 1 Peter 3:18–20). On the third day, a Sunday, he returned to his body and took it up again. He was the first to overcome death. The prophecy had been fulfilled that "he must rise again from the dead" (John 20:9).

Shortly after his resurrection, the Savior appeared to the Nephites and established his church. He taught the people and blessed them. This moving account is found in 3 Nephi 11 through 28.

WHAT DOES THE SAVIOR'S LIFE MEAN FOR US?

Jesus taught that "greater love hath no man than this, that a man lay down his life for his friends. Ye are my friends if ye do whatsoever I command you" (John 15:13–14). He willingly and humbly went through the sorrow in Gethsemane and the suffering on the cross. He will have died in vain for our sins if we do not obey him. He asks only that we repent, come unto him, and love him with all our hearts. He has said: "And this is the gospel which I have given unto you—that I came into the world to do the will of my Father, because my Father sent me. And my Father sent me that I might be lifted up upon the cross; and after that I had been lifted up upon the cross, that I might draw all men unto me . . . that they may be judged according to their works . . . for the works which ye have seen me do that shall ye also do. . . . Therefore, what manner of men ought ye to be? Verily, verily I say unto you, *even as I am.*" (3 Nephi 27:13–27.)

Imagine that you had a large debt but could not pay it. How would you feel about a person who offered to pay the debt for you? Compare this to the sacrifice of Jesus.
Sing "Christ the Lord is Risen Today," "How Great the Wisdom and the Love."

ADDITIONAL SCRIPTURES
2 Nephi 25:12 (the Only Begotten of the Father in the flesh)
Moses 6:57 (Jesus Christ named as the Only Begotten)
Matthew, Mark, Luke, John (life and teachings of Jesus Christ)
Matthew 10:1–8; Luke 9:1–2 (Apostles ordained with power and authority)
Matthew 26, 27, 28; Mark 14, 15; Luke 22–23 (Jesus in garden, betrayed and crucified)

THE ATONEMENT

Jesus Christ "came into the world . . . to be crucified for the world, and to bear the sins of the world, and to sanctify the world, and to cleanse it from all unrighteousness, that through him all might be saved" (D&C 76:41–42). The great sacrifice that he made in order to pay for our sins and overcome death is called the *Atonement*. It is the most important event that has ever occurred in the history of mankind: "For it is expedient that an atonement should be made; for according to the great plan of the Eternal God there must be an atonement made, or else all mankind must unavoidably perish; . . . yea, all are fallen and are lost, and must perish except it be through the atonement" (Alma 34:9).

Sing "How Great the Wisdom and the Love."
Why did Jesus come to the earth?

THE ATONEMENT WAS NECESSARY FOR OUR SALVATION

The fall of Adam brought two kinds of death into the world—physical death and spiritual death. Physical death is separation of the body and the spirit. Spiritual death is separation from the Lord. If these two kinds of death had not been overcome by Jesus' atonement, two consequences would have resulted: our bodies and our spirits would be separated forever, and we could not live again with our Heavenly Father. But our wise Heavenly Father prepared a wonderful, merciful plan to save us from both physical and spiritual death. He planned that a savior would come to earth to ransom (redeem) us from our sins and death. Because of our sins and the weakness of our mortal bodies we could not ransom (redeem) ourselves (see Alma 34:10–12). The one who would be our savior would need to be sinless and to have power over death.

Compare our earthly bodies to a hand with a glove on it. Take off the glove. Explain that this is like physical death—the spirit (the hand) and the body (the glove) are separated.

CHRIST WAS THE ONLY ONE WHO COULD ATONE FOR OUR SINS

There are several reasons why Jesus Christ was the only person who could become our savior. One reason is that he was the one chosen by our Heavenly Father to be the savior. He was the Only Begotten Son of God, and thus had power over death. Jesus explained: "I lay down my life, that I might take it up again. No man taketh it from me, but I lay it down of myself. I have power to lay it down, and I have power to take it again" (John 10:17–18). Jesus also qualified to be our Savior because he is the only person who has ever lived on the earth who did not sin. This made him a worthy sacrifice to pay for the sins of others.

Have someone list the reasons why Jesus was the only one who could atone for our sins.

CHRIST SUFFERED AND DIED TO ATONE FOR US

The Savior atoned for us by suffering in Gethsemane and by giving his life on the cross. It is impossible for us to fully understand how Christ suffered for the sins of all men. In the Garden of Gethsemane, the weight of our sins caused him to feel such agony and heartbreak that he bled from every pore (see D&C 19:18–19). Later, as he hung upon the cross, Jesus suffered painful death by one of the most cruel methods known to man.

How Jesus must have loved us, to suffer such spiritual and physical agony for our sake! How great the love of Heavenly Father that he would send his Only Begotten Son to suffer and die for the rest of his children. "For God so loved the world, that he gave his only begotten Son, that whosoever

In the Garden of Gethsemane, Christ atoned for the sins of all mankind.

Christ died on the cross.

believeth in him should not perish, but have everlasting life'' (John 3:16).

Ask the members to imagine themselves in the Garden of Gethsemane as witnesses of the suffering of Jesus Christ. Have someone read the account in Luke 22:39-44.

CHRIST'S ATONEMENT AND RESURRECTION BRINGS RESURRECTION TO ALL

On the third day after his crucifixion, Christ took up his body again and became the first person to be resurrected. When his friends went to seek him, the angels who guarded his tomb told them: ''He is not here; for he is risen, as he said'' (Matthew 28:6). His spirit had reentered his body, never to be separated again.

Christ thus overcame physical death. Because of his atonement all persons born on this earth will be resurrected (see 1 Corinthians 15:21-22). In the same way Jesus was resurrected, so our spirits will be reunited with our bodies, ''that they can die no more; [our] spirits uniting with [our] bodies, never to be divided'' (Alma 11:45). This condition is called *immortality*. All men who have ever lived will be resurrected, ''both old and young, both bond and free, both male and female, both the wicked and the righteous'' (Alma 11:44).

Refer again to the hand and glove. Explain that because Jesus Christ atoned for our sins, all people will someday be resurrected. (Put glove on hand.) Our bodies and our spirits will reunite.

THE ATONEMENT MAKES IT POSSIBLE FOR THOSE WHO REPENT TO BE SAVED FROM THEIR SINS

Christ's atonement makes it possible for us to overcome spiritual death. Although all mankind will be resurrected with a body of flesh and bone, only those who accept Christ's atonement will be saved from spiritual death. We accept Christ's atonement by repenting of our sins, being baptized, receiving the gift of the Holy Ghost, and obeying all of the commandments. In this way we are cleansed from sin and we become worthy to return and live forever with our Heavenly Father. The Savior tells us: ''For behold, I, God, have suffered these things for all, that they might not suffer even as I'' (D&C 19:16-17). Christ did his part to atone for our sins. Each of us must repent and obey to make Christ's atonement effective in our lives.

Elder Boyd K. Packer of the Council of the Twelve gave the following illustration to show how Christ's atonement makes it possible to be saved from sin *if* we do our part.

"Let me tell you a story—a parable.

There once was a man who wanted something very much. It seemed more important than anything else in his life. In order for him to have his desire, he incurred a great debt.

"He had been warned about going into that much debt, and particularly about his creditor. But it seemed so important for him to do what he wanted to and to have what he wanted right now. He was sure he could pay for it later.

"So he signed a contract. He would pay it off some time along the way. He didn't worry too much about it, for the due date seemed such a long time away. He had what he wanted now, and that was what seemed important.

"The creditor was always somewhere in the back of his mind, and he made token payments now and again, thinking somehow that the day of reckoning really would never come.

"But as it always does, the day came, and the contract fell due. The debt had not been fully paid. His creditor appeared and demanded payment in full.

"Only then did he realize that his creditor not only had the power to repossess all that he owned, but the power to cast him into prison as well.

" 'I cannot pay you, for I have not the power to do so,' he confessed.

" 'Then,' said the creditor, 'we will exercise the contract, take your possessions and you shall go to prison. You agreed to that. It was your choice. You signed the contract, and now it must be enforced.'

" 'Can you not extend the time or forgive the debt?' the debtor begged. 'Arrange some way for me to keep what I

Chapter 12

have and not go to prison. Surely you believe in mercy? Will you not show mercy?'

"The creditor replied, 'Mercy is always so one-sided. It would serve only you. If I show mercy to you, it will leave me unpaid. It is justice I demand. Do you believe in justice?'

" 'I believed in justice when I signed the contract,' the debtor said. 'It was on my side then, for I thought it would protect me. I did not need mercy then, nor think I should need it ever. Justice, I thought, would serve both of us equally as well.'

" 'It is justice that demands that you pay the contract or suffer the penalty,' the creditor replied. 'That is the law. You have agreed to it and that is the way it must be. Mercy cannot rob justice.'

"There they were: One meting out justice, the other pleading for mercy. Neither could prevail except at the expense of the other.

" 'If you do not forgive the debt there will be no mercy,' the debtor pleaded.

" 'If I do, there will be no justice,' was the reply.

"Both laws, it seemed, could not be served. They are two eternal ideals that appear to contradict one another. Is there no way for justice to be fully served, and mercy also?

"There is a way! The law of justice *can* be fully satisfied and mercy *can* be fully extended—but it takes someone else. And so it happened this time.

"The debtor had a friend. He came to help. He knew the debtor well. He knew him to be shortsighted. He thought him foolish to have gotten himself into such a predicament. Nevertheless, he wanted to help because he loved him. He stepped between them, faced the creditor, and made this offer.

" 'I will pay the debt if you will free the debtor from his contract so that he may keep his possessions and not go to prison.'

70

"As the creditor was pondering the offer, the mediator added, 'You demanded justice. Though he cannot pay you, I will do so. You will have been justly dealt with and can ask no more. It would not be just.'

"And so the creditor agreed.

"The mediator turned then to the debtor. 'If I pay your debt, will you accept me as your creditor?'

" 'Oh yes, yes,' cried the debtor. 'You saved me from prison and show mercy to me.'

" 'Then,' said the benefactor, 'you will pay the debt to me and I will set the terms. It will not be easy, but it will be possible. I will provide a way. You need not go to prison.'

"And so it was that the creditor was paid in full. He had been justly dealt with. No contract had been broken.

"The debtor, in turn, had been extended mercy. Both laws stood fulfilled. Because there was a mediator, justice had claimed its full share, and mercy was satisfied." ("The Mediator," *Ensign*, May 1977, pp. 54–55.)

Without Jesus Christ, who is our Savior and Mediator, we would all pay for our sins, which are our spiritual debts, by suffering spiritual death. But because of him, if we will keep his terms, which are to repent and keep his commandments, we may return to live with our Heavenly Father.

It is wonderful that Christ has given us a way to be healed from our sins. He said: "Behold, I have come unto the world . . . to save the world from sin. Therefore, whoso repenteth and cometh unto me as a little child, him will I receive, for of such is the kingdom of God. Behold, for such I have laid down my life, and have taken it up again; therefore repent, and come unto me ye ends of the earth, and be saved" (3 Nephi 9:21-22).

Read Acts 2:38.
What must we do to show that we accept the Atonement?
Read D&C 19:16–17.
What is the penalty for those who do not accept the atonement of the Savior?
Sing "Behold the Great Redeemer Die."

ADDITIONAL SCRIPTURES

Alma 34:9-16 (Atonement necessary)
Romans 5:12-17 (by one came death, by one came life)
Helaman 14:15-18 (purpose of Jesus' death)
Third article of faith (all may be saved)
Alma 34:9-16 (sacrifice of God)
1 Peter 1:18-20 (Jesus foreordained)
Matthew 16:21 (his sacrifice necessary)
Luke 22:39-46 (suffering in the garden)
1 John 1:7 (Jesus cleanses from sin)
2 Nephi 9:21-22 (Savior suffered for all men)
John 10:17-18 (power of resurrection in the Savior)
Mosiah 16:6-8 (resurrection only possible through Jesus)
Alma 11:40-45; Mormon 9:12-14 (all to resurrect)
Isaiah 1:18 (sins shall be made white)
1 Corinthians 15:21-22; 40-44 (resurrection of all mankind)

Chapter 13

THE PRIESTHOOD

WHAT IS THE PRIESTHOOD?

Our Heavenly Father has great power. This power is called the priesthood. By his priesthood power the heavens and the earth were created. By this power, the universe is kept in perfect order.

Our Heavenly Father shares his priesthood power with his children on the earth. It is the power and authority by which those who are ordained to this power act in his name to do his work (see D&C 121:36).

WHY DO WE NEED THE PRIESTHOOD ON THE EARTH?

We must have priesthood authority to act in the name of God to perform the sacred ordinances of the gospel, such as baptism, confirmation, administration of the sacrament, and temple marriage. If a man does not have the priesthood, even though he may be sincere, the Lord will not recognize ordinances performed by him (see Matthew 7:21–23). These important ordinances must be performed on the earth by men holding the priesthood.

Men need the priesthood to preside in The Church of Jesus Christ of Latter-day Saints and to direct the work of the Church in all parts of the world. When Christ lived on the earth, he chose his apostles and ordained them so that they could lead his church. He gave them the power and authority of the priesthood to act in his name (see Mark 3:13–15; John 15:16).

Another reason the priesthood is needed on the earth is so that we can understand the will of the Lord and carry out his purposes. God reveals his will to his authorized priesthood representative on the earth, the prophet. The prophet, who is president of the Church, serves as the spokesman for God to all the members of the Church and all people on the earth.

Name some things that can only be done by persons who hold the priesthood. Discuss the need for priesthood authority.

HOW DO MEN RECEIVE THE PRIESTHOOD?

The Lord has prepared an orderly way for his priesthood to be given to his sons on the earth. A worthy male member of the Church receives the priesthood by "the laying on of hands, by those who are in authority to preach the Gospel and administer in the ordinances thereof" (fifth article of faith).

This is the same way that men received the priesthood long ago, even in the days of Moses: "And no man taketh this honour unto himself, but he that is called of God, as was Aaron" (Hebrews 5:4). Aaron received the priesthood from his priesthood leader, who was the prophet, Moses (see Exodus 28:1). Only those who hold the priesthood can ordain others.

Men cannot buy and sell the power and authority of the priesthood, and they cannot take this authority for themselves. In the New Testament we read of a man named Simon who lived when Christ's apostles were the priesthood leaders presiding over the Church. Simon became converted and was baptized into the Church. Becase he was a very skillful magician, the people believed he had the power of God. But Simon did not have the priesthood and he knew it.

Simon knew that the apostles and the other priesthood leaders of the Church had the true power of God. He saw them use their priesthood to do the Lord's work, and he wanted this power for himself. He offered to buy the priesthood. But Peter, the chief apostle, said: "Thy money perish with thee,

Moses conferred the priesthood on Aaron by the laying on of hands.

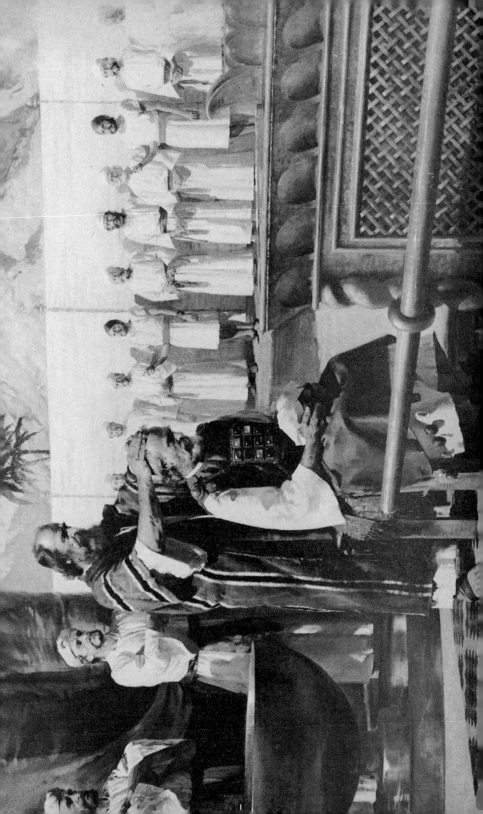

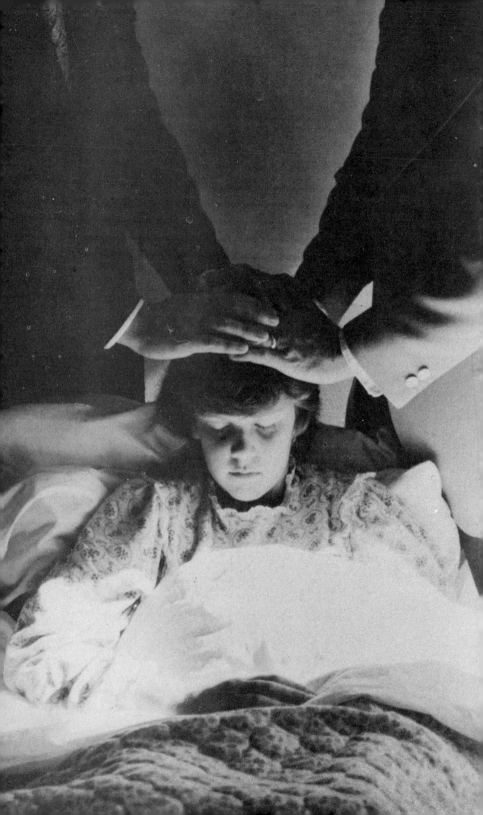

because thou hast thought that the gift of God may be purchased with money" (Acts 8:9–21).

Have someone read or quote the fifth article of faith.
Who is given the priesthood? How is it given?
Who may ordain a male member to the priesthood?

HOW DO MEN PROPERLY USE THE PRIESTHOOD?

The priesthood should be used to bless the lives of our Heavenly Father's children here on earth. Priesthood holders
should preside in love and kindness. They should not force
their families and others to obey them. The Lord has told us
that the power of the priesthood cannot be controlled except
in righteousness (see D&C 121:36). When we try to use the
priesthood to unrighteously gain wealth or fame or for any
other selfish purpose, "behold, the heavens withdraw themselves; the Spirit of the Lord is grieved; and when it is withdrawn, Amen to the priesthood or the authority of that man"
(D&C 121:37).

When a man uses the priesthood "by persuasion, by longsuffering, by gentleness and meekness, and by love un-
feigned" (D&C 121:41), he can do many wonderful things
for his family and others. He can baptize and confirm, administer the sacrament, bless the sick. He can give priesthood
blessings to his family members to encourage and protect
them when they have special needs. He can also help other
families with these ordinances and blessings when asked to
do so.

Men can use the priesthood authority to preside in the
Church in such callings as branch presidents, bishops, quorum presidents, or stake and mission leaders. The women
who hold positions in the Church as officers and teachers
work under the direction of the priesthood.

Read D&C 121:34–40. How should the priesthood not be used?
Read D&C 121:41–44. How should the priesthood be used?

WHAT BLESSINGS COME WHEN WE USE
THE PRIESTHOOD PROPERLY?

The Lord has promised great blessings to righteous priesthood holders who use the priesthood to bless others: "Then

The sick are blessed by the laying on of hands.

shall thy confidence wax strong in the presence of God; and the doctrine of the priesthood shall distil upon thy soul as the dews from heaven. The Holy Ghost shall be thy constant companion, and thy scepter an unchanging scepter of righteousness and truth; and thy dominion shall be an everlasting dominion, and without compulsory means it shall flow unto thee forever and ever'' (D&C 121:45–46).

A great latter-day prophet, David O. McKay, promised to every man who faithfully uses the priesthood in righteousness ''[He] will find his life sweetened, his discernment sharpened to decide quickly between right and wrong, his feelings tender and compassionate, yet his spirit strong and valiant in defense of right; he will find the priesthood a never-failing source of happiness—a well of living water springing up unto eternal life'' (David O. McKay, *Instructor,* Oct. 1968, p. 378).

What are some of the blessings you have received through the priesthood?
What are some of the blessings you can receive through the priesthood?
Sing ''We Thank Thee O God, For a Prophet'' and ''Praise to the Man.''

ADDITIONAL SCRIPTURES
D&C 107:1–100 (revelation on priesthood)
D&C 20:38–67 (duties of priesthood explained) (Also see *Priesthood Leader's Guidebook for Group or Small Branch* [PBMP0054].)

PRIESTHOOD ORGANIZATION

The Church of Jesus Christ of Latter-day Saints is governed by the priesthood. The priesthood, which is always associated with God's work, "continueth in the church of God in all generations, and is without beginning of days or end of years" (D&C 84:17). It is upon the earth today. Men young and old are baptized into the Church, and when they are judged worthy, they are ordained to the priesthood. They are given the authority to act for the Lord and to do his work on the earth.

TWO DIVISIONS OF PRIESTHOOD

The priesthood is divided into two parts, the Melchizedek Priesthood and the Aaronic Priesthood (see D&C 107:1). The greater priesthood is the Melchizedek Priesthood. Long ago, it was called "the Holy Priesthood, after the Order of the Son of God." But the name was changed so that the name of the Lord would not be used so often. The Church in ancient days called the priesthood "the Melchizedek Priesthood," after a great high priest who lived during the time of Abraham (see D&C 107:2–4).

The lesser priesthood is an appendage to the Melchizedek Priesthood. It is called the Aaronic because it was conferred upon Aaron and his sons throughout all their generations. Those who hold the Aaronic Priesthood have authority to administer the outward ordinances of faith, repentance, and baptism (D&C 107:13–14, 20).

Those holding the Melchizedek Priesthood have the power and authority to lead the Church and to direct the preaching of the gospel in all parts of the world. They are in charge of all the spiritual work of the Church (see D&C 84:19–22). They direct the work done in the temples; they preside over wards, branches, stakes, and missions; they heal the sick, bless the babies, give special blessings to Church members. The Lord's chosen prophet, the President of the Church, is the presiding high priest over the Melchizedek Priesthood (D&C 107:65–67).

Read D&C 107:1–4.
What are the two divisions of the priesthood?
How did the Melchizedek Priesthood get its name?

KEYS OF THE PRIESTHOOD

"There is a difference between priesthood and the 'keys' of the priesthood. A priest in a ward has power sufficient to baptize, yet he has not the right to perform this ordinance until he has been authorized by the bishop. The bishop has the 'keys' to administer to the affairs belonging under his ecclesiastical jurisdiction. Therefore, he is the person who can tell a priest to baptize.

"The president and prophet of the Church has the 'keys' of the priesthood to administer in all spiritual and temporal affairs of the Church. It is his right to delegate stake presidents, bishops, patriarchs and others, as holders of the 'keys' pertaining to specific offices in certain geographical areas.

"President Joseph F. Smith taught on this subject:

" 'Every man ordained to any degree of the priesthood has this authority delegated to him. But it is necessary that every act performed under this authority shall be done at the proper time and place, in the proper way, and after the proper order. The power of directing these labors constitutes the keys of the priesthood.' (*Gospel Doctrine*, p. 136)" (Melvin R. Brooks, *L.D.S. Reference Encyclopedia*, p. 393).

What is the difference between the priesthood and the keys of the priesthood?

THE OFFICES AND DUTIES OF THE AARONIC PRIESTHOOD

When the Aaronic Priesthood is conferred on a man or a boy, he is ordained to an office in that priesthood. Offices of the priesthood are called *appendages* to the priesthood (see D&C 84:29–30; 107:5). Each office carries duties and responsibilities that may be given to those who meet in priesthood groups or quorums. Each group or quorum is presided over by a group leader or quorum president who teaches the members their duties and asks them to fill assignments.

The offices in the Aaronic Priesthood are *deacon, teacher, priest,* and *bishop.* Some men join the Church or become active after they have passed the usual age to receive the offices of the priesthood. No matter what their age, they usually start as deacons and can be advanced to higher offices if they are worthy.

DEACON

When a boy has been baptized and confirmed a member of the Church and is worthy, he may be ordained to the office of deacon when he is twelve years old. The deacons are usually assigned to pass the sacrament to members of the Church, act as ushers, keep Church buildings and grounds in good order, act as messengers for priesthood leaders, and fulfill special assignments such as collecting fast offerings.

TEACHER

A worthy boy may be ordained a teacher when he is fourteen years old or older. Teachers have all the duties, rights, and powers of the office of deacon plus additional ones. Teachers in the Aaronic Priesthood are to help Church members live the commandments (see D&C 20:53–59). To help fulfill this responsibility, they are usually assigned as home teachers. They visit the homes of Church members and encourage them to live the principles of the gospel. They have been commanded to teach the truths of the gospel from the scriptures (see D&C 42:12). Teachers also prepare the bread and water for the sacrament service.

PRIEST

Priests have all the duties, rights, and powers of the offices of deacon and teacher plus some additional ones (see D&C 20:46–51). A priest may baptize. He may also administer the sacrament. He may ordain other priests, teachers, and deacons. A priest may take charge of meetings when there is no Melchizedek Priesthood holder present. He is to preach the gospel to those around him. A boy must be at least sixteen years old before he can be ordained a priest.

BISHOP

A bishop is ordained and set apart to preside over the Aaronic Priesthood in a ward. He is the president of the priest's quorum (see D&C 107:87–88). When he is acting in his Aaronic Priesthood office, a bishop deals primarily with temporal matters, such as buildings, collecting tithes and offerings, and preparing budgets (D&C 107:68).

However, a bishop is also ordained a high priest so that he can preside over all ward affairs and all members in the ward (see D&C 107:71–73; 68:15). A bishop is a judge in Israel (see D&C 107:74). It is his right to have the gift of discernment. This is the power to discern or know all spiritual gifts, "lest there shall be any among you professing and yet be not of God" (D&C 46:27).

Read D&C 84:29–30 and D&C 107:5. Discuss how offices of the priesthood are appendages to the priesthood.
Discuss the duties of the deacon, teacher, priest, and bishop.

THE OFFICES AND DUTIES OF THE MELCHIZEDEK PRIESTHOOD

The offices of the Melchizedek Priesthood are elder, seventy, high priest, patriarch, and apostle.

ELDER

Elders are called to teach, expound, exhort, baptize, and watch over the Church (see D&C 20:42). All Melchizedek Priesthood holders are elders. They have the authority to bestow the gift of the Holy Ghost by the laying on of hands (see D&C 20:43). Elders should conduct meetings of the Church

The priesthood is conferred in our own day by the laying on of hands.

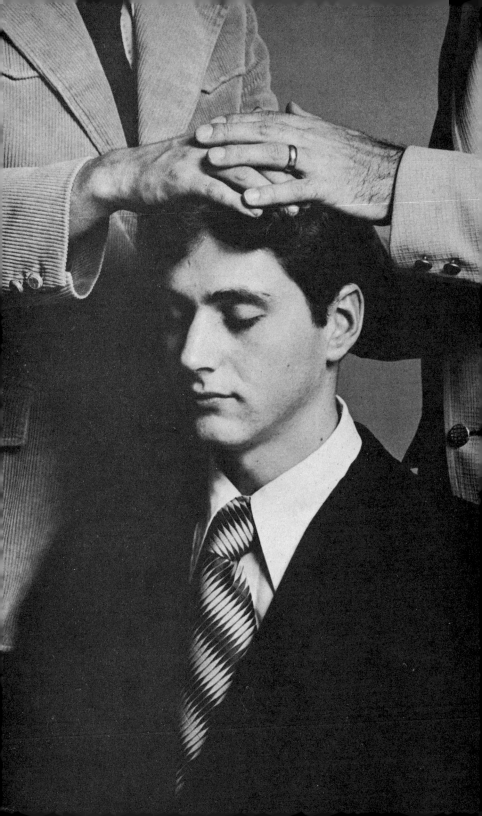

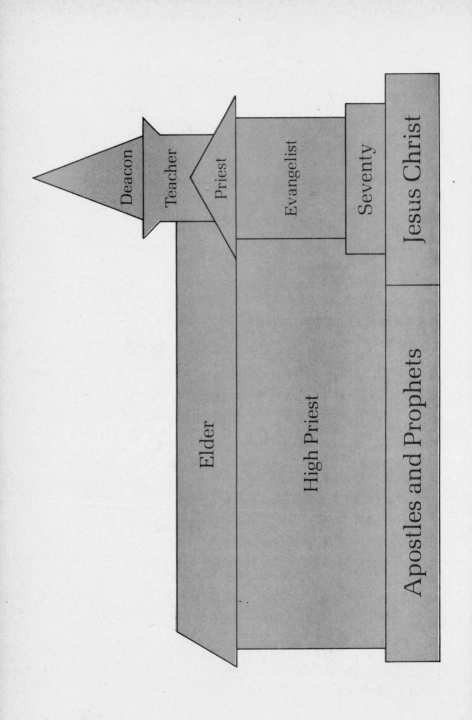

as they are led by the Holy Ghost (see D&C 20:45; 46:2). Elders may administer to the sick (see D&C 42:44). They are commanded to bless little children (see D&C 20:70). Elders may preside over Church meetings when there is no high priest present (D&C 107:11).

SEVENTY

A seventy has a special call to preach the gospel (see D&C 107:25). In the stakes of the Church, the seventies are called to be missionaries to nonmembers.

HIGH PRIEST

A high priest has the right to officiate in the Church and be in charge of spiritual things (see D&C 107:10, 12). He has the authority to officiate in all lesser offices (see D&C 68:19). Stake presidents, mission presidents, high councilors, bishoprics, and other leaders of the Church are ordained as high priests.

PATRIARCH

Patriarchs are chosen and ordained by the Apostles of the Church to give special patriarchal blessings to members of the Church in the stakes. These blessings give us some understanding of our callings on earth. They are the word of the Lord personally to us. Patriarchs are also ordained high priests (see D&C 107:39–56).

APOSTLE

An Apostle is a special witness of Jesus Christ in all the world (see D&C 107:23). The Apostles administer the affairs of the Church throughout the world. Those who are ordained to the office of Apostle in the Melchizedek Priesthood are usually set apart as members of the Council of Twelve Apostles. Each one is given all the keys of the kingdom of God on earth, but only the senior Apostle, who is President of the Church, actively exercises all of the keys. The others act under his direction.

Discuss the duties of elder, seventy, high priest, patriarch, and Apostle.

The Church of Jesus Christ is like a building with Christ as the chief cornerstone and the apostles and prophets as the foundation.

THE QUORUMS OF THE MELCHIZEDEK PRIESTHOOD

The Lord has instructed that the holders of the priesthood be organized into quorums. A quorum is a body of brethren holding the same priesthood office.

There are in the stakes of Zion the following Melchizedek Priesthood quorums:

THE QUORUMS OF ELDERS

"The elders quorum is instituted for standing ministers; nevertheless they may travel, yet they are ordained to be standing ministers." They do most of their work near their homes (see D&C 124:137). The quorum is to consist of up to ninety-six elders, presided over by a quorum presidency called by the stake president. Men who do not yet hold the Melchizedek Priesthood, now called "prospective elders," associate with the quorums of elders.

THE QUORUMS OF SEVENTY

"[The seventies] quorum is instituted for traveling elders to bear record of my name in all the world" (see D&C 124:139). The quorum contains up to seventy brethren. It is to be presided over by seven presidents. They are called by the stake president; their assignment is missionary work. They receive some guidance in their work from the First Quorum of the Seventy.

THE QUORUMS OF HIGH PRIESTS

Each quorum contains all high priests residing within the boundaries of a stake, including patriarchs and bishops. The stake president and his counselors are the presidency of this quorum.

THE QUORUMS OF THE AARONIC PRIESTHOOD

There are three quorums of the Aaronic Priesthood:

1. The deacons quorum, which consists of up to twelve deacons (see D&C 107:85). The presidency of the deacons quorum is called by the bishop, from among their members.

2. The teachers quorum, which consists of up to twenty-four members (see D&C 107:86). The presidency of the teachers quorum is called by the bishop, from among their numbers.

3. The priests quorum, which consists of up to forty-eight priests (see D&C 107:87–88). It is presided over by the bishop of the ward to which the quorum belongs.

The bishop is a high priest, and thus also belongs to the high priests quorum.

Whenever the number specified for a quorum is exceeded, the quorum should be divided.

Every holder of the priesthood should belong to a quorum. It is a sacred privilege that comes with the bestowal of the priesthood. Those who hold the priesthood are expected to be members of a quorum. (See Boyd K. Packer, "The Quorum," in *A Royal Priesthood,* Melchizedek Priesthood Personal Study Guide, 1975–76, pp. 131–136.) When ordained to the priesthood, a man or boy automatically becomes a member of a priesthood quorum. From then on through life, it is expected that he will hold membership in a quorum of the priesthood according to his office.

If a priesthood quorum functions properly, the members of the quorum are encouraged, blessed, fellowshipped, and taught the gospel by their leaders. Even though a man may be called and released from Church assignments such as teacher, officer, bishop, high councilor, or stake president, his membership in his quorum does not change. Membership in a quorum of the priesthood should be regarded as a sacred privilege.

What is a quorum? How does a quorum help strengthen the individual members? How many members make up a quorum of elders, high priests, deacons, teachers, priests?

ADDITIONAL SCRIPTURES
Alma 13:1–19 (manner after which men were ordained to the priesthood)
Hebrews 7:11–13 (Melchizedek priesthood restored at the coming of Christ)
Matthew 16:19; D&C 68:12 (Apostles given power; what they seal on earth is sealed in heaven)
D&C 20:38–67 (duties of elders, priests, teachers, deacons)
D&C 84; 107 (revelations on the priesthood)
1 Corinthians 12:14–31 (all offices of the priesthood important)

THE LORD'S COVENANT PEOPLE

From the beginning the Lord has made covenants with his children on earth. When his people make promises, or covenants, with him they will know what he expects of them and what blessings they may expect from him. When people make covenants they can become righteous enough to carry out his work on earth. The group of people who covenant with the Lord and with whom the Lord makes covenants is known as *the Lord's covenant people.* Members of the Church are part of the Lord's covenant people.

Read Deuteronomy 26:18. What is the Lord referring to when he calls his people a *peculiar people?*
Why are Latter-day Saints called a covenant people?

WHAT IS A COVENANT?

Within the gospel, a covenant means a sacred agreement or mutual promise between God and a person or a group of people. In making a covenant, God offers a blessing in exchange for obedience to particular commandments. He sets the terms of his covenants and he reveals these terms to his prophets on earth. If we choose to obey the terms of the covenant, we receive a promised blessing. If we choose not to obey, he withholds the blessing, and in some instances a penalty also is given.

For example, when we join the Church we make several covenants with God (see chapter 20, "Baptism"). We covenant with the Savior at baptism to take upon ourselves his name. He promises that "as many as . . . are baptized in my name which is Jesus Christ, and endure to the end, the same shall be saved" (D&C 18:22). We covenant with the Lord as we partake of the sacrament. We promise to remember him and to obey his commandments. We are promised that the Holy Spirit will be with us (see D&C 20:77–79). As members of the Church, we also covenant to obey the law of chastity, to keep the Sabbath day holy, and to be honest. When we enter into the eternal marriage covenant, we make other sacred promises and are promised exaltation for faithful obedience (see D&C 132; chapter 47, "Exaltation").

God has also made special covenants with particular persons or groups. He made special covenants with Adam, Enoch, Noah, children of Israel, and Lehi (see Moses 6:52; Moses 6:31–36; Genesis 9:9–17; Exodus 19:5–6; 2 Nephi 1). He made a special covenant with Abraham and his descendants that affects members of the Church today.

What is a covenant?
What kinds of covenants have we made with God?
What particular blessings has he promised for keeping certain covenants?

GOD'S COVENANT WITH ABRAHAM AND HIS DESCENDANTS

Abraham, an Old Testament prophet, was a very righteous man. He refused to worship his father's idols. He kept all of the Lord's commandments. Because of his righteousness, the Lord made a covenant with him and his descendants. Part of that covenant affects the lives of the Saints today. The Lord promised Abraham that he would have numberless descendants. He promised that all of them would be entitled to receive the gospel, the blessings of the priesthood, and all of the ordinances of exaltation. These descendants, through the power of the priesthood, would carry the gospel to all nations. Through them, all the families of the earth would be blessed (see Abraham 2:11). God further promised that if they were righteous he would establish his covenant with all generations of Abraham's children (see Genesis 17:4–8).

God made the same covenant with Abraham's son, Isaac,

and again with Isaac's son, Jacob. God changed Jacob's name to Israel. Since that time, the descendants of Jacob, called Israelites, have been known as God's Covenant People.

Read Abraham 2:9-11. List the promises that God has made to his covenant people.

MEMBERS OF THE CHURCH ARE A COVENANT PEOPLE

The blood descendants of Abraham are not the only people whom God calls his covenant people. In speaking to Abraham, God said: "As many as receive this Gospel shall be called after thy name, and shall be accounted thy seed [lineage], and shall rise up and bless thee, as their father" (Abraham 2:10). Thus, two groups of people are included in the marvelous covenant made with Abraham. These are Abraham's righteous blood descendants and those adopted into his lineage by accepting and living the gospel of Jesus Christ.

When we are baptized into the Church, we are adopted into Abraham's family and have part in the covenant the Lord made with Abraham, Isaac, and Jacob (see Galatians 3:26–29). If we are obedient, we inherit the blessings of that covenant. We have the right to receive help and guidance from the Holy Ghost. We have the right to hold the priesthood. We can gain eternal life in the celestial kingdom. There are no greater blessings than these.

However, along with the blessings we receive as the Lord's covenant people, we have great responsibilities. The Lord promised Abraham that through his descendants the gospel would be taken to all the earth. We are fulfilling our responsibility now through the full-time missionary program of the Church and the missionary work done by the members. This opportunity to preach the gospel to all the world belongs only to the Lord's church and his covenant people.

As the covenant people, we must also keep all of the Lord's commandments. When the people of the covenant break their part of the covenant by disobeying the commandments, the covenant becomes void. The Lord has said: "I, the Lord, am bound when ye do what I say; but when ye do not what I say, ye have no promise" (D&C 82:10). If we disobey the commandments after accepting the gospel, we will stand condemned before God (D&C 132:4). He has said: "Refrain from sin, lest sore judgments fall upon your heads. For of him unto whom much is given much is required; and he who sins against the greater light shall receive the greater condemnation" (D&C 82:2, 3).

Read the words of the Savior, Matthew 5:14–16. What responsibility do we have as members of the Church to be a light (example) unto the world?
What does this have to do with how we dress, act, and keep all the commandments of God?
What happens when we break a covenant we have made?

THE NEW AND EVERLASTING COVENANT

The fulness of the gospel is called *the new and everlasting covenant* by the Lord. It includes the covenants made at baptism, during the sacrament, in the temple, and at any other time. The Lord calls it "everlasting" because it is ordained by an everlasting God and because the covenant will never be changed. He gave this same covenant to Adam, Enoch, Noah, Abraham, and other prophets. In this sense it is not new. But the Lord calls it "new" because each time the gospel is restored after being taken from the earth, it is new to the people who receive it (see Jeremiah 31:31–34; Ezekiel 37:26).

When we accept the new and everlasting covenant, we agree to repent, to be baptized, to receive the Holy Ghost, to receive our endowments, to receive the covenant of marriage in the temple and to live righteously to the end of our lives. We must keep all our covenants with exactness. If we do, our Heavenly Father promises us that we will receive exaltation in the celestial kingdom (see D&C 132:20–24; chapter 47, "Exaltation").

How blessed we are to be his covenant people. To the faithful Saint, the Lord has promised: "All that my Father hath shall be given unto him'' (D&C 84:38). The greatness of that promise is hard for mortals to understand. The commandments he gives are for our benefit, and in exchange for obedience, we may forever share the blessings and beauties of heaven and earth. We may live in his presence and partake of his love, compassion, power, goodness, greatness, knowledge, wisdom, glory, and dominions.

What are the things we agree to do when we enter the new and everlasting covenant?

ADDITIONAL SCRIPTURES
1 Nephi 13:23–26 (covenants recorded in the Bible)
1 Peter 2:9–10 (peculiar people)
D&C 54:4–6 (effects of covenants kept and broken)
D&C 132:7 (covenants made by proper authority)
D&C 133:57–60 (purpose of covenants)
D&C 35:24 (promises for obedience to covenants)

THE CHURCH OF JESUS CHRIST IN FORMER TIMES

"We believe in the same organization that existed in the Primitive Church, namely, apostles, prophets, pastors, teachers, evangelists, etc." (sixth article of faith).

Jesus established his church when he was on the earth. It was called the *Church of Jesus Christ* (see 3 Nephi 27:8), and the members were called *Saints*. Through the persecution and death of Church leaders and the general wickedness of the people, the Church of Jesus Christ was taken from the earth.

Today, the Church of Jesus Christ has been restored, and the Church is called *The Church of Jesus Christ of Latterday Saints*. All of the offices and functions of the Church in the days of Jesus are present in the Church today.

Have someone read or quote the sixth article of faith. Read Ephesians 4:11. Discuss the similarity of this scripture to the article of faith.

SOME FEATURES THAT IDENTIFY THE CHURCH OF JESUS CHRIST

REVELATION

When Jesus established his church, he personally instructed and directed its leaders. He, in turn, received his instructions from his Father in Heaven. Thus the Church of Jesus Christ was directed by God and not by men (see Hebrews 1:1–2). Jesus Christ taught his followers that revelation was the "rock" upon which he would build his Church (see Matthew 16:16–18).

Before Jesus went into heaven after his resurrection, he told his apostles: "I am with you alway, even unto the end of the world" (Matthew 28:20). True to his word, he continued to guide them from heaven. He sent the Holy Ghost to be a comforter and a revelator to them (see Luke 12:12; John 14:26). He spoke to Saul in a vision (see Acts 9:3–6). He revealed to Peter that the gospel should be taught, not only to the Jews, but to the whole world (Acts 10). He revealed many glorious truths to John. These are written in the Book of Revelation. The New Testament records many other ways in which Jesus revealed his will to guide his church and enlighten his disciples.

AUTHORITY FROM GOD

The ordinances and principles of the gospel cannot be administered and taught without the priesthood. The Father gave this authority to Jesus Christ (see Hebrews 5:4–6) and Jesus Christ, in turn ordained his apostles and gave them the power and authority of the priesthood (see Luke 9:1–2; Mark 3:14). He reminded them: "Ye have not chosen me, but I have chosen you, and ordained you" (John 15:16).

That there might be order in his church, Jesus gave the greatest responsibility to the twelve apostles. Peter was appointed chief apostle, and Jesus gave to him the keys to seal blessings both on earth and in heaven (Matthew 16:19). Jesus ordained other officers also with specific duties to perform. After he ascended to heaven, the pattern of appointment and ordination was continued. Others were ordained to the priesthood, but only by those who had already received that authority. Jesus made it known through the Holy Ghost that he approved of those ordinations (Acts 1:24).

THE CHURCH ORGANIZATION

The Church of Jesus Christ was a carefully organized unit. It was compared to a perfectly formed building which was "built upon the foundation of the apostles and prophets, Jesus Christ himself being the chief cornerstone" (Ephesians 2:20).

Jesus appointed other priesthood leaders to assist the apostles in the work of the ministry. He sent officers called *seventies* in pairs to preach the gospel (see Luke 10:1). Other officers in the Church were evangelists (patriarchs), pastors (presiding leaders), high priests, elders, bishops, priests, teachers, and deacons (see chapter 14, "Priesthood Organization"). These officers were all necessary in order to do missionary work, to perform the ordinances, and to instruct and inspire Church members. They helped the members to "a unity of the faith and of the knowledge of the Son of God" (Ephesians 4:11-13).

The Bible does not tell us everything concerning the priesthood or the organization and government of the Church. However, enough of the Bible has been preserved to show the beauty and perfection of the Church organization. The apostles were commanded to go into all the world and preach. They could not stay in any one city to supervise new converts. Therefore, local priesthood leaders were called and ordained, and the Apostles presided over them. The apostles visited and wrote letters to the leaders in the various branches. Thus, our New Testament contains letters written by the apostles Paul, Peter, James, John, and Jude giving counsel and instruction to the local priesthood leaders.

The New Testament shows that this Church organization was intended to continue. For example, the death of Judas left only eleven Apostles. Soon after Jesus had ascended to heaven, the eleven apostles met together. They wanted to choose someone to take the place of Judas. Through revelation from the Holy Ghost they chose Matthias (see Acts 1:23-26). Later, other Apostles died or were killed. Paul, Barnabas, and James, the brother of the Lord, were all ordained in their places. Jesus had set a pattern for twelve apostles to govern the Church. It seemed clear that the organization was to continue as he had established it.

Jesus Christ ordained apostles.

FIRST PRINCIPLES AND ORDINANCES

The apostles preached the gospel wherever they went. They taught the people two basic principles: faith in the Lord Jesus Christ and repentance. After new converts had faith in Jesus Christ as the Son of God and their Redeemer and had repented of their sins, they received two basic ordinances: baptism by immersion and the laying on of hands for the gift of the Holy Ghost. These were the first principles and ordinances of the gospel. They applied to every person who desired to be a member of the Church of Jesus Christ. Jesus had taught them: "Except a man be born of water and of the Spirit, he cannot enter into the kingdom of God" (John 3:5). Everyone needed these saving ordinances of baptism and the gift of the Holy Ghost.

ORDINANCES PERFORMED FOR THE DEAD

The Church of Jesus Christ provided for everyone to accept the gospel, whether it was preached to them on earth or after death. Between the time of his death and his resurrection, Jesus went among the spirits of those who had died. He organized missionary work among those who were dead. He appointed righteous messengers and gave them power to teach the gospel to all the spirits of men. This gave them an opportunity to accept the gospel (see 1 Peter 3:18–20; 4:6; see also Joseph F. Smith—Vision of the Redemption of the Dead [Pearl of Great Price]). Living members of his church then performed ordinances in behalf of the dead (1 Corinthians 15:29). Such ordinances as baptism and ordinations must be done on the earth.

SPIRITUAL GIFTS

All faithful members of the Church were entitled to receive gifts of the Spirit. These were given to them according to their individual needs, capacities, and assignments. Some of these gifts were faith, including both the power to heal and to be healed; prophecy; and visions. The gifts of the Spirit are discussed in more detail in chapter 22. Spiritual gifts always exist in the true church of Jesus Christ (see 1 Corinthians

12:4–11). Jesus told his disciples that these signs or spiritual gifts always follow them that believe (Mark 16:17–18). In his name, many of his disciples did perform miracles, prophesied, or beheld visions through the power of the Holy Ghost.

THE CHURCH OF JESUS CHRIST IN THE AMERICAS

After Jesus was resurrected, he visited the people in America and organized his church among them (see 3 Nephi 11–28). Then he left them and ascended into heaven. For over 200 years, they lived righteously and were among the happiest people who had been created by the hand of God (see 4 Nephi 16).

List the features that identify the Church of Jesus Christ. Are all of these features found in any other church?

APOSTASY FROM THE TRUE CHURCH

Throughout history, evil men have tried to destroy the work of God. This happened while the apostles were still alive and supervising the young, growing Church. Some of the members taught ideas from their old pagan or Jewish beliefs instead of the simple truths taught by Jesus. In addition to this, there was persecution from outside the Church. Church members were tortured and killed for their beliefs. One by one, the apostles were killed. Because of the persecution, surviving apostles could not meet to choose and ordain men to replace those who were dead. Eventually, local priesthood leaders were the only ones who had authority to direct the various, scattered branches of the Church. The perfect organization of the Church no longer existed, and confusion resulted. More and more error crept into Church doctrine, and soon the destruction of the Church was complete. The period of time when the true church no longer existed on earth is called the *Great Apostasy*.

Soon pagan beliefs dominated the thinking of those called "Christians." The Roman emperor adopted this false "Christianity" as the state religion. This church was very different from the church Jesus organized. Members of this church believed that God was a being without form or substance.

These people lost the understanding of his love for us. They did not know that we are his children. They did not understand the purpose of life. Many of the ordinances were changed, because the priesthood and revelation were no longer on the earth.

The emperor chose his own leaders and called them by the same titles used by priesthood leaders in the true Church of Christ. Church officers were given honor and wealth. Bishops and archbishops fought among themselves to gain more power. There were no apostles or other priesthood leaders with power from God and no spiritual gifts. The prophet Isaiah had foreseen that this condition would come about. He had prophesied: "The earth also is defiled under the inhabitants thereof; because they had transgressed the laws, changed the ordinance, broken the everlasting covenant" (Isaiah 24:5). It was the Church of Jesus Christ no longer; it was a church of men. Even the name had been changed. In the Americas, apostasy also occurred (see 4 Nephi).

What does the term apostasy mean?
Have someone review the story of the apostasy.
What were some of the signs of the apostasy?

A RESTORATION FORETOLD

God had foreseen what would happen, and he had prepared for the gospel to be restored. The apostle Peter spoke of this to the Jews: "He shall send Jesus Christ, which before was preached unto you: Whom the heaven must receive until the times of restitution of all things, which God hath spoken by the mouth of all his holy prophets since the world began" (Acts 3:20–21).

John the Revelator had also foreseen the time when the gospel would be restored. He said: "I saw another angel fly in the midst of heaven, having the everlasting gospel to preach unto them that dwell on the earth, and to every nation, and kindred, and tongue, and people" (Revelation 14:6).

Read Daniel 2:44-45. What did Daniel see? Explain that the Church is the "stone" mentioned in this scripture.
Sing "High on the Mountain Top."

ADDITIONAL SCRIPTURES

Ephesians 2:19 (members called Saints)
1 Corinthians 12:12-31 (Church likened to a perfect body)
Hebrews 11:6 (faith necessary)
Luke 10:1; Acts 14:23; Titus 1:7; 1 Timothy 2:7 (officers of Church identified)
John 8:26-29 (the Father directs Jesus)
Luke 9:1; James 1:17; 5:14-15 (spiritual gifts)
2 Peter 2:1; Matthew 24:9-12; John 16:1-3; Amos 8:11; 2 Thessalonians 2:3-4 (apostasy predicted)
Daniel 2:44-45; Matthew 24:14; Micah 4:1; Isaiah 2:2-4 (restoration predicted)

Chapter 17

THE CHURCH OF JESUS CHRIST TODAY

When Jesus Christ lived on the earth, he established his church, the only true church. He organized his church so that the truths of the gospel could be taught to all people and the ordinances of the gospel could be administered correctly with authority. Using this organization, Christ could bring the blessings of salvation to mankind.

After the Savior ascended to heaven, men changed the ordinances and doctrines that he and his apostles had established. Because of apostasy, there was no direct revelation from God. The true Church of Jesus Christ was no longer on the earth. Men organized different churches. Each church claimed to be true but they taught conflicting doctrines. There was much confusion and contention over religion. The Lord had foreseen these conditions, saying there would be "a famine in the land, not a famine of bread, nor a thirst for water, but of hearing the words of the Lord . . . they shall seek . . . the word of the Lord, and shall not find it" (Amos 8:11, 12).

What does it feel like to go without food or water? Read Amos 8:11–12.
What kind of famine is spoken of in this scripture? Compare the famine to the period of time before the restoration.

THE LORD PROMISED TO RESTORE HIS TRUE CHURCH

The Savior promised that he would restore his church in the latter days. He said: "I will proceed to do a marvellous work among this people, even a marvellous work and a wonder" (Isaiah 29:14).

For many years people lived in spiritual darkness. About 1700 years after Christ, people were becoming more and more interested in knowing the truth about God and religion. Some of them could see that the gospel Jesus taught was no longer on the earth. Some recognized that there was no revelation and no true authority and that the church Christ organized did not exist on the earth. The time had arrived for the true Church of Jesus Christ to be restored to the earth. The Lord was about to do ''a marvellous work and a wonder'' and restore his church.

Read Isaiah 29:14. What is the ''marvellous work'' spoken of in Isaiah?

NEW REVELATION FROM GOD

In the spring of 1820, one of the most important events in the history of mankind occurred. The time had come for the marvelous work and wonder of which the Lord had spoken to come to pass. As a young boy, Joseph Smith wanted to know which of all the churches was the true church of Christ. He went into the woods near his home and prayed humbly and intently to his Heavenly Father, asking which church he should join. On that morning, a miraculous thing happened. Heavenly Father and Jesus Christ appeared to Joseph Smith. The Savior told him that he should not join any church, because the true church was not on the earth. He also said that the teachings of present churches were ''an abomination in his sight'' (see Joseph Smith 2:7–20). Beginning with this event, there was once more direct revelation from the heavens. The Lord had chosen a new prophet. Since that time the heavens have not been closed. Revelation continues to this day through each of his chosen prophets. Joseph was to be the one to help restore the true gospel of Jesus Christ.

Have a class member read Joseph Smith 2:7-21 or tell in his own words the Joseph Smith story.
Sing ''Oh, How Lovely Was the Morning.''

AUTHORITY FROM GOD WAS RESTORED

In restoring the gospel, the priesthood was given again to men on earth. John the Baptist came in 1829 to ordain Jo-

The Father and the Son visited Joseph Smith.

seph Smith and Oliver Cowdery to the Aaronic Priesthood (see D&C 13; 27:8). Then Peter, James, and John, the presidency of the Church in ancient times, came and gave Joseph and Oliver the Melchizedek Priesthood (see D&C 27:12–13) and the keys of the kingdom of God. Later, additional keys of the priesthood were restored by heavenly messengers such as Moses, Elias, and Elijah (see D&C 110:11–16). Through the Restoration the priesthood was returned to the earth. Those who hold this priesthood today have the authority to perform ordinances such as baptism. They also have the power to direct the affairs of the Lord's kingdom on the earth.

Have a member of the class tell about the restoration of the priesthood. Include the following: the restoration of the Aaronic Priesthood, the restoration of the Melchizedek Priesthood, and the effect of these restorations on the Lord's work.

CHRIST'S CHURCH WAS ORGANIZED AGAIN

On 6 April 1830, the Savior again directed the organization of his church on the earth (see D&C 20:1). His church is called The Church of Jesus Christ of Latter-day Saints (see D&C 115:4). Christ is the head of his church today, just as he was in ancient times. The Lord has said that it is "the only true and living church upon the face of the whole earth, with which I, the Lord, am well pleased" (D&C 1:30).

Joseph Smith was sustained as prophet and "first elder" of the Church (see D&C 20:2–4). Later the First Presidency was organized, and he was sustained as President. At the time the Church was first organized, only the framework was set up. The organization was perfected during the next several years.

The Church was organized with the same offices as were in the ancient Church of Jesus Christ. The organization of the ancient Church of Jesus Christ included apostles, prophets, seventies, evangelists (patriarchs), pastors (presiding officers), high priests, elders, bishops, priests, teachers, and deacons. These same offices are in his church today (see sixth article of faith).

A prophet acting under the direction of the lord leads the Church. This prophet is also the President of the Church. He holds all of the authority necessary to direct the work (see D&C 107:65, 91). Two counselors assist the President. The Church has twelve Apostles who are special witnesses of Jesus Christ. They carry the gospel to all parts of the world. Other general officers of the Church with special assignments are the patriarch, the Presiding Bishopric, and the First Quorum of the Seventy.

Throughout the Church, the offices of the priesthood include apostles, patriarchs, high priests, seventies, elders, priests, teachers, and deacons. These are the same offices that existed in the original Church of Jesus Christ.

The Church has grown much larger than it was in the days of Jesus. As it has grown, the Lord has revealed additional units of organization within the Church. When the Church is fully organized in an area, it has local divisions called *stakes*. A stake president and his two counselors preside over each stake. The stake has twelve high councilors who help carry out Church programs in the stake. Melchizedek Priesthood quorums are organized in the stake under the direction of the stake president (see this manual, chapter 14, "Priesthood Organization). Each stake is divided into smaller areas called *wards*. A bishop and his two counselors preside over each ward. In areas of the world where the Church is developing, there are missions which are divided into the smaller units of districts and then branches, small branches, groups, and families.

Read the testimony of Joseph Smith contained in the preface to Doctrine and Covenants 20.

FIRST PRINCIPLES AND ORDINANCES WERE RESTORED

The Church of Jesus Christ today teaches the same principles and performs the same ordinances as were performed in the days of Jesus. The first principles and ordinances of the gospel are faith in the Lord Jesus Christ, repentance, baptism by immersion, and the laying on of hands for the gift of the Holy Ghost. These precious truths were returned in their fulness when the Church was restored to the earth. Through the gift and power of God, Joseph Smith translated the Book of Mormon, which contains the plain and precious truths of the gospel. Many other revelations followed and have been recorded as scripture in the Doctrine and Covenants and the Pearl of Great Price (see this manual, chapter 10, "Scriptures").

Read the fourth article of faith. Discuss what this means to members of the Church.

OTHER IMPORTANT TRUTHS WERE RESTORED

Other important truths that the world had lost and did not possess at the time of the restoration are taught in The Church of Jesus Christ of Latter-day Saints. These include the following:

1. Our Heavenly Father is a real person with a tangible body of flesh and bones.

2. We existed in premortal life as spirit children of God.

3. The priesthood is necessary to administer the ordinances of the gospel.

4. Men will be punished for their own sins and not for Adam's transgression.

5. Little children do not need to be baptized until they are accountable (eight years old).

6. There are three degrees of glory in the heavens and men will be rewarded according to their actions on earth.

7. Family relationships can be eternal, through the sealing power of the priesthood.

8. The temple endowment and sealings are available for both the living and the dead.

THE CHURCH OF JESUS CHRIST WILL NEVER BE DESTROYED

Since its restoration in 1830, The Church of Jesus Christ of Latter-day Saints has grown rapidly in membership. There are members in nearly every country in the world. The Church will continue to grow. As Christ said: "This Gospel of the Kingdom shall be preached in all the world, for a witness unto all nations" (Joseph Smith 1:31). The Church will never again be taken from the earth. Its mission is to take the truth to every person. Thousands of years ago, the Lord said that he would "set up a kingdom, which shall never be destroyed: and the kingdom shall not be left to other people, . . . and it shall stand for ever" (Daniel 2:44).

Read D&C 84:76. What can you do to help spread the kingdom of God?

ADDITIONAL SCRIPTURES
Revelation 14:6; Daniel 2:44-45; Isaiah 2:2-4; 2 Nephi 3:6-15 (restoration foretold)
D&C 110; D&C 128:19-21; D&C 133:36-39, 57-58 (restoration of gospel)
Ephesians 2:20 (Jesus Christ the cornerstone of the Church)
D&C 20:38-67 (duties of officers of Church)
Matthew 24:14 (gospel to be preached to all nations)
D&C 84:76 (duty to preach gospel)

FAITH IN JESUS CHRIST

Faith in the Lord Jesus Christ is the first principle of the gospel. It is necessary to our salvation. The righteous King Benjamin declared: "Salvation cometh to none . . . except it be through repentance and faith on the Lord Jesus Christ" (Mosiah 3:12).

Sing "I Know That My Redeemer Lives" and "I Know My Father Lives."
Read the fourth article of faith.

WHAT IS FAITH?

Faith is confidence in things that are not seen but that are true (see Hebrews 11:1; Alma 32:21). The Prophet Joseph Smith taught that faith motivates our day to day activities. He said that faith is a principle of power and the moving cause of action within us.

Would we try to study and learn if we did not believe that we could obtain wisdom and knowledge? Would we work each day if we did not hope that by doing so we could accomplish something? Would a farmer plant if he did not expect to harvest? Our food, our clothing, our homes exist because of our faith. Each day we act upon things we hope for, when we cannot see the end result. This is faith (see Hebrews 11:3).

Many scriptural incidents tell how great things were accomplished through faith.

In faith Noah built an ark and saved his family from the flood (see Hebrews 11:7). Moses parted the waters of the Red Sea (see Hebrews 11:29). Elijah called down fire from heaven

We must have faith in Jesus Christ.

Chapter 18

(see 1 Kings 18:17–40). Nephi called for a famine (see Helaman 11:3–5). He also asked the Lord to end the famine (see Helaman 11:9–17). Seas have been calmed, visions opened, and prayers answered, all through the power of faith.

If we carefully study the scriptures we learn that faith is a strong belief of truth within our souls that motivates us to do good. This causes us to ask: In whom should we have faith?

Ask the group to think about their everyday activities. How does faith move you to action?

WHY SHOULD WE HAVE FAITH IN JESUS CHRIST?

Faith must be centered in the Lord Jesus Christ.

The Apostle Paul preached that "there is none other name under heaven given among men, whereby we must be saved" (Acts 4:10–12). Jacob taught that men must have ". . . perfect faith in the Holy One of Israel [Jesus Christ], or they cannot be saved in the kingdom of God" (2 Nephi 9:23). Through faith in the Savior and through repentance, his atonement becomes effective in our lives. Through faith we can receive strength to overcome temptations (see Alma 37:33).

We cannot have faith in Jesus Christ without also having faith in our Heavenly Father. If we have faith in them, we will also have faith that the Holy Ghost, whom they send, will teach us all truth and will comfort us.

Read Acts 4:10–12 and Alma 37:33. Why do we need to have faith in Jesus Christ?

HOW CAN WE INCREASE OUR FAITH IN JESUS CHRIST?

Knowing of the many blessings that can be ours if we exercise faith in Jesus Christ, we should *strive* to increase our faith in him. The Savior said: "If ye have faith as a grain of mustard seed, . . . nothing shall be impossible unto you" (Matthew 17:20). A mustard seed is very small, but it grows into a large tree.

How can we increase our faith? The same way we increase or develop any other skill. How do we develop skills in wood-carving, weaving, painting, cooking, making pottery or play-

The prophet Noah foresaw the great flood and in faith built an ark, on which he saved a few faithful people.

ing a musical instrument? We study and practice and work at it. As we do so, we improve. So it is with faith. If we want to increase our faith in Jesus Christ, we must work at it. The Prophet Alma compares increasing our faith to planting a seed. He said:

"But behold, if ye will awake and arouse your faculties, even to an experiment upon my words, and exercise a particle of faith, yea, even if ye can no more than desire to believe, let this desire work in you, even until ye believe in a manner that ye can give place for a portion of my words.

"Now, we will compare the word unto a seed. Now, if ye give place, that a seed may be planted in your heart, behold, if it be a true seed, or a good seed, if ye do not cast it out by your unbelief, that ye will resist the Spirit of the Lord, behold, it will begin to swell within your breasts; and when you feel these swelling motions, ye will begin to say within your-selves—It must needs be that this is a good seed, or that the word is good, for it beginneth to enlarge my soul; yea, it be-ginneth to enlighten my understanding. . . .

"Now behold, would not this increase your faith?" (Alma 32:27–29)

So we can increase our faith by acting on our desire to have faith in God.

We can also exercise our faith by praying to our Heavenly Father about our hopes, our desires, and our needs (see Alma 34:17–25). But we must not suppose that all we have to do is ask. We are told in the scriptures that "faith, if it hath not works, is dead, being alone" (James 2:17). The following is an example of a man who combined faith and works.

This man wanted to study the scriptures, but he could not read. He prayed to his Heavenly Father to help him learn to read. In time a teacher came to his village, and he asked the teacher to help him. He learned the alphabet. He studied sounds and learned to put the letters together to make words. Soon he was reading simple words. The more he practiced, the more he learned. He thanked the Lord for sending the teacher and for helping him learn to read. This man has increased his faith, humility, and knowledge to such a degree that he has served as a branch president in the Church.

President Spencer W. Kimball explains: "There must be works with faith. How foolish it would be to ask the Lord to *give* us knowledge, but how wise to ask the Lord's help to acquire knowledge, to study constructively, to think clearly, and to retain things that we have learned" (*Faith Precedes the Miracle,* p. 205).

Faith involves doing everything we can to bring about the things we hope and pray for. President Kimball has said: "In faith we plant the seed, and soon we see the miracle of the blossoming. Men have often misunderstood and have reversed the process." He continued by explaining that many of us want to have health and strength without keeping the health laws. We want to have prosperity without paying our tithes. We want to be close to the Lord but we don't want to fast and pray. We want to have rain in due season and to have peace in the land without observing the Sabbath as a holy day and without keeping the other commandments of the Lord (see *Faith Precedes the Miracle,* p. 4).

An important way to increase our faith is to hear and study the word of the Lord. We hear the word of the Lord at our Church meetings. We can study his word in the scriptures. "And as all have not faith, seek ye diligently and teach one another words of wisdom; yea, seek ye out of the best books words of wisdom; seek learning, even by study and also by faith" (D&C 88:118).

Read James 2:17.
Why did President Kimball say "faith involves doing everything we can"?
Discuss ways to make faith stronger. (Pray, fast, study the scriptures, obey commandments.) Challenge the class members to use these ways.

WHAT ARE SOME BLESSINGS THAT FOLLOW FAITH?

By faith, miracles are wrought, angels appear, the gifts of the Spirit are given, prayers are answered and men become the sons of God (see Moroni 7:25-26; 36-37). The Prophet Joseph Smith said:

"When faith comes it brings . . . with it—apostles, prophets, evangelists, pastors, teachers, gifts, wisdom, knowledge, miracles, healings, tongues, interpretation of tongues, etc. All these appear when faith appears on the earth, and disappear when it disappears from the earth; for these are the effects of faith, . . . And he who possesses it will, through it, obtain all necessary knowledge and wisdom, until he shall know God, and the Lord Jesus Christ, whom he has sent—whom to know is eternal life. Amen." (*Lectures on Faith,* p. 69.)

Tell a story about how showing faith made a person stronger, or use a faith story from the additional scripture list.

ADDITIONAL SCRIPTURES
Hebrews 11; Alma 32 (nature of faith explained)
Exodus 14:19-22 (parting the waters of the Red Sea)
Genesis 6-8 (Noah and the flood)
1 Kings 18:17-39 (Elijah—fire from heaven)
Matthew 8:5-33 (sick healed, tempest, miracles of faith)
Mark 5:25-34 (healed by faith)

REPENTANCE

There has been the need for repentance in the world from the time of Adam to the present day. In the very beginning, the Lord instructed Adam: "Wherefore, teach it unto your children, that all men, everywhere, must repent, or they can in nowise inherit the kingdom of God, for no unclean thing can dwell there, or dwell in his presence" (Moses 6:57).

WE ALL NEED TO REPENT

We come to this earth for the purpose of growing and progressing. This is a lifetime process. During this time, we all sin. We all have need to repent. Sometimes we sin because of ignorance; sometimes because of our weaknesses; and sometimes because of willful disobedience. But all of us are guilty of sin to some degree. In the Bible we read that "there is not a just man upon the earth, that doeth good, and sinneth not" (Ecclesiastes 7:20) and that "if we say that we have no sin, we deceive ourselves, and the truth is not in us" (1 John 1:8).

What is sin? The Apostle James said: "To him that knoweth to do good, and doeth it not, to him it is sin" (James 4:17). Another apostle described sin as "all unrighteousness" (1 John 5:17).

That is why the Lord has said that "all men, everywhere must repent" (Moses 6:57). Except for Jesus Christ, who lived a perfect life, everyone who has lived upon the earth has sinned. Our Heavenly Father in his great love has provided the principle of repentance to help us overcome our sins.

Why do all people need to repent?

WHAT IS REPENTANCE?

It is the way provided for us to become free from our sins and to receive forgiveness for them. Sins slow our spiritual progression and can even stop it. Repentance makes it possible for us to grow and develop spiritually again. To repent, we must feel sincere sorrow for our sins. We must stop sinning and begin keeping the commandments.

The privilege of repenting is made possible through the atonement of Jesus Christ. In a way we do not fully understand, Jesus Christ paid for our sins. President Joseph Fielding Smith said of this event:

"I have suffered pain, you have suffered pain, and sometimes it has been quite severe; but I cannot comprehend pain . . . that would cause the blood, like sweat, to come out upon the body. It was something terrible, something terrific. . . .

"There was *no man ever born into this world that could have stood under the weight of the load that was upon the Son of God, when he was carrying my sins and yours* and making it possible that we might escape from our sins" (*Doctrines of Salvation,* 1:130–31).

Repentance sometimes requires great courage; much strength; many tears; unceasing prayers; and untiring efforts to live the commandments of the Lord.

What does the word *repentance* mean to you?

HOW DO WE REPENT?

President Spencer W. Kimball has declared: "There is *no royal road to repentance,* no privileged path to forgiveness. Every man must follow the same course whether he be rich or poor, educated or untrained, tall or short, prince or pauper, king or commoner. . . . There is only one way. It is a long road spiked with thorns and briars and pitfalls and problems" (*The Miracle of Forgiveness,* p. 149).

We must repent of our sins.

WE MUST RECOGNIZE OUR SINS

The first step on the road to repentance is to admit to ourselves that we have sinned. If we do not admit to ourselves that we have done wrong, we cannot repent.

Alma counseled his son Corianton, who had been unfaithful in his missionary calling and had committed a serious sin: "Let your sins trouble you, with trouble which shall bring you down unto repentance. . . . Do not endeavor [try] to excuse yourself in the least point" (Alma 42:29–30). The scriptures advise us further not to justify our sinful practices (see Luke 16:15–16).

As we learn truth from error, we must examine our lives and admit the things we do that are wrong.

WE MUST FEEL SORROW FOR OUR SINS

In addition to recognizing our sins, we must also have feelings of sincere sorrow for what we have done. We must come to feel that our sins are disgusting and loathsome. We must want to unload and abandon them. The scriptures tell us: "All those who humble themselves before God, and desire to be baptized, and come forth with broken hearts and contrite spirits and . . . have truly repented of their sins . . . shall be received by baptism into his church" (D&C 20:37).

WE MUST FORSAKE OUR SINS

Our sincere sorrow should lead us to forsake (stop) our sinning. It does little good to admit that we have sinned if we do not stop doing the evil thing. If we truly repent of our sins, we will do them no more. If a person has stolen, he will steal no more. If he has lied, he will lie no more. If he committed adultery, he will stop this evil practice. The Lord said to the Prophet Joseph Smith: "By this ye may know if a man repents of his sins—behold, he will confess them and forsake them" (D&C 58:43).

WE MUST CONFESS OUR SINS

Confessing our sins is very important. The Lord has commanded that we confess them. It relieves a heavy burden from the sinner. We cannot hide any act of our lives from ourselves or from the Lord. We must confess all our sins to him. In addition, serious sins, such as adultery, fornication, and robbery, which might affect our standing in the Church must be confessed to the proper priesthood authority. If we have sinned against another person, we should confess to the person we have injured. Some less serious sins involve no one but ourselves and the Lord. These may be confessed privately to the Lord. The Lord has promised: "I, the Lord, forgive sins, and am merciful unto those who confess their sins with humble hearts" (D&C 61:2).

WE MUST MAKE RESTITUTION

Part of repentance is to make restitution. This means that insofar as possible we must make right any wrong that we have done. For example, a thief should give back what he has stolen. A liar should make the truth known. A gossip, who has slandered the character of a person, should work to restore the good name of the person he has harmed. If we do these things, then when we are judged by God our sins will not be mentioned to us (see Ezekiel 33:15–16).

WE MUST FORGIVE OTHERS

A vital part of repentance is to forgive those who have sinned against us. The Lord will not forgive us unless our hearts are fully cleansed of all hate, bitterness, and bad feelings against our fellowmen (see 3 Nephi 13:14–15). Wherefore, I say unto you, that ye ought to forgive one another; for he that forgiveth not his brother his trespasses standeth condemned before the Lord; for there remaineth in him the greater sin" (D&C 64:9).

WE MUST KEEP THE COMMANDMENTS OF GOD

To make our repentance complete we must always keep the commandments of the Lord (see D&C 1:32). A person is not fully repentant who does not pay his tithes or does not keep the Sabbath day holy or refuses to obey the Word of Wisdom. He is not repentant if he does not sustain the authorities of the Church and does not love the Lord or his fellowmen. A man who fails to have his family prayers and who is unkind to his family and others is surely not repentant. When a person is repentant, his life changes. President Kimball said, "Repentance means not only to convict yourselves of the horror of the sin, but to confess it, abandon it, and restore to all who have been damaged to the total extent possible; then spend the balance of your lives trying to live the commandments of the Lord so he can eventually pardon you and cleanse you" (*The Miracle of Forgiveness,* p. 200).

Discuss the steps of repentance.

HOW REPENTANCE HELPS US

As a result of repentance, the atonement of Jesus Christ becomes effective in our lives, and our sins are forgiven. We become free from the bondage of our sins, and we find happiness and joy.

Alma shared with us his experience in repenting from his sinful past:

"My soul was harrowed up [troubled] to the greatest degree and racked with all my sins.

"Yea, I did remember all my sins and iniquities, for which I was tormented with the pains of hell; yea, I saw that I had rebelled against my God, and that I had not kept his holy commandments.

". . . So great had been my iniquities, that the very thought of coming into the presence of my God did rack my soul with inexpressible horror.

". . . It came to pass that as I was . . . harrowed up by the memory of my many sins, behold, I remembered also to have heard my father prophesy . . . concerning the coming of one Jesus Christ, a Son of God, to atone for the sins of the world.

"Now, as my mind caught hold upon this thought, I cried within my heart: O Jesus, thou Son of God, have mercy on me. . . .

". . . And . . . behold, when I thought this, I could remember my pains no more . . . ."

"And oh, what joy, and what marvelous light I did behold; yea, my soul was filled with joy as exceeding as was my pain!

". . . There can be nothing so exquisite and sweet as was my joy" (Alma 36:12-21).

Read Alma 36:10-28. Discuss the agony Alma suffered remembering his sins, his repentance, and how forgiveness brought him joy.

WHEN SHOULD WE REPENT?

The prophets have declared that "this life is the time for men to prepare to meet God" (Alma 34:32). We should repent now, every day. When we get up in the morning, we should examine ourselves to see whether the Spirit of God is with us. At night before we go to sleep, we should review our acts and words of the day and ask the Lord to show us the things for which we need to repent. By repenting every day and having the Lord forgive our sins we will experience the daily process of perfecting ourselves. Like Alma, our happiness and joy can be sweet and exquisite.

Discuss how difficult it is to learn something new all at once. By contrast, discuss how easy it is to practice each day until we gain mastery. How is this like repentance?
Sing "How Gentle God's Commands."

ADDITIONAL SCRIPTURES
Matthew 9:10-13; Luke 13:3; Ezekiel 18:30 (repent or perish)
2 Corinthians 7:9-10 (godly sorrow)
Mosiah 4:10-12 (steps to repentance)
Isaiah 1:18; Mosiah 26:28-32 (repentance brings forgiveness)
D&C 58:42 (sins remembered no more)
2 Nephi 9:23 (repentance necessary to salvation)
2 Nephi 2:21 (repent while in the flesh)

BAPTISM

Today, as in the days of Jesus, there are certain principles and ordinances of the gospel which the Lord said we must learn and obey. A principle is a belief or a teaching. An ordinance is a rite or a ceremony. The first two principles of the gospel are faith in the Lord Jesus Christ and repentance. Baptism is the first ordinance of the gospel. One of the instructions the Lord gave to his apostles was, "Go ye therefore, and teach all nations, baptizing them in the name of the Father, and of the Son, and of the Holy Ghost: Teaching them to observe all things whatsoever I have commanded you" (Matthew 28:19–20).

Sing "The Spirit of God like a Fire."
How does a principle of the gospel differ from an ordinance of the gospel?

WHY MUST WE BE BAPTIZED?

WE MUST BE BAPTIZED FOR THE REMISSION OF OUR SINS

If we repent, and are baptized, our sins are forgiven through the atonement of Jesus Christ.

From the scriptures we learn that John the Baptist did "baptize in the wilderness, and preach the baptism of repentance for the remission of sins" (Mark 1:4). The Apostle Peter taught: "Repent, and be baptized every one of you in the name of Jesus Christ for the remission of sins" (Acts 2:38). Following Paul's conversion, Ananias said to him: "Arise, and be baptized, and wash away thy sins" (Acts 22:16).

We must be baptized by immersion for the remission of sins.

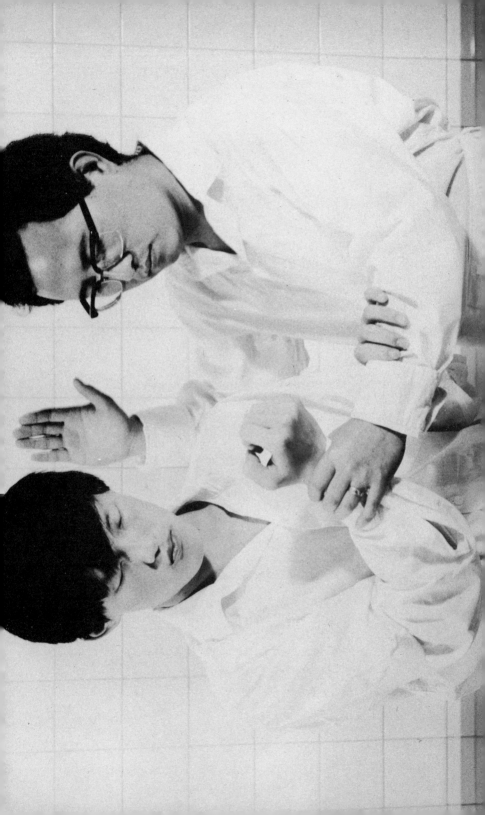

Chapter 20

WE MUST BE BAPTIZED TO BECOME MEMBERS OF THE CHURCH OF JESUS CHRIST

"All those who humble themselves before God, and desire to be baptized . . . that . . . have truly repented of all their sins . . . shall be received by baptism into his church" (D&C 20:37).

WE MUST BE BAPTIZED BEFORE WE CAN RECEIVE THE GIFT OF THE HOLY GHOST

The Lord said: "If thou wilt turn unto me, and . . . repent of all thy transgressions [sins], and be baptized, even in water, in the name of mine Only Begotten Son . . . ye shall receive the gift of the Holy Ghost" (Moses 6:52).

WE MUST BE BAPTIZED TO SHOW OBEDIENCE

Jesus Christ was without sin, yet he was baptized. He said that his baptism was necessary "to fulfill all righteousness" (see Matthew 3:13–15). The Prophet Nephi explained that the voice of the Lord said: "Follow me, and do the things which ye have seen me do . . . with full purpose of heart, acting no hypocrisy and no deception before God, but with real intent, repenting of your sins, witnessing unto the Father that ye are willing to take upon you the name of Christ by baptism" (2 Nephi 31:12–13).

WE MUST BE BAPTIZED TO ENTER THE CELESTIAL KINGDOM

Jesus said: "Whoso believeth in me, and is baptized . . . shall inherit the kingdom of God. And whoso believeth not in me, and is not baptized, shall be damned" (3 Nephi 11:33–34). Baptism is the gateway through which we enter the celestial kingdom. There is no other way.

Discuss five reasons why we need to be baptized.

HOW SHOULD WE BE BAPTIZED?

There is only one correct mode of baptism. Jesus revealed to the Prophet Joseph Smith that a person having the proper priesthood authority to perform baptism "shall go down into the water with the person who has presented himself or her-

Alma baptized in the waters of Mormon.

self for baptism. . . . Then shall he immerse him or her in the water, and come forth again out of the water" (D&C 20:73-74). Immersion is necessary. The apostle Paul taught that being immersed in water and coming out again is symbolic of death and resurrection. Our sinful life ends when we are baptized. After baptism we start a new life. Paul said, "Know ye not, that so many of us as were baptized into Jesus Christ were baptized into his death? Therefore we are buried with him by baptism into death: that like as Christ was raised up from the dead by the glory of the Father, even so we also should walk in newness of life. For if we have been planted together in the likeness of his death, we shall be also in the likeness of his resurrection" (Romans 6:3-5).

Baptism by immersion by one having the proper authority is the only true and acceptable way of being baptized.

Read D&C 20:72-74. Why is authority to perform a baptism important?

WHO SHOULD BE BAPTIZED?

Every person who has reached eight years of age and is accountable, or responsible, for his actions should be baptized. Some churches teach that little children should be baptized. This is not in keeping with the teachings of the Savior. When Jesus spoke of little children he said, "Of such is the kingdom of heaven" (Matthew 19:14). The prophet Mormon said that it is mockery before God to baptize little children for they are not capable of sinning; baptism is not required of persons who are mentally incapable of knowing right and wrong (see Moroni 8:9-22). All other persons are to be baptized. There is no other way. We must receive the ordinance of baptism and remain true to the covenant we make at that time. Unless we remain true to these covenants we cannot live with our Heavenly Father again.

Ask: Why does the Apostle Paul liken our baptism to the burial of the Savior?
Read Moroni 8:11-20. Why do we not baptize little children?

WE MAKE COVENANTS WHEN WE ARE BAPTIZED

Many scriptures teach about baptism. In one of these scriptures, (Mosiah 18:7-17) the prophet Alma taught that faith and repentance are steps which prepare us for baptism. He taught that when we are baptized we actually make a covenant with the Lord. We promise to do certain things, and God promises to bless us in return. When we are baptized, we show that we have made covenants with God.

Alma explained that we must want to be called the people of God. We must be willing to help each other and to comfort each other. We must stand as witnesses of God at all times and in all things and in all places. He said that if we do these things and are baptized, we will have our sins forgiven. Then we will come forth in the first resurrection. We will have eternal life. Alma concluded: "Behold, here are the waters of Mormon . . . if this be the desire of your hearts, what have you against being baptized in the name of the Lord, as a witness before him that ye have entered into a covenant with him, that ye will serve him and keep his commandments, that he may pour out his Spirit more abundantly upon you?" The people clapped their hands for joy and said that it was their desire to be baptized. Alma baptized them in the waters of Mormon.

Alma taught that when we are baptized we make covenants with the Lord to—

1. Come into the fold of God.

2. Be called his people.

3. Bear one another's burdens.

4. Stand as witnesses of God at all times and in all places all of our lives.

5. Serve God and keep his commandments.

When we are baptized and keep the covenants of baptism the Lord promises to—

1. Forgive our sins.

2. Pour out his Spirit more abundantly upon us.

3. Give us daily guidance and help of the Holy Ghost.

4. Let us come forth in the first resurrection.

5. Give us eternal life.

Review the baptismal covenants. List and discuss the promises we make and those made by our Heavenly Father. How can we help each other keep these covenants?

BAPTISM GIVES US A NEW BEGINNING

With baptism we begin a new way of life. That is why we call it a rebirth. Jesus said that unless a man is born again he cannot enter the kingdom of God. He further explained that except a man is born of the water and of the spirit he cannot enter the kingdom of God (see John 3:3–5). This principle was explained clearly to Adam: "Inasmuch as ye were born into the world by water, and blood, and the spirit, which I have made, and so became of dust a living soul, even so ye must be born again into the kingdom of heaven, of water, and of the Spirit, and be cleansed by blood, even the blood of mine Only Begotten" (Moses 6:59).

The Apostle Paul said that following our baptism we should begin a new life: "We are buried with him by baptism . . . even so we also should walk in newness of life" (Romans 6:4).

One of the great blessings of baptism is that it provides us with a new start as we strive for our eternal goal.

Why is baptism a new beginning?

ADDITIONAL SCRIPTURES
2 Nephi 31:4–7 (purpose and necessity of baptism)
3 Nephi 11:21–27 (how to perform a baptism)
Acts 21:38–39 (baptism required of all who repent)
D&C 20:71 (baptism not required of children)
3 Nephi 27:16 (baptism a covenant)
Alma 7:14–16; Colossians 2:12 (be baptized, cleansed)

THE GIFT OF
THE HOLY GHOST

Joseph Smith said that we believe in the gift of the Holy Ghost being enjoyed now as much as it was enjoyed in the days of the first apostles. We believe in this gift in all its fullness, power, greatness, and glory (see "The Prophet Speaks," *Friend,* Apr. 1977, inside front cover).

In chapter 7 we learned that the Holy Ghost is a member of the Godhead. He is a spirit in the form of a man. He does not have a body of flesh and bones. He can be in only one place at a time, but his influence can be every place at the same time. His mission is to bear witness of the Father and the Son and to bear witness to all truth.

There is a difference between the Holy Ghost and the *gift* of the Holy Ghost. In this chapter, we will learn what the gift of the Holy Ghost is and how we can receive this great gift from God.

Have someone tell what they know about the Holy Ghost (see this manual, chapter 7).

WHAT IS THE GIFT OF THE HOLY GHOST?

The gift of the Holy Ghost is the privilege given to a baptized person, after he has been confirmed a member of the Church, to receive guidance and inspiration from the Holy Ghost. Of course, the members of the Church must be worthy to receive revelation and enjoy the companionship of the Holy Ghost (see Joseph F. Smith, *Gospel Doctrine,* pp. 60–61).

A person may be temporarily guided by the Holy Ghost without receiving the gift of the Holy Ghost. But this guidance will not continue with him if he does not receive baptism and the laying on of hands for the gift of the Holy Ghost. We read in Acts 10 that the Roman soldier Cornelius received inspiration from the Holy Ghost so that he knew the gospel of Jesus Christ was true. But Cornelius did not receive the gift of the Holy Ghost until after he was baptized. The Prophet Joseph Smith taught that if Cornelius had not received baptism and the gift of the Holy Ghost, the Holy Ghost would have left him (see *Teachings of the Prophet Joseph Smith,* p. 199).

Today many nonmembers of the Church learn, by the power of the Holy Ghost, that the Book of Mormon is true (see Moroni 10:4–5). But that flash of testimony leaves them if they do not receive the gift of the Holy Ghost. They do not receive the continuing assurance that comes to those who have the gift of the Holy Ghost.

Discuss the difference between inspiration by the Holy Ghost and the gift of the Holy Ghost.

HOW DO WE RECEIVE THE GIFT OF THE HOLY GHOST?

Those persons who have been baptized and confirmed are given the gift of the Holy Ghost. This gift is given through the laying on of hands by the elders of the Church. The Lord has said: "Whoso having faith you shall confirm in my church, by the laying on of the hands, and I will bestow the gift of the Holy Ghost upon them" (D&C 33:15).

Every worthy elder of the Church when authorized may give the gift of the Holy Ghost to another person. However, there is no guarantee that the person will receive inspiration and guidance from the Holy Ghost just because the elders have laid their hands on his head. Each person must "receive the Holy Ghost." This means that the Holy Ghost will only come to a person when he is worthy and desires help from this heavenly messenger (see Bruce R. McConkie, *Mormon Doctrine,* p. 313).

We must receive the gift of the Holy Ghost by the laying on of hands.

To be worthy to have the help of the Holy Ghost, a person must be striving to obey all of the commandments of God. He must keep his thoughts and actions pure. President David O. McKay, the ninth president of the Church, said: "One chief purpose of life is to overcome evil tendencies, to govern our appetites, to control our passions—anger, hatred, jealousy, immorality. We have to overcome them; we have to subject them, conquer them because God has said: '. . . the Spirit of the Lord doth not dwell in unholy temples—' (Helaman 4:24), nor will it '. . . always strive with man' (2 Nephi 26:11)" (David O. McKay, "Emotional Maturity," *Instructor*, Sept. 1959, p. 281).

What must we do to receive the constant companionship of the Holy Ghost?

ONE OF GOD'S GREATEST GIFTS

The gift of the Holy Ghost is one of God's greatest gifts to man. Through the Holy Ghost we may know that God lives, that Jesus is the Christ, and that his Church has been restored to the earth. We may have the promptings of the Holy Ghost to tell us all the things we should do (see 2 Nephi 32:5). We may enjoy the gifts of the Spirit (see this manual, chapter 22). This great gift from our Heavenly Father can also bring peace to our hearts and an understanding of the things of God (1 Corinthians 2:9–12).

In what ways does the Holy Ghost help us?

ADDITIONAL SCRIPTURES
1 Corinthians 3:16–17, D&C 130:21–23 (the Holy Ghost dwells with the worthy)
Moroni 8:25–26 (how to receive the Holy Ghost)
Moroni 10:5 (the Holy Ghost a witness to truth)

SUGGESTED SONG
"The Spirit of God like a Fire"

THE GIFTS
OF THE SPIRIT

Following baptism, each of us had hands laid on our heads to receive the gift of the Holy Ghost. If we are faithful, we can have his influence constantly with us. Through him, each of us can be blessed with certain spiritual powers called *gifts of the Spirit.* These gifts are only given to those who are obedient to God's laws. They help us know and teach the truths of the gospel. They will help us to bless others. They will guide us back to our Heavenly Father. In order to use our gifts wisely, we need to know what they are, how we can develop them, and how to recognize Satan's imitations of them.

Discuss the reasons the Lord has given us special spiritual gifts.

THE GIFTS OF THE SPIRIT

The scriptures mention many gifts of the Spirit. These gifts of the Spirit have been given to members of the true church whenever it has been on the earth. Their presence is proof that this is the true church (see Mark 16:16–18). However, because they are easily imitated, gifts of the Spirit are not the *only* proof of the true Church.

THE GIFT OF TONGUES (D&C 46:24)

Sometimes it is necessary to communicate the gospel in a language we have not learned. When this happens, the Lord can bless us with the ability to speak that language. Many missionaries have received the gift of tongues when there was a great need for it. For example, Elder Alonzo A. Hinckley was a missionary in Holland who understood and spoke very little Dutch even though he had prayed and studied hard. When he returned to a home he had visited before, a lady opened the door and spoke to him very angrily in Dutch. To his amazement he could understand every word. He felt a strong desire to bear his testimony to her in Dutch. He began to speak, and the words came out very clearly in Dutch. But when he returned to show his mission president that he could speak Dutch, the ability had left him. Many faithful members have been blessed with the gift of tongues (see Joseph Fielding Smith, *Answers to Gospel Questions,* 2:32–33).

THE GIFT OF INTERPRETATION OF TONGUES (D&C 46:25)

This gift is sometimes given to us when we do not understand a language and we need to receive an important message from God. For example, President David O. McKay had a great desire to speak to the Saints in New Zealand without an interpreter. He told them that he hoped that the Lord would bless them that they could understand him. He spoke in English. His message lasted about forty minutes. As he spoke, he could tell by the expression on many of their faces and the tears in their eyes that they were receiving his message (see *Answers to Gospel Questions,* 2:30–31).

THE GIFT OF TRANSLATION (D&C 5:4)

If we have been called by the leaders of the Church to translate the word of the Lord, we can receive a gift to translate beyond our natural ability. As with all gifts, we must live righteously, study hard, and pray to receive it. When we do these things, the Lord causes us to feel a burning inside concerning the correctness of the translation (D&C 9:8–9). Joseph Smith had the gift of translation when he translated the Book of Mormon. This gift came to him only when he was in tune with the Spirit.

THE GIFT OF WISDOM (D&C 46:17)

Some of us have been blessed with the ability to understand people and the principles of the gospel as they apply in our

Joseph Smith translated the Book of Mormon by the power of the Spirit.

lives. We are told: "If any of you lack wisdom, let him ask of God, that giveth to all men liberally, and upbraideth not; and it shall be given him. But let him ask in faith, nothing wavering. For he that wavereth is like a wave of the sea driven with the wind and tossed. For let not that man think that he shall receive any thing of the Lord" (James 1:5–7). The Lord has said: "Seek not for riches but for wisdom, and behold, the mysteries of God shall be unfolded unto you" (D&C 6:7).

THE GIFT OF KNOWLEDGE (D&C 46:18)

All who become like our Heavenly Father eventually know all things. The knowledge of God and his laws is revealed by the Holy Ghost (D&C 121:26). We cannot be saved if we are ignorant of these laws (D&C 131:6). The Lord has said: "If a person gains more knowledge and intelligence in this life through his diligence and obedience than another, he will have so much the advantage in the world to come" (D&C 130:19). He has commanded us to learn as much as we can about his work. He wants us to learn about the heaven, the earth, things which have happened or will happen, things at home and in foreign lands (D&C 88:78–79). However, there are those who try to gain knowledge by their own study alone. They do not ask for the help of the Holy Ghost. They are those who are always learning, but never arriving at the truth (2 Timothy 3:7). When we receive knowledge by revelation from the Holy Ghost, his Spirit speaks to our minds and our hearts and we feel the truth burn within us (D&C 8:2).

What kinds of things should we learn about? (Read also D&C 90:15.)

Read 2 Nephi 9:28–29; D&C 88:118. What is the right way to gain knowledge?

THE GIFT OF TEACHING WISDOM AND KNOWLEDGE (Moroni 10:9–19)

Some people are given a special ability to explain and testify to the truths of the gospel. This gift can be used when we teach a class. It can be used by parents to teach their children. This gift also helps us instruct others so they can come to an understanding of the gospel.

Why must we have the Spirit of the Lord to teach? (see D&C 42:14).

138

THE GIFT OF KNOWING THAT JESUS CHRIST IS THE SON OF GOD (D&C 46:13)

This has been the gift of prophets and apostles who have been called as special witnesses of Jesus Christ. However, others are also given this gift. Every person can have a testimony. It may come through the whispering of the Holy Spirit or in a dream or a vision. These things are so sacred that they are seldom talked about. Elder Orson F. Whitney saw a vision of the Savior in Gethsemane. He saw the great suffering of the Savior, and it caused him to weep. Then the Savior took him into his arms and blessed him (see Bryant S. Hinckley, *The Faith of Our Pioneer Fathers*, pp. 211–13).

THE GIFT OF BELIEVING THE TESTIMONY OF OTHERS (D&C 46:14)

By the power of the Holy Ghost we may know the truth of all things. If we want to know whether someone else is speaking the truth we must ask God in faith. If the thing we are praying about is true, the Lord will speak peace to our minds (see D&C 6:22–23). In this way we can know when someone else, even the prophet, has received revelation. Nephi asked the Lord to let him see, feel, and know that his father's dream was true (see 1 Nephi 10:17–19).

How can we receive a testimony that another person is speaking the truth?

THE GIFT OF PROPHECY (D&C 46:22)

Those who receive true revelations about the past, present, or future have the gift of prophecy. Prophets have this gift, but we too can have it to help us govern our own lives (see 1 Corinthians 14:39). We may receive revelations from God for ourselves and our own callings, but never for the Church or its leaders. It is contrary to the order of heaven for a person to receive revelation for one higher in authority than himself. If we truly have the gift of prophecy, we will not receive any revelation which does not agree with what the Lord has said in the scriptures (see Joseph Fielding Smith, *Doctrines of Salvation*, 3:203–04).

Read 1 Corinthians 14. Who can receive the gift of prophecy?

THE GIFT OF HEALING (D&C 46:19-20)

Some have the faith to heal and others have the faith to be healed. We can all exercise the faith to be healed when we are ill (see D&C 42:48). Many who hold the priesthood have the gift of healing the sick. Others may be given a knowledge of how to cure illness.

Read D&C 42:43-44. What should we do when we are ill?

THE GIFT OF WORKING MIRACLES (D&C 46:21)

The Lord has blessed his people many times in miraculous ways. When the Utah pioneers planted their first crops, a plague of locusts nearly destroyed them. The pioneers prayed very hard that the Lord would save them and he sent sea gulls to eat the locusts. When we are in great need of help and we ask in faith, if it is for our good the Lord will work miracles for us (see Matthew 17:20; D&C 24:13-14).

THE GIFT OF FAITH (Moroni 10:11)

The Brother of Jared had the gift of great faith. Because of his faith, he received other gifts. His faith was so great that the Savior appeared to him (see Ether 3:9-15). Without faith, no other gift can be given. Moroni promises: "Whoso believeth in Christ, doubting nothing, whatsoever he shall ask the Father in the name of Christ it shall be given him" (Mormon 9:20-21). We should seek to increase our faith, find out our gifts, and use them.

Some people are so lacking in faith that they deny that these gifts of the Spirit actually exist. Moroni says to them: "And again I speak unto you who deny the revelations of God, and say that they are done away, that there are no revelations, nor prophesies, nor gifts, nor healings, nor speaking with tongues, and the interpretation of tongues; Behold I say unto you, he that denieth these things knoweth not the gospel of Christ; yea, he has not read the scriptures; if so he does not understand them" (Mormon 9:7-8).

WE CAN DEVELOP OUR GIFTS

The Lord has said: "For all have not every gift given unto

The brother of Jared had such great faith that he saw the finger of the Lord.

them; for there are many gifts, and to every man is given a gift by the Spirit of God. To some is given one, and to some is given another, that all may be profited thereby" (D&C 46:11–22).

To develop our gifts, we must find out which gifts we have. We do this by praying and fasting. We should seek after the best gifts (see D&C 46:8). Sometimes patriarchal blessings will tell us which gifts we have been given.

We must be obedient and faithful to be given our gifts. We then should use these gifts to do the work of the Lord. They are not given to satisfy our curiosity or to prove anything to us because we lack faith. If we ever demand and received a sign without faith or humility, it will be held against us (see Alma 30:50). Our gifts are to be used to build up the kingdom of God and to strengthen our testimonies.

Discuss ways we can discover our spiritual gifts.
How will Satan tempt us to misuse them?

SATAN IMITATES THE GIFTS OF THE SPIRIT

Satan can imitate the gifts of tongues, prophecy, visions, healings, and other miracles. Moses had to compete with Satan's imitations in Pharaoh's court (see Exodus 7:8–22). Satan wants us to believe in his false prophets, false healers, and false miracle workers. They may appear to be so real to us that the only way we have of knowing is to ask God for the gift of discernment. The devil himself can appear as an angel of light. Satan wants to blind us to the truth and keep us from seeking the true gifts of the Spirit. Mediums, astrologers, fortune tellers, and sorcerers are inspired by Satan even if they claim to follow God. Their works are abominable to the Lord (see Isaiah 47:12–14; Deuteronomy 18:9–10). We should avoid all associations with the powers of Satan.

How can we discern between the true gifts of the Spirit and Satan's imitations?

WE MUST BE CAREFUL WITH OUR GIFTS OF THE SPIRIT

The Lord says: "A commandment I give unto them, that they shall not boast themselves of these things, neither speak them before the world; for these things are given unto you for your profit and for salvation" (D&C 84:73). We must remember that spiritual gifts are sacred.

The Lord asks only one thing in return for giving us these gifts. He says: "Ye must give thanks unto God in the Spirit for whatsoever blessing ye are blessed with" (D&C 46:32).

How do we keep our spiritual gifts sacred?

ADDITIONAL SCRIPTURES
3 Nephi 29:6-7 (fate of those who deny gifts)
Moroni 10:7-19 (gifts depend on faith)
1 Corinthians 12:1-31 (spiritual gifts)
Acts 10 (a gift given at baptism)
D&C 46:9-26 (gifts of the Spirit)

SUGGESTED SONGS
"Oh Say, What Is Truth?," "The Spirit of God like a Fire"

THE SACRAMENT

Our Savior wants us to remember his great atoning sacrifice and to keep his commandments. To help us do so, he has commanded us to meet often and partake of the sacrament.

The sacrament is a holy priesthood ordinance that helps remind us of the atonement of the Savior. During the sacrament, we partake of bread and water. We do this in remembrance of his flesh and his blood which were given as a sacrifice for us. As we partake of the sacrament, we renew sacred covenants with our Heavenly Father.

Sing "Jesus, the Very Thought of Thee."
What is the sacrament?
What is the purpose of the sacrament?

CHRIST INTRODUCED THE SACRAMENT

Shortly before his crucifixion, Jesus gathered his Apostles around him in an upstairs room. He knew he would soon die on the cross. This was the last time he would meet with these beloved men before his death. He wanted them to always remember him so that they could be strong and faithful to his teachings. To help them remember, he introduced the sacrament. He broke bread into pieces and blessed it. Then he said: "Take, eat; this is in remembrance of my body which I give a ransom for you." Next he took a cup of wine, blessed it, and gave it to his apostles to drink. He said: "Drink ye all of it. For this is in remembrance of my blood . . . which is shed for as many as shall believe on my name, for the remission of their sins" (Inspired Version, Matt. 26:22–24. See

Jesus administered the sacrament at the last supper with his apostles.
Print © Providence Lithograph Co.

also King James Version, Matt. 26:26–28; Mark 14:22–23; Luke 22:15–20).

After his resurrection, Jesus came to the Americas, where he taught the Nephites the same ordinance (3 Nephi 18:1–11). After the Church was restored in the latter days, Jesus once again commanded his people to partake of the sacrament in remembrance of him, saying: "It is expedient that the church meet together often to partake of bread and wine in the remembrance of the Lord Jesus" (D&C 20:75).

Read Matthew 26:26–28. Ask each class member to think about the Lord's Supper the next time he partakes of the sacrament.

HOW THE SACRAMENT IS ADMINISTERED

Modern scriptures explain exactly how the sacrament is to be administered. Members of the Church meet each Sabbath day to worship and partake of the sacrament (see D&C 20:75). The sacrament is administered by those who hold the necessary priesthood authority. A priest or elder breaks bread into pieces, kneels, and blesses it (D&C 20:76). The sacrament bread is then passed to members of the Church. Then the priest or elder blesses water, and it too is passed to the members. Christ gave his disciples wine when he introduced the sacrament. However, in a modern revelation he has said that it doesn't matter what we eat and drink during the sacrament as long as we remember him (D&C 27:2–3). Today, Latter-day Saints drink water instead of wine.

Jesus has given us the exact words for both prayers. We should listen carefully to these beautiful prayers and try to understand what we are promising and what is being promised to us. Here is the prayer said over the bread:

"O God, the Eternal Father, we ask thee in the name of thy Son, Jesus Christ, to bless and sanctify this bread to the souls of all those who partake of it, that they may eat in the remembrance of the body of thy Son, and witness unto thee, O God, the Eternal Father, that they are willing to take upon them the name of thy Son, and always remember him and keep his commandments which he has given them; that they may always have his Spirit to be with them. Amen" (D&C 20:77).

Here is the prayer said over the water:

"O God, the Eternal Father, we ask thee in the name of thy Son, Jesus Christ, to bless and sanctify this wine [water] to the souls of all those who drink of it, that they may do it in remembrance of the blood of thy Son, which was shed for them; that they may witness unto thee, O God, the Eternal Father, that they do always remember him, that they may have his Spirit to be with them. Amen." (D&C 20:79).

The ordinance of the sacrament is performed very simply and reverently.

Read the sacrament prayers one sentence at a time. Discuss the meaning of each sentence. Challenge each member to memorize the prayers.

THE COVENANTS THAT WE RENEW DURING THE SACRAMENT

Each time we partake of the sacrament, we renew covenants with the Lord. A covenant is a sacred promise between the Lord and his children. The covenants we make are clearly stated in the sacramental prayers. It is important to know what those covenants are and what they mean.

We covenant to take upon ourselves the name of Jesus Christ. By this, we show we are willing to be identified with him and his church. We promise that we will never do anything that will bring shame or reproach upon that name.

We covenant to remember Jesus Christ. All our thoughts, feelings, and actions will be influenced by him and his mission.

We promise to keep all of his commandments.

We take these obligations upon ourselves when we are baptized (see D&C 20:37; Mosiah 18:6–10). Thus, when we partake of the sacrament, we renew the covenants we made when we were baptized. Worthy partakers of the sacrament put themselves in perfect harmony with the Lord (see 3 Nephi 18:1–12). The Lord said they gain "the remission of their sins" (Inspired Version, Matthew 26:24).

The Lord promises that if we keep our covenants, we will always have his Spirit to be with us. A person guided by the Spirit will have the knowledge, faith, power, and righteousness to gain eternal life.

Refer to D&C 20:77 again.
What are the promises we make during the sacrament?

OUR ATTITUDE WHEN TAKING THE SACRAMENT

Before partaking of the sacrament, we must prepare ourselves spiritually. The Lord has made it clear that no one should partake of the sacrament unworthily. That means we must repent of our sins before taking the sacrament. The scriptures say: "If any have trespassed, let him not partake until he makes reconciliation" (D&C 46:4). The scriptures also say: "Ye shall not suffer anyone knowingly to partake of my flesh and blood unworthily, when ye shall minister it. For whoso eateth and drinketh my flesh and blood unworthily eateth and drinketh damnation to his soul" (3 Nephi 18:28–29).

During the sacrament service we should dismiss from our minds all worldly thoughts. We should feel prayerful and reverent. We should think of the atonement of our Savior and be grateful for it. We should examine our lives and look for ways to improve. We should also renew our determination to keep the commandments.

We do not need to be perfect before partaking of the sacrament, but we must have the spirit of repentance in our hearts. The attitude with which we partake of the sacrament influences our experience with it. If we partake of the sacrament with a pure heart, we receive the promised blessings of the Lord.

Ask someone to tell how we should properly prepare ourselves to partake of the sacrament.
What things can we think about during the sacrament to help us be more reverent?

ADDITIONAL SCRIPTURES
D&C 20:75–79 (how to administer sacrament)
1 Corinthians 11:27–29 (partake of sacrament worthily)

THE SABBATH DAY

"Remember the Sabbath day, to keep it holy" (Exodus 20:8; see also D&C 68:29).

WHAT IS THE SABBATH DAY?

The word *Sabbath* comes from the Hebrew word meaning *day of rest.* The Sabbath day commemorates God's day of rest after he finished the creation. We read in the book of Genesis that God created the heavens and the earth in six periods of time which he called "days": "And on the seventh day God ended his work which he had made; and he rested on the seventh day from all his work which he had made. And God blessed the seventh day, and sanctified it" (Genesis 2:2–3).

The Sabbath day is every seventh day. It is a holy day ordained by God for us to rest from our daily labors and worship him.

What is the Sabbath day?

PURPOSE OF THE SABBATH DAY

Jesus Christ taught that the Sabbath day was made to benefit man (see Mark 2:27). The purpose for the Sabbath is to give us a certain day of the week on which to direct our thoughts and actions toward God. It is not a day merely to rest from work. It is a sacred day to be spent in worship and reverence. As we rest from our usual daily activities, our minds are freed to ponder on spiritual matters. On this day we may renew our covenants with the Lord and feed our souls on the things of the Spirit (see Mark 2:27).

Sunday is a day for studying the scriptures.

What is the Lord's purpose for the Sabbath day?

HISTORY OF THE SABBATH

The seventh day was consecrated by God as a Sabbath in the beginning of the earth (see Genesis 2:2-3). Since earliest times, the tradition of a sacred seventh day has been preserved among various peoples of the earth. God renewed a commandment concerning this day to the Israelites, saying: "Remember the sabbath day, to keep it holy" (Exodus 20:8). Keeping the Sabbath day was also a sign that the Israelites were his covenant people (see Exodus 31:12-17; Isaiah 56:1-8; Jeremiah 17:19-27).

However, some Jewish leaders made many unnecessary rules about the Sabbath. They decided how far a person could walk, what kind of knot he could tie, and so forth. When certain Jewish leaders criticized Jesus Christ for healing sick people on the Sabbath, Jesus reminded them that the Sabbath was made for the benefit of man.

The Nephites on the Western Hemisphere also observed the Sabbath day according to the commandments of God (see Jarom 5).

In modern times, the Lord has repeated his commandment that we should remember the Sabbath day and keep it holy (see D&C 68:29).

Have someone tell about the history of the Sabbath using the scriptures: Genesis 2:2-3; Exodus 20:8; Isaiah 56:1-8; Jarom 5; Mark 2:27; D&C 68:29.)

THE LORD'S DAY

Until the resurrection of Jesus Christ, he and his disciples honored the seventh day as the Sabbath. After his resurrection, Sunday was held sacred as the Lord's Day in remembrance of his resurrection on that day (see Acts 20:7; 1 Corinthians 16:2). From that time on his followers appointed the first day as their Sabbath. In either case, there were six days of labor and one for rest and devotion.

The Lord has given us a direct commandment in these days that we, too, should honor Sunday, the Lord's day, as our Sabbath (see D&C 59:12).

Chapter 24

Why was the Sabbath changed from the seventh day to the first day?
What special event does the first day commemorate?

HOW DO WE KEEP THE SABBATH DAY HOLY?

The Lord asks us, first, to *sanctify* the Sabbath day. In a revelation given to Joseph Smith in 1831, the Lord commanded the Saints to go to the house of prayer and offer up their sacraments, rest from their labors, and pay their devotions to the Most High (D&C 59:9–12).

Second, he asks us to rest from daily work. This means that we should perform no labor that would keep us from giving our full attention to spiritual matters. The Lord told the Israelites: "Thou shalt not do any work, thou, nor thy son, nor thy daughter, thy manservant, nor thy maidservant"; even the animals were to rest on the Sabbath (see Exodus 20:10). Our prophets have told us that we should not shop, hunt, fish, attend sports events, or participate in any similar activities on that day.

President Spencer W. Kimball has cautioned, however, that if we merely lounge about doing nothing on the Sabbath, we are not keeping the day holy; the Sabbath calls for constructive thoughts and acts (see *The Miracle of Forgiveness,* pp. 96–97).

What kinds of things *may* we do on the Sabbath? The Lord has told us to prepare only simple foods on that day, keeping the purpose of the Sabbath in mind (see D&C 59:13). The prophet Isaiah suggested that we should turn away from doing our own pleasure and should "call the Sabbath a delight, the holy of the Lord, honourable" (Isaiah 58:13). We should do righteous things. We will keep the Sabbath day holy by—

1. Attending Church meetings.

2. Reading the scriptures and the words of our Church leaders.

3. Visiting the sick, aged, and our loved ones.

4. Listening to uplifting music and singing hymns.

5. Praying to our Heavenly Father with praise and thanksgiving.

6. Performing Church service that we have been assigned to do.

7. Preparing genealogical records and personal and family histories.

8. Telling faith-promoting stories and bearing our testimony to family members, and sharing spiritual experiences with them.

9. Writing letters to loved ones.

10. Fasting with a purpose.

11. Sharing time with children and others in the home.

In deciding what other activities we should properly engage in on the Sabbath, we should ask ourselves: Will it uplift and inspire me?

There may be times when we are required to work on the Sabbath. We should avoid this whenever possible, but when it is absolutely necessary, we can still maintain the spirit of Sabbath worship in our hearts to some extent.

Read D&C 59:9-13.
What things can we do to draw nearer to our Heavenly Father?

BLESSINGS FOR OBSERVING THE SABBATH

If we honor the Sabbath day in a righteous manner, we may receive great spiritual and temporal blessings. The Lord has said that if we keep the Sabbath day with thanksgiving and cheerful hearts, we will be full of joy. He has promised that "the fulness of the earth is yours . . . whether for food or for raiment, or for houses, or for barns, or for orchards, or for gardens, or for vineyards; yea, all things which come of the earth, in the season thereof, are made for the benefit and use of man, both to please the eye and to gladden the heart; yea for food and for raiment, for taste and for smell, to strengthen the body and to enliven the soul" (D&C 59:13-19).

Read together D&C 59:15-19.
Discuss some of the blessings that come from keeping the Sabbath day holy.

ADDITIONAL SCRIPTURES

Exodus 31:14-17 (under Mosaic law Sabbath kept under pain of death)
Mosiah 18:23; Mosiah 13:16-19; Exodus 35:1-3 (observe Sabbath as a holy day)
Hebrews 8:1-13 (old covenant superseded by new)
Luke 6:1-11 (lawful to do good on the Sabbath)
Luke 13:11-17; John 5:1-18 (Jesus' example of doing good on Sabbath)

SUGGESTED SONG

"How Gentle God's Commands"

FASTING

Since the time of Adam, men have fasted to help them draw near to our Heavenly Father and to worship him. Jesus showed the importance of fasting by his own example (see Luke 4:1–4). Through latter-day revelation we learn that the Lord still expects his people to fast and pray often (see D&C 88:76).

Sing "In Humility, Our Savior."
Read D&C 88:76. Discuss why fasting is given as a commandment.

HOW TO FAST PROPERLY

Fasting means to go without food and drink (see Joseph F. Smith, *Gospel Doctrine,* p. 243). Occasional fasting is good for our bodies and helps our minds become more active (see *Principles of the Gospel,* p. 175). The Savior taught us that purposeful fasting is more than just going without food and drink. We must also concentrate on spiritual matters.

WE SHOULD PRAY WHEN WE FAST

Prayer is a necessary part of fasting. Throughout the scriptures, prayer and fasting are mentioned together. Our fasting should be accompanied by sincere prayer, and we should begin and end our fasting with prayer.

WE SHOULD FAST WITH A PURPOSE

Fasting can have many purposes. We can overcome weaknesses or problems by fasting and praying. Sometimes we may wish to fast and pray for help or guidance for others; such as a family member who is ill and needs a blessing (see

Fasting and prayer bring blessings.

Mosiah 27:22–23). Through fasting we can come to know the truth of things just as did the prophet Alma in the Book of Mormon. He said: "I have fasted and prayed many days that I might know these things of myself. And now I do know of myself that they are true; for the Lord God hath made them manifest unto me by his Holy Spirit" (Alma 5:46). We can fast for our nonmember friends to become converted to the truth. Fasting can help comfort us in times of sorrow and mourning (see Alma 28:4–6). Fasting can help us to become humble and feel closer to our Heavenly Father (see Helaman 3:35). Our purpose in fasting should not be to impress others. "Moreover when ye fast, be not, as the hypocrites, of a sad countenance: for they disfigure their faces, that they may appear unto men to fast. Verily I say unto you, they have their reward. But thou, when thou fastest, anoint thine head, and wash thy face; that thou appear not unto men to fast" (see Matthew 6:16–18). We should be cheerful when we fast and not advertise our fasting to others.

What things should we do to make our fasting more spiritual? What things do we need to fast for? After a few minutes of meditation, ask if anyone wants to share some ideas.

THE FAST DAY

One Sunday each month Latter-day Saints observe a fast day. On this day we neither eat nor drink for two consecutive meals, thus making a fast of twenty-four hours. If we were to eat our evening meal on Saturday, then we would not eat or drink until the evening meal on Sunday.

Everyone who can do so should fast. "Many are subject to weakness, others are delicate in health, and others have nursing babies; of such it should not be required to fast. Neither should parents compel their little children to fast" (*Gospel Doctrine,* p. 244).

We should encourage our children to fast after they have been baptized, but we should never force them. The fast day is a special day for us to humble ourselves before the Lord in fasting and prayer. It is a day to pray for forgiveness from our sins and for the power to overcome our faults and to forgive others.

On Fast Sunday, members of the Church meet together and partake of the sacrament. They strengthen themselves and one another by bearing testimony in the fast meeting.

FAST OFFERINGS

The Lord asks us to fast one Sunday each month to help the poor. Every member who fasts should give through the proper priesthood authority either food or the money he would have spent on food for the two meals. We should give as generously as we are able. Through our fast offerings we become partners with the Lord in administering to the needs of our less fortunate brothers and sisters.

What should we do on fast day to make fasting more meaningful?
What are some of the reasons we pay fast offerings?

WE ARE BLESSED WHEN WE FAST

Isaiah, a prophet of the Old Testament, has told us that rich promises are made by the Lord to those who fast and help the needy. We are promised peace, increased health, and spiritual guidance. Isaiah tells us that when we fast, "then shall thy light break forth as the morning, and thine health shall spring forth speedily; and thy righteousness shall go before thee; the glory of the Lord shall be thy reward. Then shalt thou call, and the Lord shall answer; thou shalt cry, and he shall say, Here I am" (Isaiah 58:8–9).

Fasting improves our lives and gives us added strength. It helps us live other principles of the gospel because it draws us nearer to the Lord.

FASTING TEACHES SELF-CONTROL

Fasting helps us gain strength of character. This reason alone makes fasting important (see David O. McKay, *True to the Faith,* p. 81). When we fast properly, we will learn to control our appetites, our passions, and our tempers. Solomon, a great and wise king, said: "He that is slow to anger is better than the mighty; and he that ruleth his spirit than he that taketh a city" (Proverbs 16:32). Even fasting for only two meals can give us a feeling of success. We are a little stronger by having proved to ourselves that we have self-control. If we teach our children to fast they will develop the willpower to overcome greater temptations later in their lives.

FASTING GIVES US SPIRITUAL POWER

When we fast wisely and prayerfully, we develop our faith. With that faith we will have greater spiritual power. For example, Alma (the Book of Mormon prophet) tells the story of meeting again with the sons of Mosiah many years after their miraculous conversion. He felt great joy when he learned that these, his friends, had strengthened their faith and had developed great spiritual power. They had gained this power because "they had given themselves to much prayer, and fasting; therefore they had the spirit of prophecy and the spirit of revelation" (Alma 17:3). The sons of Mosiah had been preaching for fourteen years to the Lamanites. Because the sons of Mosiah had fasted and prayed, the Spirit of the Lord increased the power of their words. This gave them great success in their missionary work (see Alma 17:4).

The Savior has said to those who fast properly: "Thy Father, which seeth in secret, shall reward thee openly" (Matthew 6:18).

Why is it important to have self control?
How does fasting give or increase our spiritual power?
Have someone tell how they have been blessed by observing a proper fast.

ADDITIONAL SCRIPTURES
Luke 2:37; Alma 45:1; D&C 59:13-14 (worshipping God through fasting)
Purposes of fasting:
Mosiah 27:19, 23 (for the sick)
3 Nephi 27:1-3; Exodus 34:27-28 (for revelation and testimony)
Alma 6:6; 17:9 (for nonmembers)
Acts 13:2-3 (for selection of Church officers)

SACRIFICE

Sacrifice is the crowning test of the gospel. It means consecrating our time, our earthly possessions and our energies to further the work of God. The Lord commanded: "Seek ye first the kingdom of God and his righteousness" (Matthew 6:33). Men have always been tried and tested to see if they will put the things of God first in their lives.

Have each member think of a favorite thing they possess.
How would you feel if you were asked to give it up?
Consider the sacrifice of many people as you read Matthew 19:29, Romans 12:1-2.

ANIMAL SACRIFICE WAS AN ORDINANCE OF THE GOSPEL

From the time of Adam and Eve to the time of Jesus Christ the people practiced the law of animal sacrifice (see Moses 5:5). It was an ordinance of the gospel. They were commanded to offer as sacrifices the firstlings of their flocks. These animals had to be perfect, without blemish. The ordinance was given to remind the people that Jesus Christ, the first born of the Father, would come into the world. He would be perfect in every way and he would offer himself as a sacrifice for our sins (see Moses 5:5-8).

Jesus did come and did offer himself as a sacrifice just as the people had been taught he would. Because of his sacrifice everyone will be saved from physical death by the resurrection and all can be saved from their sins by repentance (see this manual, chapter 12, "The Atonement").

Christ's atoning sacrifice marked the end of blood sacrifices. Blood sacrifice was replaced by the ordinance of the sacrament. The ordinance of the sacrament was also given to remind us of the Savior's great sacrifice. We should partake often of the sacrament. The emblems of bread and water remind us of the Savior's bruised body and of his blood which he shed for us (see this manual, chapter 23, "The Sacrament").

Read Moses 5:5–7.
What did the sacrifice of a lamb represent in ancient times?
What event brought blood sacrifice to an end?
What ordinance was given to replace the ancient law of sacrifice?

WE STILL MUST SACRIFICE

Even though blood sacrifice was ended, the Lord still asks us to sacrifice. But now he requires a different kind of offering. He said: "Ye shall offer up unto me no more the shedding of blood, . . . and your burnt offerings shall be done away. And ye shall offer for a sacrifice unto me a broken heart and a contrite spirit" (3 Nephi 9:19–20). A broken heart and a contrite spirit means that we offer deep sorrow for our sins and that we humble ourselves and repent of our sins. Unless we do so, the atoning sacrifice of the Savior will have little effect upon us.

How do we observe the law of sacrifice today?

WE MUST BE WILLING TO SACRIFICE EVERYTHING WE HAVE TO THE LORD

The Apostle Paul wrote that we should become living sacrifices, holy and acceptable unto God (see Romans 12:1).

If we are to be a living sacrifice, we must, if asked, be willing to give up everything we have for The Church of Jesus Christ of Latter-day Saints.

A rich young ruler asked the Savior: "What shall I do to inherit eternal life?" Jesus answered: "Thou knowest the commandments, Do not commit adultery, Do not kill, Do not steal, Do not bear false witness, Honour thy father and thy mother." And the rich man said: "All these have I kept from

The rich young ruler lacked the faith to sacrifice his possessions and to follow Jesus.
Print Courtesy of The Riverside Church

my youth. . . ." When Jesus heard this, he said: "Yet lackest thou one thing: sell all that thou hast, and distribute unto the poor, and thou shalt have treasure in heaven; and come, follow me." When the young man heard this, he was sorrowful. He was very rich and had his heart set upon his riches (see Luke 18:18–23).

The young ruler was a good man. But when he was put to the test, he was not willing to sacrifice his worldly possessions. On the other hand, the Lord's disciples Peter and Andrew were willing to sacrifice everything for the sake of the kingdom of God. When Jesus said unto them: "Follow me, . . . they straightway left their nets, and followed him" (Matthew 4:19–20).

Like the disciples, we must offer our daily activities as a sacrifice to the Lord. We must say, "Thy will be done." Abraham did this. He lived on the earth before Christ in the days when blood sacrifices and burnt offerings were required. As a test of his obedience, Abraham was commanded by the Lord to offer up his son, Isaac, as a sacrifice (see Genesis 22:1–14). Isaac was the only son of Abraham and Sarah. To offer him as a sacrifice was difficult and extremely painful for Abraham. Nevertheless, he and Isaac made the long journey to Mount Moriah, where the sacrifice was to be made. They traveled for three days. Imagine Abraham's thoughts and his heartache. His son was to be sacrificed to the Lord. All too soon they reached Mount Moriah. Isaac carried the wood and Abraham carried the fire and the knife to the place where they were to build the altar. Isaac said: "My father . . . behold the fire and the wood: But where is the lamb for the burnt offering?" Abraham answered: "My son, God will provide himself a lamb." Then Abraham built an altar and arranged the wood on it. He bound Isaac and laid him upon the wood. He then took the knife to kill Isaac. At that moment an angel of the Lord stopped him, saying: "Abraham . . . lay not thine hand upon the lad, neither do thou anything unto him: for now I know that thou fearest God, seeing thou has not withheld thy son, thine only son from me." Abraham must have

Abraham had such great faith that he was prepared to sacrifice his son Isaac at the Lord's command.

been overcome with joy that he was no longer required to sacrifice his son. But he loved the Lord so much that he was willing to do anything the Lord asked.

Have someone tell the story of Abraham, found in Genesis 22:1–14, and have someone tell the story of the rich young ruler, found in Luke 18:18–23.
Ask that each person think what he might have done in these situations.

SACRIFICE HELPS PREPARE US TO LIVE IN THE PRESENCE OF GOD

Only through sacrifice can we become worthy to live in the presence of God. God has ordained it is through sacrifice that men should enjoy eternal life. Many who have lived before us have sacrificed all they had. We must be willing to do the same if we would earn the rich reward they enjoy (see Joseph Smith, *Lectures on Faith,* p. 58).

We may not be asked to sacrifice all things. But like Abraham, we should be willing to sacrifice everything to become worthy to live in the presence of the Lord.

The Lord's people have always sacrificed greatly and in many different ways. Some have suffered hardship and ridicule for the gospel. Some new converts to the Church have been cut off from their families because they joined the Church. Lifetime friends have turned away. Some members have lost their jobs, some have lost their lives. But the Lord has said that our sacrifices will not go unnoticed. He promised: ''And everyone that hath forsaken houses, or brethren, or sisters, or father, or mother, or wife, or children, or lands, for my name's sake, shall receive an hundredfold, and shall inherit everlasting life'' (Matthew 19:29). As our testimonies of the gospel increase, we become able to make greater sacrifices to the Lord. Note the sacrifices made in these true examples:

A member of the Church in East Germany saved his tithing for years until someone with priesthood authority could come and accept his tithing.

A Relief Society visiting teacher served for thirty years without missing an assignment.

A group of Saints in South Africa rode for three days, standing up, to be able to hear and see the prophet of the Lord.

At an area conference in Mexico, members of the Church slept on the ground and fasted during the days of the conference. They had used all their money just to get to the conference and had nothing left for food and shelter.

One family sold their car to get the money for a temple building fund.

Another family sold their home to get money to go to the temple.

Many faithful Latter-day Saints have very little to live on, yet they pay their tithes and offerings.

One brother sacrificed his job because he refused to work on Sunday.

In one branch, the youth gave freely and willingly of their time to care for the young children while their parents helped build the meetinghouse.

Young men and women give up good job opportunities to serve as missionaries.

And the list goes on and on—many, many sacrifices to the Lord. Yet a place in our Heavenly Father's kingdom is worth any sacrifice we have to make of our time, talents, our energy, our money, and our lives. Through sacrifice we can obtain a knowledge from the Lord that we are acceptable to him (D&C 97:8).

Have someone tell of the sacrifices he or his family members have made for the gospel. Tell some of the blessings they have received as a result of the sacrifice.

ADDITIONAL SCRIPTURES
Luke 12:16-34 (where treasure is, there is heart)
Luke 9:57-62 (sacrifice to be fit for the kingdom)
D&C 64:23; D&C 97:12 (today a day of sacrifice)
D&C 98:13-15 (those who lose life for Lord, find it)
Alma 24 (the people of Ammon sacrifice their lives rather than break their oath to the Lord)
Alma 24 (the people of Ammon offer to become slaves in payment of their sins)

SUGGESTED SONG
"Come, Come, Ye Saints" (verses 1 and 4)

WORK AND PERSONAL RESPONSIBILITY

WORK IS AN ETERNAL PRINCIPLE

Our Heavenly Father and Jesus Christ have shown us by their examples and teachings that work is an important activity in heaven and on earth. God worked to create the heavens and the earth. He caused the seas to gather in one place and the dry land to appear. He caused grass, herbs, and trees to grow on the land. He created the sun, the moon, and the stars. He created every living thing in the sea or on the land. Then he placed man on the earth to take care of it and to govern the other creatures (see Genesis 1:1–28).

Jesus Christ said: "My father worketh hitherto, and I work" (John 5:17). He also said: "I must work the works of him that sent me" (John 9:4).

Read John 9:4. Why is work an eternal principle?
Who set the example for work?
Sing the hymn "Sweet Is the Work."

WE ARE COMMANDED TO WORK

Work has been the way of life on earth since Adam and Eve left the garden of Eden. The Lord said to Adam: "In the sweat of thy face shalt thou eat bread" (Genesis 3:19). Adam and Eve worked in the fields so that they could provide for their own needs and the needs of their children (see Moses 5:1).

The Lord said to the people of Israel: "Six days shalt thou labour" (Exodus 20:9).

In the early days of the Restored Church, the Lord said to the

Latter-day Saints: "Now, I, the Lord, am not well pleased with the inhabitants of Zion, for there are idlers among them" (D&C 68:31).

In this century, a prophet of God has said: "Work is to be re-enthroned as the ruling principle of the lives of our Church membership" (Heber J. Grant, Conference Report, Oct. 1936, p. 3).

Discuss what would happen if people did not work.

FAMILY RESPONSIBILITY

The Lord has provided for a division of responsibility in the family. Husbands who are physically able should provide food and shelter and other necessities for their wives and children. The Apostle Paul wrote: "If any provide not for his own, and specially for those of his own house, he hath denied the faith" (1 Timothy 5:8).

A woman puts order, love, and beauty in the home that her husband provides for her. When she does her work well, the family has a clean home and their physical needs are met. Through helping her family, she gains a sense of personal satisfaction.

When a husband or wife is left without a spouse, he or she must fill both roles. A person in this situation has much more responsibility. Our Heavenly Father remembers these people. He will give them special blessings if they ask him in faith.

Wise parents teach their children to help in the work of the family. It is necessary for children to have work assignments to fit their abilities. They need to be praised for their successes. Good work attitudes, habits, and skills are learned through successful experiences in the home.

List the responsibilites of maintaining a home. Let each member decide what he can do to share in the work.

WE CAN ENJOY OUR WORK

To some people work is the dullest of drudgery; but to others it is an exciting part of life. One way to enjoy life's fullest benefits is to learn to love work.

Not all of us can choose the kind of work we do. Some of us labor for long hours for the bare necessities. It is difficult to enjoy such work. Yet the happiest people have learned to enjoy their work, whatever it is.

We can help one another in our work. The heaviest load becomes lighter when someone shares it.

Our attitude toward our work is very important. The following story shows how one man saw beyond his daily labor. A traveler passed a stone quarry and saw three men working. He asked each man what he was doing. Each man's answer revealed a different attitude toward the same job. "I am cutting stone," the first man answered. The second replied: "I am earning three gold pieces per day." The third man smiled and said: "I am helping to build a house of God."

In any honest work we can serve God. King Benjamin, a Nephite prophet, said: "When ye are in the service of your fellow beings ye are only in the service of your God" (Mosiah 2:17). If our work provides only enough for necessities for ourselves or our families, we are still helping some of God's children.

How does our attitude affect our work?
What can we do to improve our attitude?

GOD CONDEMNS IDLENESS AND GAIN FROM EVIL PRACTICES

The Lord has told us that he is not pleased with those who are lazy or idle. He said: "The idler shall not have place in the church, except he repent and mend his ways" (D&C 75:29). He also commanded: "Thou shalt not be idle; for he that is idle shall not eat the bread nor wear the garments of the laborer" (D&C 42:42).

From the earliest days of the Church our prophets have taught Latter-day Saints to be independent and self-sustaining and to avoid idleness. "No true Latter-day Saint will, while physically able, voluntarily shift from himself the burden of his own support. So long as he can, under the inspiration of the Almighty and with his own labor, he will supply himself with the necessities of life" (*Welfare Plan Handbook of Instructions*, 1952, p. 2).

As far as they are able, all Church members should also accept the responsibility to care for their relatives who are unable to provide for themselves.

God also condemns idleness and gain from evil and idle pursuits. President Spencer W. Kimball said: "I feel strongly that men who accept wages or salary and do not give . . . [fair] time, energy, devotion, and service are receiving money that is not clean." He also said that money obtained by evil or idle practices such as theft, gambling (including lotteries), graft, illegal drugs, oppression of the poor, and the like is unclean money. President Kimball defined the difference between honorable work and evil work: "Clean money is that . . . [pay] received for a full day's honest work. It is that reasonable pay for faithful service. It is that fair profit from the sale of goods, commodities, or service. It is that income received from transactions where all parties profit. Filthy lucre is . . . money . . . obtained through theft and robbery . . . gambling . . . sinful operations . . . bribery, and from exploitation" (Conference Report, Oct. 1953, p. 52).

Discuss the effects of idleness in your community. Discuss the effects of idleness on an individual or family.
How can idleness lead people into sinful practices?

WORK, REST, AND RELAXATION

We should each find the proper balance between work, rest, and relaxation. There is an old saying: "Doing nothing is the hardest work of all, because one can never stop to rest." Without work, rest and relaxation have no meaning.

Not only is it pleasant and necessary to rest, but we are commanded to rest (see Exodus 20:10). The Sabbath is our day of rest (see D&C 59:9–12). This day of rest after each six days of labor brings refreshment for the days that follow. The Lord also promises the "fulness of the earth" to those who observe the Sabbath day (see D&C 59:16–20; also see this manual, chapter 24).

On other days of the week, we should schedule some time

when we can visit with family, friends, and relatives. We may spend time to improve our talents and enjoy our hobbies, recreation, or other activities that will refresh us.

Why is it important to rest and relax from work?
Why is it important to keep a balance in life between work, play, rest, and education?

THE BLESSINGS OF WORK

The law that God gave Adam, "In the sweat of thy face shalt thou eat bread," was a law also for the salvation of his soul. There is no real division between spiritual, mental, and physical work. Work is essential to each of us for growth, for character, for development, and for a hundred satisfactions which the idle never know. "The happiest man is he who has toiled hard and successfully in his life work. The work may be done in a thousand different ways; with the brain or the hands, in the study, the field, or the workshop; if it is honest work, honestly done and well worth doing, that is all we have a right to ask" (Theodore Roosevelt, *A Nation of Pioneers,* quoted by Richard L. Evans, *Improvement Era,* Nov. 1963, p. 984). President David O. McKay said: "Let us realize that the privilege to work is a gift, that the power to work is a blessing, that the love of work is success" (quoted by Franklin D. Richards, "The Gospel of Work," *Improvement Era,* Dec. 1969, p. 103).

"Men are, that they might have joy" (2 Nephi 2:25). Work is a key to full joy in the plan of God. If we are righteous, we will return to live with our Heavenly Father, and we will have work to do. As we become like him, our work will become like his work. His work is "to bring to pass the immortality and eternal life of man" (Moses 1:39).

List the blessings that come from work.
Discuss the many blessings that we enjoy because of honest labor.
Copy the statement by President David O. McKay. Place it where it may be read often.

ADDITIONAL SCRIPTURES
Moses 4:23–25 (Adam told that he would work all his life for his food)
D&C 56:16–17 (God warns the rich and poor alike against greed, envy, and laziness)
D&C 58:26–29 (men should be anxiously engaged in a good cause)
Matthew 25:14–30 (parable of the talents)
Ephesians 4:28 (steal no more but rather labor)
1 Thessalonians 4:11–12 (work with your own hands)
2 Nephi 5:17 (Nephi taught his people to work and be industrious)

Chapter 28

SERVICE

Jesus said: "I am among you as he that serveth" (Luke 22:27). As true followers of Jesus we also must serve others.

Service is helping others who need assistance. Christlike service grows out of genuine love and concern for those we help. Love is more than a feeling; when we love others, we want to help them.

All of us must be willing to serve, no matter what our income, age, condition of health, or social position. Some people believe that only the poor and lowly should serve. Other people think service should only be given by the rich. But Jesus taught otherwise. When the mother of two of his disciples asked him to honor her sons in his kingdom, Jesus replied: "Whosoever will be great among you, let him be your minister; And whosoever will be chief among you, let him be your servant." (Matthew 20:26–27.)

HOW WE CAN SERVE

There are many ways to serve. We can help others economically, socially, physically, and spiritually. For example, we can give money, food, or other articles to those who need them. We can be a friend to a newcomer. We can plant a garden for an elderly person or care for someone who is sick. We can teach the gospel to someone who needs the truth or comfort someone who grieves.

We can do small acts of service as well as large. We should never fail to help someone because we are unable to do

Jesus blessed and healed the sick.
Print © Providence Lithograph Co.

175

great things. A widow tells of two children who came to her door shortly after she had moved to a new town. The children brought her a lunch basket and a note which read: "If you want anyone to do errands, call us." The widow was gladdened by the small kindness and never forgot it.

Sometimes, however, we must sacrifice greatly to serve someone. The Savior gave up his life in serving us.

Have someone tell how they have benefited at some time from some kind acts of service. Ask each person to list as many ways to serve as they can.

WHY THE SAVIOR WANTS US TO SERVE OTHERS

It is through the service of men and women and boys and girls that God's work is done. President Spencer W. Kimball explained: "God does notice us, and he watches over us. But it is usually through another person that he meets our needs" (*Ensign,* Dec. 1974, p. 5).

Throughout our lives all of us depend on others for help. When we were infants our parents fed, clothed, and cared for us. Without this care we would have died. When we grew up, other people taught us skills and attitudes. Many of us have needed nursing care during illness or money in a financial crisis. Some of us ask God to bless suffering people and then do nothing for them. We must remember that God works through us.

When we help one another, we serve God. King Benjamin, a great and good king in Book of Mormon times, taught his people this principle by the way he lived. He served them all his life, earning his own living instead of being supported by the people. In a famous speech he explained why he loved service. He said: "When ye are in the service of your fellow beings ye are only in the service of your God . . . and if I, whom ye call your king, do labor to serve you, then ought not ye to labor to serve one another?" (Mosiah 2:17–18).

Read Matthew 25:40.
Why does the Lord want and need us to serve others?
Who benefits when we perform acts of service?

BLESSINGS WE RECEIVE THROUGH SERVICE

When we serve others we gain important blessings. Through

service we increase our ability to love. We become less selfish. As we think of the problems of others, our own problems seem less serious. We must serve others to gain eternal life. God has said that those who live with him must love and serve all his children (see Matthew 25:32-46; Romans 12:1-2).

When we consider the lives of people who serve unselfishly, we can see that they gain more than they give. One such person was a man named Paul, a Latter-day Saint man of twenty who lost the use of both legs in an accident. Some men might have become bitter and useless, but Paul chose to think of others instead. He learned a trade and earned enough money to buy a house. There he and his wife made room for many homeless, unwanted children. Some were badly handicapped. Until his death twenty years later, he served these children and others. In return he was greatly loved, and his thoughts turned away from his crippled legs. He grew close to the Lord.

Have the members name some blessings we receive through service to others. How does serving others increase our ability to love them?

OPPORTUNITIES TO SERVE

Some of us serve only those we enjoy being around and avoid all others. However, Jesus commanded us to love and serve everyone. There are many opportunities to serve.

We can serve members of our families. Husbands and wives should be aware of each other's needs. Parents should not serve their children by only feeding and clothing them; they should also teach, play, and work with them. Children can serve by helping with household chores and by helping brothers and sisters.

A husband can care for a sick baby when his wife needs rest. A wife can prepare a favorite dish for her husband. A mother and father may sacrifice to send a child on a mission. An older boy may comfort a little sister who is afraid of the dark or help her learn to read. Our prophets have told us that a family is the most important unit in society. We must serve our families well (see Mosiah 4:14-15).

We have many opportunities to serve our fellowmen—our neighbors, friends, and even strangers. If a neighbor is having difficulty harvesting crops before a storm, we can help. If a mother is ill, we can watch her children or help with the housework. If a young man is falling away from the Church, we can lead him back. If a child is ridiculed, we can befriend him and persuade others to be kind. We do not need to know the people we serve; nor do we need to be fond of them. We should look for ways to serve as many of our Heavenly Father's children as we can.

If we have special talents, we should use them to serve our fellowmen and our communities. God blesses us with talents and abilities to help improve the lives of others.

We have opportunities to serve in the Church. One purpose of the Church organization is to give us opportunities to help each other. Members of the Church serve others by doing missionary work, accepting leadership assignments, visiting other Church members, teaching classes, and doing other Church work. In The Church of Jesus Christ of Latter-day Saints, there is no professional clergy and so the lay members must carry on all of the activities of the Church.

Have each person write on a sheet of paper one way he can serve someone in his family and someone outside his family during the week. Have him place the paper where he can see it often as a reminder.

CHRIST IS THE PERFECT EXAMPLE OF SERVICE

The Savior provided the perfect example of service. He explained that he didn't come to earth to be served but to serve and to give his life for us (Matthew 20:28).

Jesus loves all of us more than we can understand. When he was on earth he served the poor, the ignorant, the sinner, the despised. He taught the gospel to all who would listen, fed crowds of hungry people who came to hear him, healed many, and raised the dead.

He is our God and Savior and Lord of the universe, yet he did many humble acts of service. Just before his crucifixion he met with his disciples. After he had taught them, he took a basin of water and a towel and washed their feet (John

Jesus washed the feet of his apostles.
Print Courtesy of Three Lions, Inc.

13:4-10). In those days washing a visitor's feet was a sign of honor and was usually done by a servant. Jesus did it as an example of love and service. When we willingly serve others in the spirit of love, we become more like Christ.

Give three people a scripture reference and have each tell of the Savior's example of service: John 13:4-10 (washing of the feet); Matthew 15:30-31 (healing); Matthew 15:32-38 (feeding of the 4,000).

ADDITIONAL SCRIPTURES
Mosiah 2 (King Benjamin's discourse on service)
D&C 81:5 (succor, lift, strengthen)
Colossians 3:23-24 (service to others as ye would serve the Lord Christ)
Galatians 5:13 (by love serve one another)
Matthew 25:40 (do service unto the least as unto Jesus)
John 13:15-16 (Jesus gave example of service)

SUGGESTED SONG
"In Humility, Our Savior"

THE LORD'S LAW OF HEALTH

One of the great blessings we received when we came to earth was to be given a physical body. We need a physical body to become like our Heavenly Father. Our bodies are so important that the Lord calls them temples of God (see 1 Corinthians 3:17). They are holy. Because our bodies are important, our Father in Heaven wants us to take good care of them. He knows that we can be happier, better people if we are healthy. The spirit of our Heavenly Father can be with us if our bodies are clean. Our Father knows that we face temptations to treat our bodies unwisely or to take harmful things into them. For this reason he has told us which things are good for our health and which things are bad. Much of the information God has given, us concerning good health is found in Doctrine and Covenants 89. This revelation is called the Word of Wisdom.

We must obey the Word of Wisdom to be worthy to enter the temple. If we do not live the Word of Wisdom, the Lord's Spirit may not dwell with us. If we defile the "temple of God" which is our body, we hurt ourselves physically and spiritually.

Read Doctrine and Covenants 89.

WE ARE COMMANDED NOT TO TAKE CERTAIN THINGS INTO OUR BODIES

The Lord commands us not to use wine and strong drinks, meaning drinks containing alcohol. President Heber J. Grant taught that strong drink often brings cruelty into the home as well as poverty, disease, and plague. It often is a cause of dishonesty, loss of chastity, and loss of good judgment. It is a curse to all who drink it (see "Message of the First Presidency," *Improvement Era*, Nov. 1942, p. 686). Expectant mothers who drink can cause physical and mental damage to their children. Many automobile accidents are caused each year by people who drink alcohol. The Lord has told us that "tobacco is not for the body" (D&C 89:8). It is harmful to our bodies and our spirits. We should not smoke cigarettes or cigars or use chewing tobacco. Scientists have shown that tobacco causes many diseases and can harm unborn children.

The Lord also counsels us against the use of "hot drinks." The leaders of the Church have said that this means coffee and tea. Coffee and tea contain harmful drugs. We should avoid all drinks that contain harmful drugs.

Through prophets in our time the Lord has told us that we should not use drugs except when they are necessary as medicine. President Spencer W. Kimball has warned that the drug habit is often more harmful than the habit of drinking. He has said that people who misuse drugs should repent of this habit.

We should avoid anything that we know is harmful to our bodies. We should not use any substance that is habit forming. The Word of Wisdom does not tell us everything to avoid, but it does give us guidelines. It is a valuable temporal law. It is also a great spiritual law. By living the Word of Wisdom, we become stronger spiritually. We purify our bodies so that the Spirit of the Lord can dwell with us.

List the things we should not take into our bodies.
Discuss why these things should not be used.

WE ARE TAUGHT THAT CERTAIN THINGS ARE GOOD FOR OUR BODIES

Fruits, vegetables, and wholesome herbs are good for us. They are to be used with wisdom and thanksgiving.

The flesh of birds and animals is also provided for our food.

However, we should eat meat sparingly (see D&C 89:12, 49:18). Fish is also good for man.

Grains are good for us. Wheat is especially good for us. Grains may also be used to make mild drinks.

According to the Word of Wisdom, what are some of the things the Lord says are good for us?

WORK, CLEANLINESS, REST, AND EXERCISE ARE IMPORTANT

In addition to Doctrine and Covenants 89, other scriptures tell us how to be healthy. They tell us that we should "cease to be idle; cease to be unclean; . . . cease to sleep longer than is needful; retire to thy bed early, that ye may not be weary; arise early, that your bodies and minds may be invigorated" (D&C 88:124). Yet we are also told: "Six days shalt thou labour and do all thy work" (Exodus 20:9). The Lord counsels us not to labor more than we have strength for (see D&C 10:4).

A modern prophet has told us that people "should learn to keep their bodies healthy by right living . . . , by inhaling pure air, taking plenty of exercise, and bathing . . . often in fresh water" (Joseph F. Smith, *Gospel Doctrine,* p. 241).

What do work, cleanliness, rest, and exercise have to do with the Lord's law of health?

BLESSINGS FOR LIVING THE LORD'S LAW OF HEALTH

Our Heavenly Father has given us health laws to teach us how to care for our bodies. The scriptures tell us about God's laws: "No temporal commandment gave I . . . for my commandments are spiritual" (D&C 29:35). This means that his commandments concerning our physical state are for our spiritual good.

When we keep the Lord's law of health and obey his other commandments, the Lord promises to bless us physically and spiritually.

Physically we have been promised good health. As a result of this good health we will be able to "run and not be weary, and shall walk and not faint" (D&C 89:18, 20). This is a great

blessing, but the spiritual blessings he has promised us are even greater than the physical ones.

The Lord promises us that we "shall find wisdom and great treasures of knowledge, even hidden treasures" (D&C 89:19). We will be taught important truths by the Holy Ghost through revelation. The Lord also promises that the destroying angel shall pass us by. President Spencer W. Kimball has said that in our time this means that we will be saved from spiritual death: "For observing the Word of Wisdom the reward is life, not only prolonged mortal life but life eternal" (*The Miracle of Forgiveness,* p. 211).

What eternal blessings come to us from living the Word of Wisdom?
Ask the members to share ideas about how they can obey the Word of Wisdom and overcome any problems they might have.

ADDITIONAL SCRIPTURES
1 Corinthians 3:16-17 (body the temple of God)
Judges 13:13-14; Proverbs 20:1; Isaiah 5:11-12; Daniel 1 (avoid strong drink)
D&C 59:16-20 (things of the earth for the benefit of man)
Proverbs 23:20-21 (warning against drunkenness, gluttony, laziness)

SUGGESTED SONGS
"The Lord Gave Me a Temple," "How Gentle God's Commands"

CHARITY

The life of the Savior reflects his pure love for all mankind. He even gave his life for us. Charity is that pure love which our Savior Jesus Christ has. He has commanded us to love one another as he has loved us. The scriptures tell us that charity is felt within the heart. We have pure love when, from the heart, we show genuine concern and compassion for all our brothers and sisters (see 1 John 3:16–24).

What is charity?

CHARITY IS THE GREATEST OF ALL VIRTUES

The prophet Moroni tells us: "Wherefore, cleave unto charity, which is the greatest of all, for all things must fail—but charity is the pure love of Christ, and it endureth forever" (Moroni 7:46–47).

The Savior gave us the example of his life to follow. He was a perfect man. He had perfect love, and he showed us how we must love. By his example, he showed us that the spiritual and physical needs of our fellowmen are as important as our own. Before he gave his life for us, he said: "This is my commandment, That ye love one another as I have loved you. Greater love hath no man than this, that a man lay down his life for his friends" (John 15:12–13).

Speaking to the Lord, Moroni said, "I remember that thou hast said that thou hast loved the world, even unto the laying down of thy life for the world. . . . And now I know that this love which thou hast had for the children of men is charity; wherefore, except men shall have charity they cannot inherit

The good Samaritan showed us by his example how to love our neighbor.

that place which thou hast prepared in the mansions of thy Father" (Ether 12:33–34).

It may not be necessary for us to give our lives as the Savior did. But we can have charity if we make him the center of our lives and follow his example and teachings. Like the Savior we too can bless the lives of our brothers and sisters here on earth.

Why is charity the greatest of all virtues?
Why is it so important that we develop this virtue?

CHARITY INCLUDES GIVING TO THE SICK, AFFLICTED, AND POOR

The Savior gave us many teachings in the form of stories or parables. The parable of the Good Samaritan (Luke 10:30–37; see also James A. Talmage, *Jesus the Christ,* pp. 430–32) teaches us that we must give to those in need, regardless of whether they are our friends or not. In the parable, the Savior said that a man (who was probably a Jew) was traveling to another city. On the road he was attacked by bandits. They stole his clothes and money and beat him, leaving him half dead. A Jewish priest came along, saw him, and passed him by. Then a Jewish temple attendant walked over, looked at him, and went on. However, a Samaritan, who was despised by the Jews, came along, and when he saw the man he felt deep compassion. Kneeling beside him, the good Samaritan bandaged his wounds and took him on a donkey to an inn. He paid the innkeeper to take care of the man until he recovered.

Jesus taught that we should give food to the hungry, shelter to those who have none, and clothes to the poor. When we visit the sick and those who are in prison, it is as if we were doing these things to him instead. He promises us that if we do these things we will inherit his kingdom. However, he tells us that if we turn away those who are sick and in prison or need food or clothing that it is just as if he had come asking for these things and we had turned him away (see Matthew 25:34–46). We should not try to decide whether someone really deserves our help or not (see Mosiah 4:16–24). If we have taken care of our own families' needs first, then we should help all who need help. In this way we will be like our Father in heaven who causes rain to fall on the just and on the unjust alike (Matthew 5:44–45).

In recent years, President Harold B. Lee has reminded us that there are those who need more than material goods. He said: "It is well to remember that there are broken hearts and wounded souls among us that need the tender care of a brother who has an understanding heart and is kind" (*Stand Ye In Holy Places,* p. 228).

Have a person tell the parable of the Good Samaritan (see Luke 10:30–37).
Discuss the attitude of those who passed the injured man and of the Samaritan who cared for him.

CHARITY COMES FROM WITHIN THE HEART

The Apostle Paul taught that even if we give to those in need, if we do not feel compassion for them, we do not have charity (see 1 Corinthians 13:3). He taught that when we have charity we are filled with special feelings for all people. We are patient and kind. We are not boastful or proud. We are not haughty, selfish, or rude. When we have charity we do not remember or rejoice in the evil others have done. Neither do we do good things just because it is to our advantage. Instead, we share the joy of those who live by truth. When we have charity, we are loyal, we believe the best of others and we defend them. When we really have charity, these good feelings stay with us forever (see 1 Corinthians 13:4–8).

The Savior was our example of how to feel toward and treat others. He despised wickedness, but he loved the sinner in spite of his sins. He had compassion for children, the elderly, the poor, and the needy. He had such great love that he could beg our Heavenly Father to forgive the soldiers who were driving the nails into his hands and feet (see Luke 23:34). He taught us that if we do not forgive others our Father in Heaven will not forgive us (see Matthew 18:33–35). He said: "I say unto you, Love your enemies, bless them that curse you, do good to them that hate you, and pray for them

189

which despitefully use you and persecute you. . . . For if ye love them which love you, what reward have ye?'' (Matthew 5:44, 46). We must learn to feel toward others as Jesus did.

Read Moroni 7:45.
What attitudes show that we have charity?
How can we love people in spite of their sins and faults?

HOW CAN WE BECOME CHARITABLE?

First, we can study the life of Jesus Christ and keep his commandments. We can study what he did in certain situations and do the same things when we are in the same kinds of situations (see Moroni 8:25–26).

Second, when we find ourselves with uncharitable feelings, we can pray to have these feelings taken away. Moroni urges us: ''Pray unto the Father with all the energy of heart, that ye may be filled with this love [charity], which he hath bestowed upon all who are true followers of his Son, Jesus Christ'' (Moroni 7:48).

Third, we can learn to love ourselves. The Savior taught that we must love others *as we love ourselves* (Matthew 22:37–39). To love ourselves, we must respect and trust ourselves. This means that we must be obedient to the principles of the gospel that we have learned. We must repent of any wrongdoings. We must forgive ourselves when we have repented. We will only come to love ourselves when we can feel the deep, comforting assurance that the Savior truly loves us.

Fourth, as we come to love ourselves, our love for others will increase. We will not think that we are better than other people. We will have patience with their faults. Joseph Smith said: ''The nearer we get to our heavenly Father, the more we are disposed to look with compassion on perishing souls; we feel that we want to take them upon our shoulders, and cast their sins behind our backs'' (*Teachings of the Prophet Joseph Smith,* p. 241).

In the Book of Mormon, we read of Enos, a young man who wanted to know that his sins had been forgiven. He tells us:

"My soul hungered; and I kneeled down before my Maker, and I cried unto him in mighty prayer and supplication for mine own soul; and all the day long did I cry unto him; yea, and when the night came I did still raise my voice high that it reached the heavens. And there came a voice unto me saying: Enos, thy sins are forgiven thee, and thou shalt be blessed" (Enos 4–5).

The Lord explained to Enos that because of his faith in Christ, his sins had been forgiven. When Enos heard these words he no longer was concerned about himself. He knew that the Lord loved him and would bless him. He began instead to feel concern for the welfare of his friends and relatives, the Nephites. He poured out his whole soul unto God for them (see Enos 7–9). The Lord answered and said that they would be blessed according to their faithfulness in keeping the commandments which they had already been given. Enos' love increased even further after these words and he prayed with many long strugglings for the Lamanites who were the enemies of the Nephites. The Lord granted him his desires and he spent the rest of his life trying to save the souls of the Nephites and the Lamanites. Enos was so grateful for the love and forgiveness the Lord had given him that he willingly spent the rest of his life helping others to receive this same gift (see Enos 11–23). Enos had become truly charitable. We, too, can do so. In fact, we must do so to inherit the place which has been prepared for us in our Father's kingdom.

Read Moroni 8:25–26, and 2 Peter 1:5–7.
What can we do to become charitable?

ADDITIONAL SCRIPTURES
Colossians 3:12–14 (charity the bond of perfectness)
Alma 34:28 (prayers not answered unless we act charitably)
1 John 3:16–24 (charity—actions with a pure heart)
1 Corinthians 12:29–31; 13:1–3 (charity greater than any spiritual gift).
2 Peter 1:5–7 (add one virtue to another to develop charity)
Matthew 25:34–40 (rewards for charity).
D&C 121:45–46 (charity necessary to have the companionship of the Holy Ghost)

SUGGESTED SONGS
"Come, Follow Me," "There Is Beauty All Around"

HONESTY

The thirteenth article of faith says: "We believe in being honest." The Book of Mormon tells us about a group of people who were "distinguished for their zeal towards God, and also towards men; for they were perfectly honest and upright in all things; and they were firm in the faith of Christ, even unto the end" (Alma 27:27). Because of their honesty, these people were noted by their fellowmen as well as by God. It is important to learn what honesty is, how we are tempted to be dishonest, and how we can overcome this temptation.

Read Alma 27:27.
What would a society be like where everyone was perfectly honest?

HONESTY IS A PRINCIPLE OF SALVATION

Complete honesty is necessary for our salvation. An Apostle of the Lord has said: "Honesty is a principle of salvation in the kingdom of God. . . . Just as no man or woman can be saved without baptism, so no one can be saved without honesty" (Mark E. Petersen, Conference Report, Oct. 1971, p. 63).

God is honest and just in all things (Alma 7:20). We too must be honest in all things to become like him. The Brother of Jared testified: "Yea, Lord, I know that thou . art a God of truth, and canst not lie" (Ether 3:12). In contrast, the devil is a liar. In fact, he is the father of lies. (2 Nephi 9:9.) "Those who choose to cheat and lie and deceive and misrepresent become his slaves" (Mark E. Petersen, Ensign, Dec. 1971, p. 73).

Why is honesty a principle of salvation?

WHAT IS AN HONEST PERSON?

An honest person loves truth and justice. He is honest in his words and actions. He does not lie, steal, or cheat.

TO LIE IS DISHONEST

Lying is intentionally deceiving others. The Lord gave this commandment to the children of Israel: "Thou shalt not bear false witness against thy neighbour" (Exodus 20:16). Jesus also taught this when he was on earth (see Matthew 19:18). Bearing false witness is a form of lying. There are many ways of lying. When we speak untruths, we are guilty of lying. We can also intentionally deceive others by a gesture or a look, by silence, or by telling only part of the truth. Whenever we lead people in any way to believe something that is not true, we are not being honest. The Lord is not pleased with such dishonesty, and we will have to account for our lies. Satan would have us believe that it is all right to lie. He says: "Yea, lie a little, . . . there is no harm in this" (2 Nephi 28:8). Satan encourages us to justify our lies to ourselves. An honest person will recognize Satan's temptations and will speak the whole truth, even if it seems to be to his disadvantage.

TO STEAL IS DISHONEST

Jesus taught while he was on earth, "Thou shalt not steal" (Matthew 19:18). Stealing is taking something that does not belong to us. When we take what belongs to someone else or to a store or to the community without permission, we are stealing. Taking merchandise or supplies from an employer is thievery. Accepting more change or goods than one should is dishonest. Taking more than our share of anything is stealing.

TO CHEAT IS DISHONEST

We cheat when we give less than we owe, or when we get something we do not deserve. Some employees cheat their employers by not working their full time, yet accept full pay. Some employers are not fair to their employees; they pay them less than they deserve. Satan says: "Take the advantage of one because of his words, dig a pit for thy neighbor"

(2 Nephi 28:8). Taking unfair advantage is a form of dishonesty. Providing inferior service or merchandise is cheating.

Have three people tell how we can be honest. Discuss lying, stealing, and cheating.

WE MUST NOT EXCUSE OUR DISHONESTY

Many excuses are used for being dishonest. People lie to protect themselves and to have others think well of them. Some excuse themselves for stealing, thinking that they deserve what they took, intend to return it, or need it more than the owner. Some cheat to get better grades in school, or because "everyone else does it," or to get even. These excuses and many more are given as reasons for dishonesty. In the Lord's eyes, there are no acceptable reasons. President Kimball has told us that when we excuse ourselves we cheat ourselves, and the Spirit of God ceases to strive with us. We become more and more unrighteous (see *Faith Precedes the Miracle*, p. 234).

What happens to us spiritually when we excuse our dishonesty?

WE CAN BE COMPLETELY HONEST

To become completely honest, we must look carefully at our lives and have the courage to face the whole truth. If there are ways in which we are being even the least bit dishonest, we should begin at once to repent of them.

When we are completely honest, we cannot be corrupted. We are true to every trust, duty, agreement, or covenant, even if it costs us money, friends, or our lives. Then we can face the Lord, ourselves, and others without shame. President Joseph F. Smith counseled us: "Let every man's life be so that his character will bear the closest inspection, and that it may be seen as an open book, so that we will have nothing to shrink from or be ashamed of" (*Gospel Doctrine*, p. 252).

What does it mean to be completely honest? What must we do to be completely honest?

ADDITIONAL SCRIPTURES

D&C 50:17 (speak only by the spirit of truth)
D&C 76:103–106 (destination of liars)
D&C 42:27 (commandment not to speak evil of neighbors)
Exodus 20:15–16 (commandment not to steal or bear false witness)
D&C 42:20, 84–85; D&C 59:6 (forbidden to steal)
D&C 3:2 (God is honest)
D&C 10:25–28 (Satan deceives)

SUGGESTED SONGS
"Oh Say, What Is Truth?"
"Do What Is Right"

The Lord requires us to be honest in all our dealings.

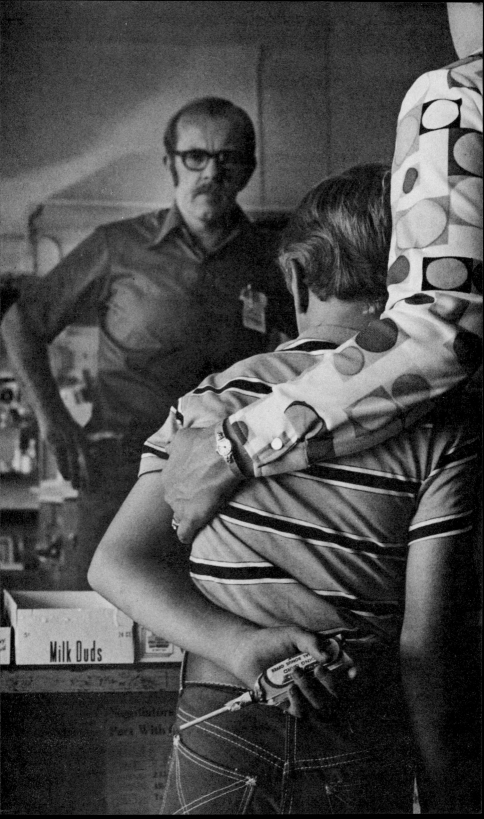

Chapter 32

TITHES AND OFFERINGS

Our Heavenly Father knows all of the things we need. He has given us this commandment and promise: "seek ye first the kingdom of God, and his righteousness; and all these things shall be added unto you" (Matthew 6:33).

We have been given commandments to help us prepare in every way to live in the presence of our Heavenly Father. He has given us a way to thank him for our blessings. Willingly paying tithes and offerings is one way that we thank him. As we pay these offerings we show the Savior that we love him and will obey his counsel: "And verily it is a day of sacrifice, and a day for the tithing of my people" (D&C 64:23).

How do we show our gratitude to our Heavenly Father for all his blessings to us?

OBEYING THE LAW OF TITHING

Anciently Abraham and Jacob obeyed the commandment to pay a tithe of one-tenth of their increase (see Hebrews 7:1–10; Genesis 28:20–22).

In modern times the Prophet Joseph Smith prayed: "O Lord, show unto thy servants how much thou requirest of the properties of thy people for a tithing" (see preface to D&C 119). The Lord answered: "And this shall be the beginning of the tithing of my people. And after that those who have thus been tithed shall pay one-tenth of all their interest annually, and this shall be a standing law unto them forever" (D&C 119:3–4).

A tithe is one-tenth of our increase. This means that we give one-tenth of all we earn before we pay for our own needs

Each year we attend tithing settlement to declare to our bishop or branch president whether we are full tithe payers.

197

such as food, clothing, and shelter. If our increase is in the form of flocks, herds, or crops rather than money, we give one-tenth of those things (see Leviticus 27:30–32).

When we pay tithing we show our faithfulness to the Lord. We also teach our children the value of this law. They will want to follow our example and pay tithing on any money that they earn for chores or small jobs.

What is an honest tithe?
What can we do to teach our children to pay tithing?

WE SHOULD GIVE WILLINGLY

It is important to give willingly. "When one pays his tithing without enjoyment he is robbed of a part of the blessing. He must learn to give cheerfully, willingly and joyfully, and his gift will be blessed" (Stephen L Richards, *The Law of Tithing,* [pamphlet], pp. 7–8).

The apostle Paul taught that how we give is as important as what we give. He said: "Let him give; not grudgingly, or of necessity: for God loveth a cheerful giver" (2 Corinthians 9:6–7).

Read 2 Corinthians 9:6–7.
What does it mean to give grudgingly?
Discuss the importance of our attitude in giving.

OFFERINGS

As members of the Church, we give offerings to the Lord in money, goods, and time.

FAST OFFERING

"The purpose of the fast offering funds is to provide food, shelter, clothing, and medical care to those in need. Proper observance of the monthly fast consists of going without food and drink for two consecutive meals, attending the fast and testimony meeting, and making a generous offering to the bishop for the care of those in need. This generous offering is the fast offering" (*General Handbook of Instructions,* no. 21, pp. 91–92).

BUDGET

Wards, branches, and other units of the Church have budgets. A budget includes money to pay for heating and lighting our chapels and for supplies. It might also include funds for recreation and social programs. We should contribute as we are able to pay. The bishop or the presiding priesthood leader will help us decide how much we should give.

BUILDING, WELFARE, AND MISSIONARY FUNDS

We have the responsibility and privilege of sharing the cost of building chapels, stake centers, and temples. Through the Church Welfare Program, we provide work and goods for those who cannot care for themselves. When we are able, we may also make contributions to the missionary fund to assist in spreading the gospel.

How do the offerings in addition to tithing show that we are grateful to our Heavenly Father?

USES OF TITHES AND OFFERINGS

Tithes and offerings are used by the Church for many purposes. Some of these are—

1. To help the missionary program.

2. To build and maintain chapels and other buildings.

3. To educate young people in Church schools, seminaries, and institutes.

4. To print and distribute lesson materials.

5. To help in genealogy and temple work.

6. To help those in need who cannot help themselves.

How do the tithes and offerings of others help you?

WE ARE BLESSED WHEN WE GIVE TITHES AND OFFERINGS

The Lord has promised to bless us if we faithfully pay our tithes and offerings. He said, "Bring ye all the tithes into the storehouse, that there may be meat in mine house, and prove me now herewith, saith the Lord of hosts, if I will not open you the windows of heaven, and pour you out a blessing, that there shall not be room enough to receive it" (Malachi 3:10).

In D&C 64:23 we are told of another blessing for those who tithe: "Verily it is a day of sacrifice, and a day for the tithing of my people; for he that is tithed shall not be burned at his coming."

The blessings we have been promised are both material and spiritual. If we give willingly Heavenly Father will help us to take care of our daily needs for food, clothes, and shelter. He will also help us grow "in a knowledge of God, in a testimony, in the power to live the gospel and to inspire our families to do the same" (Heber J. Grant, *Gospel Standards,* p. 58).

Those who pay their tithes and offerings are greatly blessed. They have a good feeling that they are helping to build the kingdom of God on the earth.

Name three blessings we receive from being obedient to the law of tithing.

ADDITIONAL SCRIPTURES
D&C 119:1–4 (the law of tithing)
Genesis 14:19–20; Alma 13:13–16 (Abraham paid tithes)
2 Chronicles 31:5–6, 12; Nehemiah 10:37–38 (children of Israel paid tithing)
3 Nephi 24:8–10 (will a man rob God?)

MISSIONARY WORK

The Lord himself revealed to Adam the gospel plan: "And thus the Gospel began to be preached, from the beginning" (Moses 5:58). Later, when men had become wicked, Adam's righteous sons were sent to preach the gospel to the others on the earth: "They . . . called upon all men, every where, to repent; and faith was taught unto the children of men" (Moses 6:23).

All the prophets have been missionaries. Each in his day was commanded to preach the gospel message. Whenever the priesthood has been on the earth the Lord has needed missionaries to preach the eternal principles of the gospel to his children.

When was the gospel message first preached to man on the earth?

THE LORD'S CHURCH IS A MISSIONARY CHURCH

The Lord's church has always been a missionary church. When the Savior lived on the earth, he ordained Apostles and Seventies and gave them the authority and responsibility to preach the gospel. Most of their preaching was to their own people, the Jews (see Matthew 10:5-6). After Jesus was resurrected, he sent Apostles to preach the gospel to the Gentiles. He commanded the Apostles: "Go ye into all the world, and preach the gospel to every creature" (Mark 16:15).

The Apostle Paul was a great missionary sent to the Gentiles. After he was converted to the Church, he spent the remainder of his life preaching the gospel to them. At different times during his mission, he was whipped, stoned, and imprisoned. Yet the moment he escaped from his persecutors, he preached the gospel as diligently as before (see Acts 23:10–12; Acts 26).

Missionary work began again when the Lord's church was restored through the Prophet Joseph Smith. Today the Apostles and Seventies have been given the chief responsibility for preaching the gospel and seeing that it is preached in all the world. The Lord told Joseph Smith: "Proclaim my gospel from land to land, and from city to city . . . Bear testimony in every place, unto every people" (D&C 66:5, 7). In June 1830, Samuel Harrison Smith, the Prophet's brother, began the first missionary journey for the Church.

Since that time thousands of missionaries have been called and sent forth to preach the gospel. The message they take to the world is that Jesus Christ is the Son of God and the Savior of mankind. They testify that the gospel has been restored to the earth through a prophet of God (see David O. McKay, *Gospel Ideals,* p. 132). The missionaries are given the responsibility to preach the gospel to all people, to baptize them, and to teach them to do all things which the Lord has commanded (see Matthew 28:19–20). Latter-day Saint missionaries go at their own expense to all parts of the world to preach the gospel message.

What are the two important messages the missionaries teach and testify of?

THE GOSPEL WILL BE PREACHED TO ALL THE WORLD

We have been told by modern revelation that we must take the restored gospel to every nation and people in the world (see D&C 133:37). The Lord never gives us a commandment without preparing a way for us to accomplish that which we are commanded to do (see 1 Nephi 3:7). The Lord will prepare a way for us to teach the gospel in the nations that are now closed to us. President Spencer W. Kimball has asked members of the Church to pray that these nations may be opened to missionary work.

President Kimball has also told us that many wonderful inventions will come forth to further the missionary work. Some

Jesus commanded the apostles to preach the gospel in all the world.

of these will enable our brothers and sisters in all parts of the world to hear the gospel in their own language (see "When the World Will Be Converted," *Ensign,* Oct. 1974, pp. 10–11). "For, verily, the sound must go forth from this place into all the world, and unto the uttermost parts of the earth—the gospel must be preached unto every [person]" (D&C 58:64). We who have the fullness of the gospel have the responsibility to share it with others.

Who needs to hear the gospel? Have each member think of one person with whom he could share the gospel.

MISSIONARY WORK IS IMPORTANT

"This is our first interest as a church—to save and exalt the souls of the children of men" (Ezra Taft Benson, Conference Report, Apr. 1974, p. 151). Missionary work is necessary in order to give the people of the world an opportunity to hear and accept the gospel. They need to learn the truth, turn to God, and receive forgiveness from their sins.

Many of our brothers and sisters on earth are blinded by the false teachings of men and "are only kept from the truth because they know not where to find it" (D&C 123:12). Through the missionary work we will bring them the truth.

The Lord has commanded us: "Labor ye in my vineyard for the last time—for the last time call upon the inhabitants of the earth" (D&C 43:28). As we teach the gospel to our brothers and sisters we are preparing the way for the second coming of the Savior (see D&C 34:6).

Why is it so important for each person to hear and understand the gospel?

WE SHOULD ALL BE MISSIONARIES

Every member of the Church is to be a missionary. We should be missionaries even if we are not formally called and set apart. We have the responsibility to teach the gospel by word and deed to all of our Heavenly Father's children. The Lord has told us: "It becometh every man who hath been warned to warn his neighbor" (D&C 88:81). We have been told by a prophet that we should show our neighbors that we

Thousands of missionaries are preaching the gospel around the world.

love them before we warn them. They need to experience our friendship and fellowship.

The sons of Mosiah, as it is told in the Book of Mormon, willingly accepted their responsibility to teach the gospel. When they were converted to the Church their hearts were filled with compassion for their fellowman. They wanted to preach the gospel to their enemies the Lamanites, "for they could not bear that any human soul should perish." The thought that anyone should have to suffer the punishment for his sins caused them to quake and tremble (see Mosiah 28:1–3). As the gospel fills our lives with joy we will feel this kind of love and compassion for our brothers and sisters. We will want to share the message of the gospel with everyone who desires to listen.

Why do we feel a desire to share the gospel with others when we are truly converted?

HOW CAN WE ALL BE MISSIONARIES?

There are many ways we can share the gospel. Here are some suggestions:

1. We can show our friends and others the joy we experience from living the truths of the gospel. In this way we will be a light to the world (see Matthew 5:16).

2. We can overcome our natural shyness by being friendly to others and doing kind things for them, whenever the opportunity arises. We can help them to see that we are sincerely interested in them and not seeking personal gain.

3. We can explain the gospel to our nonmember friends and others.

4. We can invite our friends who are interested in learning more about the gospel into our homes to be taught by the missionaries. If our nonmember friends live too far away we can request that missionaries in their areas visit them.

5. We can teach our children the importance of sharing the gospel, and we can prepare them spiritually and financially to go on missions.

6. We can pay our tithing and contribute to the missionary fund. These donations are used for furthering missionary work.

7. We can help support financially a missionary whose family is unable to support him.

8. We can do genealogical research and temple work to assist in helping our ancestors become members of the Church.

9. We can invite nonmembers to activities in the Church such as family home evening, socials, conferences, and meetings.

Our Heavenly Father will help us to be effective missionaries when we have the desire to share the gospel and pray for guidance. He will help us to find ways to share the gospel with those around us.

Ask each person to decide on a way to share the gospel with the individual he chose earlier in the lesson.

THE LORD PROMISES US BLESSINGS FOR DOING MISSIONARY WORK

The Prophet Joseph Smith was told in a revelation from the Lord that missionaries would receive great blessings. In this revelation the Lord said to the elders who were returning from their missions: "Ye are blessed, for the testimony which ye have borne is recorded in heaven for the angels to look upon; and they rejoice over you" (D&C 62:3).

The Lord has told us: "If it so be that you should labor all your days in crying repentance unto this people, and bring, save it be one soul unto me, how great shall be your joy with him in the kingdom of my Father"; and also: "If your joy will be great with one soul that you have brought unto me into the kingdom of my Father, how great will be your joy if you should bring many souls unto me!" (D&C 18:15–16).

Why is it so important to bear testimony to the truth of the gospel?
What blessings come from sharing the gospel?

ADDITIONAL SCRIPTURES
D&C 1:17–23 (Joseph Smith commanded to preach)
D&C 34:4–6; Acts 5:42 (Gospel to be preached)
D&C 60:1–2 (The Lord warns those who are afraid to preach the gospel)
Matthew 24:14 (Gospel to be preached before end shall come)
Abraham 2:9 (Priesthood to be given to all nations)

SUGGESTED SONG
"It May Not Be on the Mountain Height"

DEVELOPING OUR TALENTS

We all have special talents and abilities given to us by our Heavenly Father. When we were born, we brought these talents and abilities with us (see this manual, chapter 2). Each of us has been given at least one special talent.

WE ALL HAVE DIFFERENT TALENTS AND ABILITIES

The prophet Moses was a great leader, but he had no talent for public speaking. Aaron, his brother, was chosen to help Moses because he had the ability to speak well (see Exodus 4:14–16). Some of us are leaders like Moses or good speakers like Aaron. Some of us can sing well or play an instrument. Others of us may be good in sports or able to work well with our hands. Other talents we might have are understanding others, patience, cheerfulness, or ability to teach others.

Ask each member to identify a talent of the person sitting beside him.

WE SHOULD USE AND IMPROVE OUR TALENTS

Our Heavenly Father has told us that it is up to us to receive the gifts he has given us (D&C 88:33). This means we must develop and use our talents. Sometimes we think that we do not have many talents or that others have been blessed with more abilities than we possess. Sometimes we do not use our talents because we are afraid that we might fail or be criticized by others. We should not hide our talents. We should use them. Then others can see our good works and glorify our Heavenly Father (see Matthew 5:16).

Why should we improve our talents?

The Lord expects us to develop our special gifts and talents.

HOW CAN WE DEVELOP OUR TALENTS?

There are certain things that we must do to develop our talents. First, we must discover our talents. We should examine ourselves to find our strengths and abilities. Our family and friends can help us do this. We should also ask our Heavenly Father to help us learn about our talents.

Second, we must be willing to spend the time and effort to develop the talent we are seeking.

Third, we must have faith that our Heavenly Father will help us, and we must have faith in ourselves.

Fourth, we must learn the skill necessary for us to develop our talents. We might do this by taking a class, getting a friend to teach us, or reading a book.

Fifth, we must practice using our talent. Every talent takes effort and work to develop. The mastery of a talent must be earned.

Sixth, we must share our talent with others. It is by using our talents that they grow (Matthew 25:29).

All of these steps are easier if we pray and seek the help of the Lord. He wants us to develop our talents, and he will help us.

Name a talent or a skill you possess. How can a person develop this talent or skill? Have someone in the group explain how he has developed his talent or skill.

WE CAN DEVELOP OUR TALENTS IN SPITE OF OUR WEAKNESSES

Sometimes the Lord gives us weaknesses so that we will work hard and overcome them. With his help, our weaknesses can become our strengths (see Ether 12:27). "Beethoven, a great composer, wrote his greatest works after he was stone deaf. Demosthenes overcame weak lungs and a lisp to become one of the greatest orators of all time" (Paul H. Dunn, *I Challenge You*, p. 65).

Some great athletes have had to overcome a handicap before they have succeeded in developing their talents. Shelly Mann was such an example. "At the age of five she had polio. . . . Her parents took her daily to a swimming pool where they hoped the water would help hold her arms up as she tried to use them again. When she could lift her arm out of the water with her own power, she cried for joy. Then her goal was to swim the width of the pool, then the length, then several lengths. She kept on trying, swimming, enduring, day after day, until she won the gold medal for the butterfly stroke—one of the most difficult of all swimming strokes'' (Marvin J. Ashton, *Ensign,* May 1975, p. 86).

Heber J. Grant overcame many of his weaknesses and turned them into talents. He had as his motto: "That which we persist in doing becomes easier for us to do; not that the nature of the thing is changed, but that our power to do is increased" (*Gospel Standards,* p. 355).

Read Ether 12:27. How can weak things be made strong?

THE LORD WILL BLESS US IF WE USE OUR TALENTS WISELY

President Joseph F. Smith said: "Every son and every daughter of God has received some talent, and each will be held to strict account for the use or misuse to which it is put" ("The Returned Missionary," *Juvenile Instructor,* Nov. 1903, p. 689). A talent is one kind of stewardship (responsibility in the kingdom of God). The parable of the talents (Matthew 25:14–29) tells us that when we serve well in our stewardship we will be given greater responsibilities. If we do not serve well, our stewardship will eventually be taken from us.

We are also told in the scriptures that we will be judged according to our works (Matthew 16:27). By developing and using our talents for other people, we perform good works.

The Lord is pleased when we use our talents wisely. He will bless us if we use our talents to benefit other people and to build up his kingdom here on earth. Some of the blessings we gain are joy and love from serving our brothers and sisters here on earth. We also learn self-control. All of these things are necessary if we are going to be worthy to live with our Heavenly Father again.

Read and discuss the parable of the talents found in Matthew 25:14-30.

ADDITIONAL SCRIPTURES
James 1:17 (gifts come from God)
D&C 46:8-9; 1 Timothy 4:14 (develop gifts)
2 Corinthians 12:9 (weak things made strong)
Revelation 20:13; 1 Nephi 15:33; D&C 19:3 (judged by our works)
Hebrews 13:21; Matthew 5:16 (show good works)

SUGGESTED SONG:
"Ere You Left Your Room This Morning"

Chapter 35

OBEDIENCE

When Jesus was upon the earth a lawyer asked him a question:

"Master, which is the great commandment in the law?

"Jesus said unto him, Thou shalt love the Lord thy God with all thy heart, and with all thy soul, and with all thy mind.

"This is the first and great commandment.

"And the second is like unto it, Thou shalt love thy neighbor as thyself.

"On these two commandments hang all the law and the prophets" (Matthew 22:36–40).

From these scriptures we learn how important it is for us to love the Lord and our fellowmen. But how do we show our love for the Lord?

Jesus also answered this question when he said: "He that hath my commandments and keepeth them, he it is that loveth me: and he that loveth me shall be loved of my Father" (John 14:21).

WE SHOULD OBEY WILLINGLY

Each of us should ask ourselves why we live God's commandments. Is it because we fear punishment? Is it because we desire the rewards for living a good life? Is it because we love God and Jesus Christ and want to serve them?

Certainly it is better to obey the commandments because of fear of punishment than not to obey them at all. But we shall be much happier if we obey God because we *want* to rather than because we are afraid not to. When we obey him freely, he can bless us freely. He said: "I, the Lord . . . delight to honor those who serve me in righteousness and truth unto the end" (D&C 76:5). Obedience also helps us to progress and become more like our Heavenly Father. But those who do nothing until they are commanded and then keep the commandments unwillingly lose their reward (see D&C 58:26–29).

Read D&C 58:26–29. Why is it important to obey willingly rather than unwillingly?

WE CAN OBEY WITHOUT UNDERSTANDING WHY

By keeping all the commandments of God, we prepare for eternal life and exaltation. Sometimes we do not know the reason for a particular commandment. However, we show our faith and trust in God when we obey him without knowing why. Adam did this.

Adam and Eve were commanded to offer sacrifice to God. One day an angel appeared to Adam and asked why he offered sacrifice. Adam replied that he did not know the reason. He did it because the Lord commanded him to. (Moses 5:5–6).

The angel then taught Adam the gospel and told him of the Savior who was to come. The Holy Ghost fell upon Adam and he prophesied concerning the inhabitants of the earth down to the last generation (see Moses 5:9–10; D&C 107:56). This knowledge and great blessings came to Adam because he was obedient.

Discuss why we need not understand the Lord's purposes in order to be obedient.

GOD WILL PREPARE A WAY

The Book of Mormon (1 Nephi 3:1–6) tells us that Nephi and his older brothers received a very difficult assignment from the Lord. Nephi's brothers complained, saying: "It is a hard thing you require of us." But Nephi said: "I will go and do the things which the Lord hath commanded, for I know that the Lord giveth no commandments unto the children of men, save he shall prepare a way for them that they may accomplish the thing which he commandeth them" (1 Nephi 3:7). When we find it difficult to obey a commandment of the Lord, we should remember Nephi's words.

Have members learn and memorize 1 Nephi 3:7.
Ask the members to tell about times when the Lord has prepared a way for them to obey him.

NO COMMANDMENT IS TOO SMALL OR TOO GREAT TO OBEY

Sometimes we may think a commandment is not very important. The scriptures (2 Kings 5:1–4) tell us of a man named Naaman who thought that way. Naaman had a dreadful disease. He traveled from Syria to Israel to ask the prophet Elisha to heal him. Naaman was an important man in his own country. He was offended when Elisha did not greet him in person but sent his servant instead. Naaman was even more offended when he received Elisha's message: wash seven times in the river Jordan. "Are not [the] rivers of Damascus better than all the waters of Israel? may I not wash in them and be clean?" he demanded. He went away in a rage. But his servants asked him: "If the prophet had bid thee do some great thing, wouldest thou not have done it? how much rather then, when he saith to thee, Wash, and be clean?" Naaman was wise enough to understand that it was important to obey the prophet of God, even if it seemed a small matter. So he washed in the Jordan and was healed.

Sometimes we may think a commandment is too difficult for us to obey. Like Nephi's brothers, we may say: "It is a hard thing you require of us." Yet, like Nephi, we can be sure that God will give us no commandment unless he prepares a way for us to obey him.

It was a "hard thing" when the Lord commanded Abraham to offer his beloved son, Isaac, as a sacrifice (see Genesis 22:1–13; also this manual, chapter 26, "Sacrifice"). Abraham had waited many long years for the birth of Isaac—the son which God had promised him. How could he now lose his son in such a way? The deed must have been most repugnant to Abraham. Yet he disregarded his own feelings

215

and chose to obey God. The Lord accepted Abraham's willingness for the deed. He was not required to make the sacrifice.

We too should be willing to do anything God requires. The Prophet Joseph Smith said: "I made this my rule: when the Lord commands, do it" (*History of the Church,* vol. 2, p. 170). This can be our rule also.

How does obeying the commandments strengthen us?

JESUS CHRIST OBEYED HIS FATHER

Jesus Christ was the sublime example of obedience to our Heavenly Father. He said: "I came down from heaven, not to do mine own will, but the will of him that sent me" (John 6:38). His whole life was devoted to obeying his Father; yet it was not always easy for him. He was tempted in all ways as other men (Hebrews 4:15). In the garden of Gethsemane he prayed to his Father, asking if he might avoid the agony he was enduring and the suffering to come on the cross. Then he ended his prayer by saying: "Not as I will, but as thou wilt" (Matthew 26:39).

The Apostle Paul says of him: "Though he were a Son, yet learned he obedience by the things which he suffered; and being made perfect, he became the author of eternal salvation unto all them that obey him" (Hebrews 5:8-9).

Because Jesus was obedient to the Father's will in all things, he made salvation possible for all of us if we, too, will obey our Father in Heaven.

How can remembering the example of the Savior help us to be obedient?

RESULTS OF OBEDIENCE AND DISOBEDIENCE

The kingdom of heaven is governed by law, and when we receive any blessing, it is by obedience to the law upon which that blessing is based (see D&C 130:21; 132:5). The Lord has told us that through our obedience and diligence, we may gain knowledge and intelligence (see D&C 130:18-19). We may also grow spiritually (see Jeremiah 7:23-24). On the other hand, disobedience brings disappointment and results

Jesus Christ is our example of perfect obedience to Heavenly Father.

Print courtesy of Bernard Picture Company

in a loss of blessings. "Who am I, saith the Lord, that have promised and have not fulfilled? I command and men obey not; I revoke and they receive not the blessing. Then they say in their hearts: This is not the work of the Lord, for his promises are not fulfilled" (D&C 58:31–33).

When we keep the commandments of God, he fulfills his promises, as King Benjamin told his people: "He doth require that ye should do as he hath commanded you; for which if ye do, he doth immediately bless you" (Mosiah 2:24).

Read together Jeremiah 7:23–24.
What happens to those who are disobedient?

THE OBEDIENT GAIN ETERNAL LIFE

The Lord counsels us: "If you keep my commandments and endure to the end you shall have eternal life, which gift is the greatest of all the gifts of God" (D&C 14:7).

The Lord has described other blessings that will come to those who obey him in righteousness and truth until the end:

"Great shall be their reward and eternal shall be their glory.

"And to them will I reveal all mysteries, yea, all the hidden mysteries of my kingdom from days of old, and for ages to come, will I make known unto them the good pleasure of my will concerning all things pertaining to my kingdom.

"Yea, even the wonders of eternity shall they know, and things to come will I show them, even the things of many generations.

"And their wisdom shall be great, and their understanding reach to heaven. . . .

"For by my Spirit will I enlighten them, and by my power will I make known unto them the secrets of my will—yea, even those things which eye has not seen, nor ear heard, nor yet entered into the heart of man" (D&C 76:6–10).

Read 2 Nephi 31:16.
Why is it so important to endure to the end?

We must search out the names of our ancestors so that they, too, can receive the ordinances of the gospel.

ADDITIONAL SCRIPTURES
Abraham 3:25 (we came to earth to test our obedience)
1 Samuel 15:22 (obedience is better than sacrifice)
Ecclesiastes 12:13; John 14:15; Romans 6:16; D&C 78:7; D&C 132:36; Deuteronomy 4:1-40 (we should obey God)
2 Nephi 31:7 (Jesus Christ was obedient)
Proverbs 3:1-4; 6:20-22; 7:1-3; Ephesians 6:1-3; Colossians 3:20 (children should obey their parents)
D&C 21:4-6 (be obedient to the prophet)
John 8:31-32; Mosiah 2:22, 41; D&C 82:10; 1 Nephi 2:20 (blessings for obedience)
D&C 58:21-22; D&C 98:4-6; D&C 134 (obey the laws of the land)
Isaiah 60:12; D&C 1:14; D&C 93:39; D&C 132:6, 39 (consequences of disobedience)
2 Nephi 31:16; D&C 53:7; Matthew 24:13; Luke 9:62 (enduring to the end)

THE FAMILY
CAN BE ETERNAL

The first family on earth was established by our Heavenly Father when he gave Eve to Adam in marriage (see Moses 4:21–24). Since then, each of us has been commanded to marry and have children so that through our own experience we can learn to be heavenly parents. President Brigham Young explained that our families are not yet ours. The Lord has committed them to us to see how we will treat them. Only if we are faithful will they be given to us forever. What we do on earth determines whether or not we will be worthy to become heavenly parents (see this manual, chapter 2, "Our Heavenly Family").

THE IMPORTANCE OF FAMILIES

After Heavenly Father gave Eve to Adam, he commanded them to have children (see Genesis 1:28). He has also told us that the purpose of marriage is to provide mortal bodies for his spirit children. As parents, we are partners with our Heavenly Father. He wants each of his spirit children to receive a physical body and to experience earth life. When we bring children into this world, we help our Heavenly Father carry out his plan.

Every new child should be welcomed into our family with gladness. Each is a child of God. We should take time to enjoy our children, to play with them, and to teach them.

President David O. McKay said: "With all my heart I believe that the best place to prepare for . . . eternal life is in the home'' (''Blueprint for Family Living,'' *Improvement Era* Apr. 1963, p. 252). At home, with our families, we can learn self-control, sacrifice, loyalty, and the value of work. We can learn to love, to share, and to serve one another.

Fathers and mothers have the responsibility to teach their children about Heavenly Father. They should show them by example that they love him because they keep his commandments. Parents should also teach their children to pray and to be obedient to the commandments (see Proverbs 22:6).

Why did the Lord give us families?
Why is the home the best place to prepare for eternal life?

THE ETERNAL FAMILY

Our family can be together forever. To enjoy this blessing we must be married in the temple. When people are married outside the temple, the marriage ends when one of the partners dies. When we are married in the temple by the authority of the Melchizedek Priesthood, we are married for time and eternity. Death cannot separate us. If we obey the commandments of the Lord, our families will be together forever as husband, wife, and children.

Discuss the things we must do to make our families eternal.

LOVING FAMILY RELATIONSHIPS

As husbands and wives we should be thoughtful and kind to each other. We should never do or say anything to hurt the feelings of the other. We should also try to do everything possible to make each other happy (see Milton R. Hunter, Conference Report, Oct. 1971, p. 50).

It is also our responsibility as parents to teach our children to love one another. In the Book of Mormon, King Benjamin explained: ''Ye will not suffer your children . . . [to] fight and quarrel one with another. . . . But ye will teach them to walk in the ways of truth and soberness; ye will teach them to love one another, and to serve one another'' (Mosiah 4:14–15).

As family members we can help each other to feel self-confident by the encouragement and the sincere praise we give

Families are sealed together for eternity in the holy temples.

to each other. Each child should feel that he is important to us. We need to show that we are interested in what he does. We should express our love and concern for our children. This will help them know how dear they are to us. Children should likewise show their love for their parents. Children should be obedient and try to live the kind of life that will make their parents proud of them. They should bring honor to their parents and to their family name.

Read together Ephesians 4:29–32.
How can we develop harmony in our homes?

HOW TO HAVE A SUCCESSFUL FAMILY

President Harold B. Lee taught: "The most important of the Lord's work that you will ever do will be the work you do within the walls of your own home" (pamphlet, *Strengthening the Home*, p. 7).

The following story illustrates this point:

After performing a temple marriage ceremony, President Spencer W. Kimball greeted the parents of the young couple. One of the fathers said: "My wife and I are common people, and have never been successful, but we are very proud of our family." The father explained that all eight of his children had now been married in the temple. All are faithful and serve in the Church, teaching the gospel in their families.

President Kimball looked at the calloused hands and wrinkled face of the father and said: "This is the greatest success story I have heard. . . . You are fulfilling the purpose for which you were sent to this world by keeping your own lives righteous, bearing and rearing this great family, and training them in faith. Why, my dear folks, you are very successful. God bless you" (Spencer W. Kimball, Conference Report, Oct. 1971, pp. 152–53).

Satan knows how important families are to our Heavenly Father's plan. He has set out to destroy them by keeping us from drawing near to the Lord and having his spirit with us. He will tempt us to do things that will draw our families apart.

All of us want to have happy, successful families. The following things will help us achieve this:

1. Have family prayer every night and morning (see 3 Nephi 18:21).

2. Teach our children the gospel by meeting together as a family at least once a week to study gospel principles (see *Organizational Guidebook for the Family*). "There shouldn't be—there mustn't be—one family in this Church that doesn't take the time to read from the scriptures every day" (H. Burke Peterson, Conference Report, Apr. 1975, p. 79).

3. Do things together as a family, such as work projects, outings, and making family decisions.

4. Husbands and wives should kneel together each night in prayer.

5. Learn to be kind, patient, longsuffering, and charitable (see Moroni 7:45–48).

6. Attend Church meetings regularly (see D&C 59:9–10).

7. Follow the counsel of the Lord given in D&C 88:119: "Organize yourselves: Prepare every needful thing; and establish a house, even a house of prayer, a house of fasting, a house of faith, a house of learning, a house of glory, a house of order, a house of God."

8. Keep a family history and gather family genealogy.

The family is the most important unit in The Church of Jesus Christ of Latter-day Saints. The Church exists to help families gain eternal blessings and exaltation. The organizations and programs within the Church are designed to strengthen us individually and to help us to live as families forever.

Discuss some of the things we can do to have a successful family.
As a family decide which principles to work on during the weeks ahead.
Have each member set a goal to express love to their family members during the coming week.

ADDITIONAL SCRIPTURES
Moses 2:27–28 (man and woman created and blessed)
Moses 3:21–24 (woman given to Adam as wife)
Genesis 2:24 (man to cleave unto his wife)
D&C 49:15–16 (God ordained marriage)
Ephesians 6:4 (train children in righteousness)
D&C 132:15–21 (eternal marriage)
D&C 88:119–126 (instructions for a successful family)

SUGGESTED SONGS
"I Am a Child of God," "There Is Beauty All Around"

FAMILY RESPONSIBILITIES

Each person has an important place in his family. Through his prophets the Lord has explained how fathers, mothers and children should behave and feel toward one another. As husbands, wives, and children we need to learn what the Lord expects us to do in order to fulfill our purpose as a family. If we all do our part we will be able to live together as a family forever.

What is the purpose of a family?

THE RESPONSIBILITY OF THE PARENTS

In marriage neither the man nor the woman is more important than the other; they are equal partners, although the man is the head of the house.

Some responsibilities must be shared by both the husband and the wife. Parents should teach their children the gospel. The Lord has said that if parents do not teach their children about repentance, faith in Jesus Christ, baptism and the gift of the Holy Ghost, the sin will be upon the heads of the parents. Parents should also teach their children to pray and to obey all the commandments of the Lord (see D&C 68:25, 28).

One of the best ways parents can teach their children is by example. Husbands and wives should show love and respect for each other and for their children by both actions and words. It is important to remember that each member of the family is a child of God. Parents should treat their children with love and respect, being firm but kind to them.

The home is the foundation for a happy life.

Parents should understand that sometimes children will make wrong choices even after they have been taught the truth. When this happens parents should not give up or become discouraged. They should continue to teach their children, to express love for them, to be good examples to them, and to fast and pray for them. The Book of Mormon tells us how the prayers of a father helped to bring a rebellious son back to the ways of the Lord (see Mosiah 27:8–32). Alma the Younger had fallen away from the teachings of his righteous father, Alma, and had gone about seeking to destroy the Church. The father prayed with faith for his son. Alma the Younger was visited by an angel. Alma the Younger then repented of his evil way of living. He became a great and strong leader of the Church.

Parents can provide an atmosphere of reverence and respect in the home if they teach and guide their children with love. They should also provide happy experiences for them.
Discuss the responsibilities of the parents.

THE RESPONSIBILITY OF THE FATHER

The father is the patriarch of the family and has important responsibilities that are his alone. He is the head of his home and the leader of his family. He should lead and guide them with humility and kindness rather than with force or cruelty. The scriptures teach that those who hold the priesthood should lead others by persuasion, gentleness, love, and kindness (see D&C 121:41–44; Ephesians 6:4).

It is also the father's duty to earn the living for his family (see D&C 75:28). He should provide the necessary food, housing, clothing and education.

He should set a good example for his family by keeping the commandments. A family will usually follow the father's example of spirituality. The father should make sure the family prays together twice daily and holds family home evening. He should also share the blessings of the priesthood with the members of his family. When a man holds the Melchizedek Priesthood he can share these blessings by naming and blessing babies, administering to the sick, baptizing children, and giving special priesthood blessings and ordinations.

The father should spend time with each individual child. He should also teach and counsel them often. Some good examples are also found in the Book of Mormon (see 2 Nephi 1:14–32; 2 Nephi 2; 2 Nephi 3; and Alma 36–42).

THE RESPONSIBILITY OF THE MOTHER

President David O. McKay has said that motherhood is woman's noblest calling (see Treasures of Life, p. 54). It is a sacred calling, a partnership with God in bringing his spirit children into the world. A mother's most important responsibility is to bring children into the world and to care for and teach them. Bearing children is one of the greatest of all blessings. To refuse to do so is a serious sin.

Elder Boyd K. Packer praised those women who were unable to have children of their own, yet fulfilled their calling in a different way. He said: "When I speak of mothers, I speak not only of those women who have borne children, but also of those who have fostered children born to others, and of the many women who, without children of their own, have mothered the children of others" (Mothers, p. 8).

A mother must be warm and loving. She must spend time with the children and teach them the gospel. She needs to play with them and to work with them. A mother needs to help a child feel good about himself and to discover the world around him. She needs to make her home a clean and pleasant place.

The Book of Mormon (Alma 53:16–23) describes a group of young men who were able to rise to greatness because of the teachings of their mothers. These two thousand boys, led by the prophet Helaman, went into battle against their enemies. These young men were honest, brave, and trustworthy. They learned these things from their mothers. Their mothers also taught them that if they did not doubt, God would deliver them (see Alma 56:47). They all escaped being killed in the battle. Later they expressed faith in the teachings of their mothers saying: "We do not doubt our mothers knew it" (Alma 56:48). Every mother who has a testimony can have a profound effect on her children.

Why is motherhood called a partnership with God?
Assign someone to tell the story of Helaman's young warriors.

RESPONSIBILITIES OF THE CHILDREN

Children share with their parents the responsibility of building a happy home. They should obey the commandments and cooperate with other family members. The Lord is not pleased when children quarrel (Mosiah 4:14).

The Lord has commanded children to honor their parents. He has said, "Honor thy father and thy mother, that thy days may be long upon the land" (Exodus 20:12). To honor parents means to love and respect them. It also means to obey them. The scriptures tell children to "obey your parents in the Lord: for this is right" (Ephesians 6:1).

President Spencer W. Kimball has said that children should learn to work and to share responsibilities in the home and yard. They should be given assignments to keep the house neat and clean. Children may also be given assignments to take care of the garden (see *Ensign,* May 1976, p. 5).

What should children do to honor and respect their parents?

ACCEPTING RESPONSIBILITIES BRINGS BLESSINGS

A loving and happy family does not happen by accident. Each person in the family must do his part. The Lord has given responsibilities to both parents and to children. The scriptures tell us that each must be thoughtful, cheerful, and considerate of others. When we speak, pray, sing or work together, we can enjoy the blessings of harmony in our families (see Colossians 3).

Have each family member tell how he can help make home a happier place.

ADDITIONAL SCRIPTURES
Proverbs 22:6 (train up a child)
D&C 121:41–43 (loving our children)
Ephesians 6:4 (responsibility of fathers)
Ephesians 6:1–3 (children obey parents)

SUGGESTED SONG
"Teach Me to Walk in the Light"

ETERNAL MARRIAGE

Marriage is ordained of God. The Lord has said: "Whoso forbiddeth to marry is not ordained of God, for marriage is ordained of God unto man" (D&C 49:15). In the beginning, marriage was given as a law of the gospel. It was intended to last forever, not just for our mortal lives. Adam and Eve were married before there was any death in the world. Their marriage was performed by God. It was an eternal marriage. They taught this law to their children and their children's children. As the years passed, wickedness entered the hearts of the people, and eternal marriage was not performed. The authority to perform this sacred ceremony was taken from the earth. Through the restoration of the gospel, eternal marriage has been restored to earth.

When was eternal marriage first performed on the earth?

ETERNAL MARRIAGE IS ESSENTIAL FOR EXALTATION

Many people in the world consider marriage to be only a social custom, merely a legal agreement between a man and a woman to live together. But to Latter-day Saints, marriage is much more. Our exaltation depends on marriage. We believe that marriage is the most sacred relationship that can exist between a man and a woman. This sacred relationship affects our happiness now as well as in the eternities. Our Heavenly Father has given us the law of eternal marriage so that we can become like him. We must live the law of eternal marriage to become as he is—able to have spirit children. The Lord has said: "In the celestial glory there are three

heavens or degrees; And in order to obtain the highest, a man must enter into this order of the priesthood [meaning the new and everlasting covenant of marriage]; And if he does not, he cannot obtain it'' (D&C 131:1–3).

Why do we believe marriage to be the most sacred relationship between man and woman?

ETERNAL MARRIAGE MUST BE PERFORMED BY PROPER AUTHORITY IN THE TEMPLE

An eternal marriage must be performed by one who holds the sealing powers and authority. The Lord has said: ''If a man marry a wife by . . . the new and everlasting covenant . . . by him who is anointed . . . it . . . shall be of full force when they are out of the world'' (D&C 132:19).

Not only must an eternal marriage be performed by the proper priesthood authority, but it must also be done in the proper place. The proper place is in one of the holy temples of our Lord. The temple is the only place this holy ordinance can be performed.

In the temple, Latter-day Saint couples kneel at one of the sacred altars in the presence of their family and friends and two special witnesses. They make their marriage covenants before God. They are pronounced man and wife for time and all eternity. This is done by one who holds the holy priesthood of God and has the special authority to perform this sacred ordinance. He acts under the direction of the Lord and promises the couple the blessings of exaltation. He instructs them in the things they must do to receive these blessings. He reminds them that all blessings depend upon obedience to the laws of God.

If we are married by other than priesthood authority, the marriage is for this life only. After death, the marriage partners have no claim on each other or on their children. An eternal marriage gives us the opportunity to continue as families after this life.

Who has the authority to perform an eternal marriage? Why must it be done in the temple?

Every couple should begin life together in the temple of the Lord.

THE BENEFITS OF AN ETERNAL MARRIAGE

As Latter-day Saints, we are living for eternity and not just for the moment. However, the blessings of an eternal marriage can be ours now as well as for eternity.

The blessings we can enjoy in this life are as follows:

1. We know that our marriage can last forever. Death can part us from one another only temporarily. Nothing can part us forever except our own willful disobedience. This knowledge helps us work harder to have a happy, successful marriage.

2. We know that we can have our children with us throughout eternity. Because of this knowledge, we are more careful in the way we teach and train our children. We show them greater patience. We are more loving toward them. As a result, we have a happier home.

Some of the blessings we can enjoy for eternity are:

1. We can live in the highest degree of the celestial kingdom of God.

2. We can be exalted as God is now and receive a fulness of joy.

3. We can, at some future time, increase our family by having spirit children.

Have two persons discuss the benefits of an eternal marriage in this life and in eternity.

WE MUST PREPARE FOR AN ETERNAL MARRIAGE

President Spencer W. Kimball teaches that "marriage is perhaps the most vital of all the decisions and has the most far-reaching effects. . . . It affects not only the two people involved, but their children and . . . their children's children. . . . Of all the decisions, this one must not be wrong." He tells us: "We recommend . . . that all boys and girls from their infancy up plan to be married only in the temple . . . to keep their lives spotless so that this can be accomplished." (". . . The Matter of Marriage," devotional address, Salt Lake Institute of Religion, 22 Oct. 1976)

President Kimball has also said:

"We say to all youth regardless of what country is your home, and regardless of the customs in your country, your Heavenly Father expects you to marry for eternity and rear a good, strong family.

"It would be our hope that parents would train you . . . to earn some money, and to put it away for your missions and your marriages. . . .

"There will be a new spirit in Zion when the young women will say to their boyfriends: ''I am sorry, but as much as I love you, I will not marry out of the holy temple'' (''Marriage—The Proper Way,'' *New Era,* Feb. 1976, p. 4).

An eternal marriage should be the goal of every Latter-day Saint. This is true even for those already married by civil law. To prepare for an eternal marriage takes much thought and prayer. Only members of the Church who live righteously are permitted to enter the temple (see D&C 97:15–17). We do not suddenly decide one day that we want to be married in the temple, then enter the temple that day and get married. We must first meet certain requirements.

Before we can go to the temple, each of us must have been an active, worthy member of the Church for at least one year. Men must have received the Melchizedek Priesthood. We must be interviewed (questioned) by the branch president or bishop. If we are found to be worthy, we will be given a temple recommend. Once a person has received a recommend from his bishop or branch president, he must have it signed by a member of the stake presidency or the mission president. If we are not worthy, the bishop or branch president will counsel with us. He will help us set goals to become worthy to go to the temple.

The following are some of the questions that we are asked in interviews for a temple recommend:

1. Have you ever been involved in a transgression relating to

the law of chastity that has not been resolved with the proper priesthood authorities?

2. Do you sustain the President of The Church of Jesus Christ of Latter-day Saints as a Prophet, Seer, and Revelator, recognizing no other person on the earth as authorized to exercise all priesthood keys?

3. Are you a full tithe payer?

4. Do you keep the Word of Wisdom?

5. Are you totally honest in your dealings with your fellowmen?

6. Will you earnestly strive to do your duty in the Church; to attend your sacrament, priesthood, and other meetings; and to obey the rules, laws, and commandments of the Church?

7. Do you live in accordance with the teachings of the gospel? (See *General Handbook of Instructions,* no. 21, p. 53.)

When you ask for a recommend, remember that to enter the temple of our Lord is a sacred privilege. It is a serious act, not something to be taken lightly. We must be obedient to every covenant that we make in the temple of the Lord. He has said that if we are true and faithful we shall pass by the angels to our exaltation. We will become gods (see D&C 132:19-20). Temple marriage is worth any sacrifice. It is a way of obtaining eternal blessings beyond measure.

Ask each person to think about the temple interview questions as you reread them. How can we prepare for an eternal marriage?

ADDITIONAL SCRIPTURES
Genesis 1:26-28 (we should multiply and replenish the earth)
Genesis 2:21-24 (the first marriage was performed by God)
Matthew 19:3-8 (what God has joined. . . .)
D&C 132 (the eternal nature of marriage law)
D&C 131:1-4 (the highest place in the celestial kingdom is reserved)
D&C 42:24-26 (marriage vows should be kept)
Jacob 3:5-11 (Lamanites more loyal at this time than Nephites)
Matthew 22:23-30 (no marriage in the resurrection)

SUGGESTED SONG
"We'll Sing All Hail to Jesus' Name"

THE LAW
OF CHASTITY

A NOTE TO PARENTS

This chapter contains some parts that are beyond the maturity of young children. It is best to wait and teach children these parts when they are old enough to understand sexual relations and procreation. Our Church leaders have told us that our responsibility as parents is to teach our children about procreation (the process of conceiving and bearing children). We must also teach them the law of chastity.

We can begin teaching our children to have proper attitudes toward their bodies when they are very young. If we will talk to our children frankly but reverently, using the correct names for the parts and functions of their bodies, they will grow up without unnecessary embarrassment concerning their bodies.

Children are naturally curious. They want to know how their bodies work. They want to know where babies come from. If we answer all such questions immediately and clearly so that they can understand us, they will continue to come to us with their questions. However, if we answer them so that they feel embarrassed, rejected, or dissatisfied, they will probably go to someone else with their questions and perhaps get incorrect ideas and improper attitudes. It is not wise or necessary, however, to tell them everything at once. We need only to give them the information they have asked for and can understand. As we answer their questions, we can teach them the importance of respecting their bodies and the bodies of others. We should teach them to dress modestly. We must be careful to correct the false ideas and vulgar language that they learn from others. By the time they reach maturity, we should have frankly discussed procreation with them. They should understand that these powers are good and were given to us by the Lord. He expects us to use them only within the bounds he has given us.

Little children come to us pure and innocent from our Heavenly Father. As parents, we should teach them the gospel in our homes. If we pray for guidance, the Lord will inspire us to teach our children at the right time and in the right way.

THE POWER OF PROCREATION

After the creation, God commanded each living thing to reproduce after its own kind (Genesis 1:22). Reproduction was part of his plan so that all forms of life could continue to exist upon the earth. To the animals, he gave natural instincts and restrictions.

Then he placed Adam and Eve upon the earth. They were different from his other creations because they were spirit children of our Heavenly Father. God married Adam and Eve in the garden of Eden and commanded them to multiply and replenish the earth (Genesis 1:28). However, their lives were to be governed by moral laws rather than by instinct.

God wanted his spirit children to be born in a family so they could be properly cared for and taught. We, as well as Adam and Eve, are to provide physical bodies for these spirit children through sexual reproduction. The powers of procreation are sacred. He has commanded us that only in marriage are we to have sexual relations. This commandment is called the law of chastity.

Why did God give man the marriage relationship?

WHAT IS THE LAW OF CHASTITY?

We are to have sexual intercourse only with our spouse to whom we are legally married. No one, male or female, is to have sexual intercourse before marriage. After marriage, sexual relations are only permitted with our spouse.

To the Israelites the Lord said: "Thou shalt not commit adultery" (Exodus 20:14). Those Israelites who broke this commandment were put to death (see Leviticus 20:10). The Lord repeated this commandment to the prophet Joseph Smith when he said: "Thou shalt not commit adultery; and he that committeth adultery, and repenteth not, shall be cast out [meaning excommunicated]" (D&C 42:24).

We have been taught that the law of chastity encompasses more than sexual intercourse. President Kimball warned young people of other sins that are part of the law of chastity:

"Among the most common sexual sins our young people commit are necking and petting. Not only do these improper relations often lead to fornication, pregnancy, and abortions—all ugly sins—but in and of themselves they are pernicious evils, and it is often difficult for youth to distinguish where one ends and another begins. They awaken lust and stir evil thoughts and sex desires. They are but parts of the whole family of related sins and indiscretions" (*The Miracle of Forgiveness,* p. 65).

Chastity is so important that President Kimball counseled young people to fight if necessary to protect it:

"Your bodies are yours; they belong to you and no one else. As you get a little older and begin to have boy friends, you should keep these facts in mind that your body is sacred to you and precious, and through courtship, gradually there comes an affection between two people that leads to marriage. Remember, sometimes there is a tendency to get too intimate in that courtship.

"Remember this, girls, it is actually better for you to die fighting for your chastity and cleanliness, than to let any one take advantage of you and take your virtue. If you have a boy friend who insists upon using your body, fondling it with his hands, or otherwise, you tell him No! in no uncertain terms. And if he insists, then you may have to defend yourself. Remember that one of the prophets said [that] to retain your chastity is more important than your life" (*Mexico and Central America General Conference,* Aug. 1972, p. 108).

Even if we are under threat of rape, President Kimball has said: "It is better to die in defending one's virtue than to live having lost it without a struggle" (*The Miracle of Forgiveness,* p. 196). Women who are forcibly raped are under no condemnation from the Lord.

What is the law of chastity?
How can we be morally clean?

SATAN WANTS US TO BREAK THE LAW OF CHASTITY

Satan's plan is to deceive as many of us as he possibly can to prevent us from returning to live with our Heavenly Father. One of the most damaging things he can do is to entice us to break the law of chastity. He is cunning and powerful. He would like us to believe that it is no sin to break this law. Many people have been deceived. We must guard ourselves against their influences.

Satan attacks our modesty. He wants us to believe that because the human body is beautiful, it should be seen and appreciated. Our Heavenly Father wants us to keep our bodies covered so that we do not put improper thoughts into the minds of others.

Satan not only encourages us to dress immodestly, but he also encourages us to think immoral or improper thoughts. He does this with pictures, movies, stories, jokes, music, and dances which suggest immoral acts. The law of chastity requires that our thoughts as well as our actions be pure. The prophet Alma taught that when we are judged by God, "our thoughts will also condemn us; and in this awful state, we shall not dare to look up to our God" (Alma 12:14). Jesus himself taught: "Ye have heard that it was said by them of old time, Thou shalt not commit adultery: But I say unto you, That whosoever looketh on a woman to lust after her hath committed adultery with her already in his heart" (Matthew 5:27–28).

Satan sometimes tempts us through our emotions. He knows when we are lonely, confused, or depressed. He chooses this time of weakness to tempt us to break the law of chastity. Our Heavenly Father can give us the strength to pass through these trials unharmed.

The scriptures (Genesis 39:1–18) tell us about a very righteous young man named Joseph who was greatly trusted by his master, Potiphar. Potiphar had given Joseph command over everything he had. Potiphar's wife lusted after Joseph and tempted him to commit adultery with her. Joseph resisted her and fled from her.

Our Heavenly Father has promised us: "There hath no temptation taken you but such is common to man: but God is faithful, who will not suffer you to be tempted above that which ye are able; but will with the temptation also make a way to escape, that ye may be able to bear it" (1 Corinthians 10:13).

What are some ways Satan tempts us to break the law of chastity?
What promise has the Lord given us to help us overcome Satan's temptations?

BREAKING THE LAW OF CHASTITY IS EXTREMELY SERIOUS

The prophet Alma grieved because one of his sons had broken the law of chastity. He said to his son, Corianton: "Know ye not, my son, that these things are an abomination in the sight of the Lord; yea, most abominable above all sins save it be the shedding of innocent blood or denying the Holy Ghost?" (Alma 39:5). Unchastity is next to murder in seriousness.

President David O. McKay has pleaded: "Your virtue is worth more than your life. . . . preserve your virtue even if you lose your lives" (quoted in *The Miracle of Forgiveness,* p. 63).

President Heber J. Grant taught: "There is no true Latter-day Saint who would not rather bury a son or a daughter than to have him or her lose his or her virtue—realizing that virtue is of more value than anything else in the wide world" (*Gospel Standards,* p. 55).

If a child is conceived by those who break the law of chastity, they may be tempted to commit another abominable

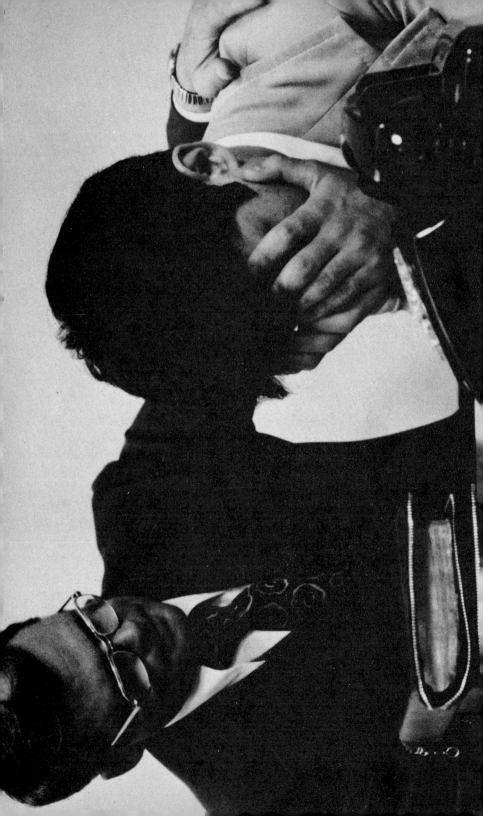

sin—abortion. There is no excuse for abortion unless the life of the mother is seriously threatened.

It is extremely important to our Heavenly Father that his children obey the law of chastity. Members of the Church who break this law may be excommunicated (see D&C 42:22–26, 80–81). All those who do not repent after committing adultery will not be able to live with our Heavenly Father and Jesus Christ, but will live in the telestial kingdom (see D&C 76:81–86, 103–105; see also this manual, chapter 46).

Read D&C 76:103–105.
Why is breaking the law of chastity such a serious transgression?
What blessings do people who break the law of chastity lose?

THOSE WHO BREAK THE LAW OF CHASTITY CAN BE FORGIVEN

Peace can come to those who have broken the law of chastity. The Lord tells us: "If the wicked will turn from all his sins that he hath committed, and keep all my statutes . . . all his transgressions that he hath committed, they shall not be mentioned unto him" (Ezekiel 18:21–22). Peace comes only through forgiveness. But forgiveness has a high price. President Kimball tells us: "To every forgiveness there is a condition. . . . The fasting, the prayers, the humility must be equal to or greater than the sin. There must be a broken heart and a contrite spirit. . . . There must be tears and genuine change of heart. There must be conviction of the sin, abandonment of the evil, confession of the error to properly constituted authorities of the Lord" (*The Miracle of Forgiveness*, p. 353).

For many, confession is the most difficult part. We must not only confess to the Lord, but also to the person we have offended, such as a husband or wife, and to the proper priesthood authority. The priesthood leader (bishop or stake president) will judge our standing in the Church. The Lord told Alma: "Whosoever transgresseth against me . . . if he confess his sins before thee and me, and repenteth in the sincerity of his heart, him ye shall forgive, and I will forgive him also" (Mosiah 26:29).

Confession of our sins is a necessary step toward forgiveness.

But President Kimball warns us: "Even though forgiveness is so abundantly promised, there is no promise nor indication of forgiveness to any soul who does not totally repent. . . . We can hardly be too forceful in reminding people that they cannot sin and be forgiven and then sin again and again and expect forgiveness" (*The Miracle of Forgiveness,* pp. 353, 360). Those who receive forgiveness and then repeat the sin are held accountable for their former sins (see D&C 82:7; Ether 2:15).

THOSE WHO KEEP THE LAW OF CHASTITY ARE GREATLY BLESSED

When we obey the law of chastity, we can be without guilt or shame. Our lives and our children's lives are blessed when we keep ourselves pure and spotless before the Lord. Our children can look to our example and follow in our footsteps.

Read D&C 76:58–60.
How will those who keep all of God's commandments, including the law of chastity, be blessed?

ADDITIONAL SCRIPTURES
Matthew 19:5–9; Genesis 2:24 (sacredness of marriage relationship)
1 John 2:16–17; Titus 2:5–12 (instructions for chastity)
Genesis 19:5; Proverbs 6:25–32; Leviticus 19:20–25; 29; Leviticus 20:13, 15–16; (perversion condemned)
1 Corinthians 7:2–5; Ephesians 5:28 (loyalty to spouse)
Alma 7:25; Revelation 14:4–5 (blessings for obedience to the law of chastity)
Proverbs 6:25–29 (warning against adulteresses)
Proverbs 31:10; Revelation 14:4–5 (virtue praised)

SUGGESTED SONG
"The Lord Gave Me a Temple"

The Salt Lake Temple
Photograph by Eldon K. Linschoten

TEMPLE WORK AND GENEALOGY

TEMPLES OF THE LORD

Temples of The Church of Jesus Christ of Latter-day Saints are special buildings dedicated to the Lord. We go there to receive sacred ordinances and to make covenants with our Heavenly Father. These ordinances and covenants are necessary for our salvation. They must be performed in the temples of the Lord.

We also go to the temple to learn more about our Heavenly Father and his Son, Jesus Christ. In the temple we gain a better understanding of our own purpose in life. We are taught about our premortal existence, the meaning of earth life, and life after death.

Show a picture of a temple. Have someone tell what it is and what happens there.

TEMPLE ORDINANCES SEAL FAMILIES TOGETHER FOR ETERNITY

All of the temple ordinances are performed by the power of the priesthood. Through this power ordinances performed on earth are sealed in heaven. The Savior taught, "Whatsoever thou shalt bind on earth shall be bound in heaven" (Matthew 16:19; see also D&C 132:7).

Marriage is one of the temple ordinances. Temple marriage seals (unites or binds) a man and woman together as husband and wife here on earth and for eternity. In addition, when parents who have been married in the temple later have children, these children are born under the cov-

The Washington Temple
Photograph by Eldon K. Linschoten

enant—automatically sealed to their parents. If a man and a woman are married civilly, they may later go to the temple to be sealed for eternity. They may also bring their children to be sealed to them.

What does it mean to be sealed?

TEMPLE ORDINANCES CAN BE PERFORMED FOR THE DEAD

To live with our Heavenly Father and with our families forever, we must be baptized. We must also receive the ordinances of the temple. This is true for everyone who has ever lived on the earth. However, millions of people have died without hearing the gospel and receiving the necessary ordinances. What will happen to them?

Heavenly Father loves all of his children. He has provided a way for everyone to have the ordinances of the gospel performed for them so that they may return and live with him. We have the opportunity to go to a temple in behalf of the dead. In the temple, we can perform all the ordinances necessary for the exaltation of those who have died. This includes temple marriage.

How do those who have died without a knowledge of the gospel receive their temple ordinances?

TEMPLE WORK IS VERY IMPORTANT

Each of us should make sure that temple work is done for ourselves and our own ancestors. The Prophet Joseph Smith taught that the greatest responsibility we have in this world is to identify our ancestors and go to the temple in their behalf (see *Teachings of the Prophet Joseph Smith,* p. 356). Another modern prophet, Joseph Fielding Smith, said: "Some may feel that if they pay their tithing, attend their regular meetings and duties, give of their substances to the poor . . . , spend one, two, or more years preaching the gospel in the world, that they are [free] from further duty. But *the greatest and grandest duty of all is to labor for the dead"* (see *Doctrines of Salvation,* 2:149).

Read D&C 128:15, 24.
How important is temple work and genealogy?

HOW TO PERFORM TEMPLE WORK FOR THE DEAD

There are three steps in doing temple work for the dead. These are researching our genealogy, submitting names, and attending the temple.

RESEARCHING OUR GENEALOGY

Temple work cannot be done for nameless people. We must identify our ancestors. We should write down their names, places of birth, date of birth, and the names of their parents. This is called genealogical research. The Genealogical Department of the Church will help us learn how to do this work.

Our Church leaders have asked us to begin doing our genealogy by gathering information about our ancestors for four generations. These four generations include ourselves, our parents, our grandparents, and our great-grandparents. After we have identified the members of our family for four generations, we should continue to search for the names and vital information about other ancestors who lived before them.

SUBMITTING NAMES

After we have identified our ancestors, we should submit their names to the proper priesthood authorities. Then temple ordinances may be performed for them. If we need help in submitting names, our priesthood leaders can help us.

ATTENDING THE TEMPLE

After we have been to the temple and received the temple ordinances for ourselves, we should return to do the ordinance work for the dead.

How do we go about doing our temple work?
Discuss the three steps listed above.
Show pictures of a family group sheet and a pedigree chart. Members may discuss the information required on these forms.

KEEPING A PERSONAL RECORD

Temple work and genealogy involves more than collecting information about our ancestors. Their purpose is to bind us

FAMILY GROUP RECORD

HUSBAND _____

Born	Place	
Chr.	Place	
Mar.	Place	
Died	Place	
Bur.	Place	

HUSBAND'S FATHER _____   HUSBAND'S MOTHER _____

HUSBAND'S OTHER WIVES _____

WIFE _____

Born	Place
Chr.	Place
Died	Place
Bur.	Place

WIFE'S FATHER _____   WIFE'S MOTHER _____

WIFE'S OTHER HUSBANDS _____

Husband

Wife

Ward Examiners 1 _____ 2 _____

Stake or Mission _____

NAME & ADDRESS OF PERSON SUBMITTING SHEET

RELATION OF ABOVE TO HUSBAND   RELATION OF ABOVE TO WIFE

FOUR GENERATION SHEET FOR FILING ONLY   YES ☐   NO ☐

DATE SUBMITTED TO GENEALOGICAL SOCIETY

LDS ORDINANCE DATA

	BAPTIZED (Date)	ENDOWED (Date)	SEALED (Date and Temple) WIFE TO HUSBAND
HUSBAND			
WIFE			

SEX M F	CHILDREN List each child (whether living or dead) in order of birth SURNAME _____ Given Names	WHEN BORN			WHERE BORN				DATE OF FIRST MARRIAGE TO WHOM	WHEN DIED			SEALED (Date and Temple) CHILDREN TO PARENTS
		DAY	MONTH	YEAR	TOWN	COUNTY	STATE OR COUNTRY			DAY	MONTH	YEAR	
1													
2													
3													
4													
5													
6													
7													
8													
9													
10													
11													

SOURCES OF INFORMATION

OTHER MARRIAGES

NECESSARY EXPLANATIONS

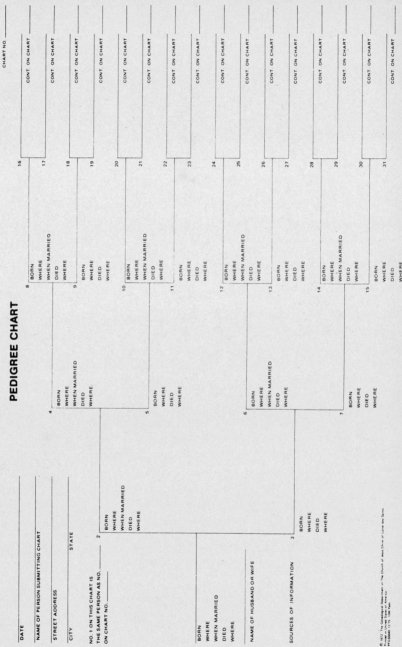

PEDIGREE CHART

DATE

NAME OF PERSON SUBMITTING CHART

STREET ADDRESS

CITY   STATE

NO. 1 ON THIS CHART IS
THE SAME PERSON AS NO.
ON CHART NO.

2

BORN
WHERE
WHEN MARRIED
DIED
WHERE

BORN
WHERE
WHEN MARRIED
DIED
WHERE

NAME OF HUSBAND OR WIFE

3

BORN
WHERE
DIED
WHERE

SOURCES OF INFORMATION

4

BORN
WHERE
WHEN MARRIED
DIED
WHERE.

5

BORN
WHERE
DIED
WHERE

6

BORN
WHERE
WHEN MARRIED
DIED
WHERE

7

BORN
WHERE
DIED
WHERE

8

BORN
WHERE
WHEN MARRIED
DIED
WHERE

9

BORN
WHERE
DIED
WHERE

10

BORN
WHERE
WHEN MARRIED
DIED
WHERE

11

BORN
WHERE
DIED
WHERE

12

BORN
WHERE
WHEN MARRIED
DIED
WHERE

13

BORN
WHERE
DIED
WHERE

14

BORN
WHERE
WHEN MARRIED
DIED
WHERE

15

BORN
WHERE
DIED
WHERE

CHART NO.

16
CONT. ON CHART

17
CONT. ON CHART

18
CONT. ON CHART

19
CONT. ON CHART

20
CONT. ON CHART

21
CONT. ON CHART

22
CONT. ON CHART

23
CONT. ON CHART

24
CONT. ON CHART

25
CONT. ON CHART

26
CONT. ON CHART

27
CONT. ON CHART

28
CONT. ON CHART

29
CONT. ON CHART

30
CONT. ON CHART

31
CONT. ON CHART

© 1972 The Genealogical Department of The Church of Jesus Christ of Latter-day Saints
Printed in United States of America
PFCS00040 (7/75 10M Part)

together with our families—the living, the dead, and those yet to be born.

In addition to genealogical research, one of the things we can do to unite our families is to keep a personal record of our own lives. This record is a personal book of remembrance. Since the time of Adam, the Lord has commanded us to keep a book of remembrance (see Moses 6:8). The prophets kept such books (see Moses 6:45–47; Malachi 3:16). By reading their records we learn about the blessings and commandments they received from Heavenly Father. We also gain strength from their testimonies. Our children and their children will benefit from reading about our experiences and testimonies.

President Spencer W. Kimball said: "Get a notebook. . . . Begin today and write in it your goings and comings, your deepest thoughts, your achievements and your failures, your associations and your triumphs, your impressions and your testimonies" ("The Angels May Quote from It," *New Era,* Oct. 1975, p. 5).

If we keep a personal record, our children and grandchildren can gain strength from our lives. This record will turn our hearts and thoughts toward our children. Then, when our descendants read our record, their minds and hearts will be turned toward us.

Discuss the things a person should include in keeping a personal journal.
Discuss and decide on ways to begin.

ADDITIONAL SCRIPTURES
D&C 124:39–40 (why build temples?)
3 Nephi 11:1 (temples in this land)
D&C 88:119 (temples to be built)
1 Peter 4:6 (gospel preached to dead)
D&C 1:8–9; D&C 132:7 (sealing power)
D&C 128:15–18; 1 Corinthians 15:29 (work for the dead)

SUGGESTED SONGS
"Redeemer of Israel," "Sweet Is the Work, My God, My King"

Each of us should keep a diary or a journal.
Photograph by Eldon K. Linschoten

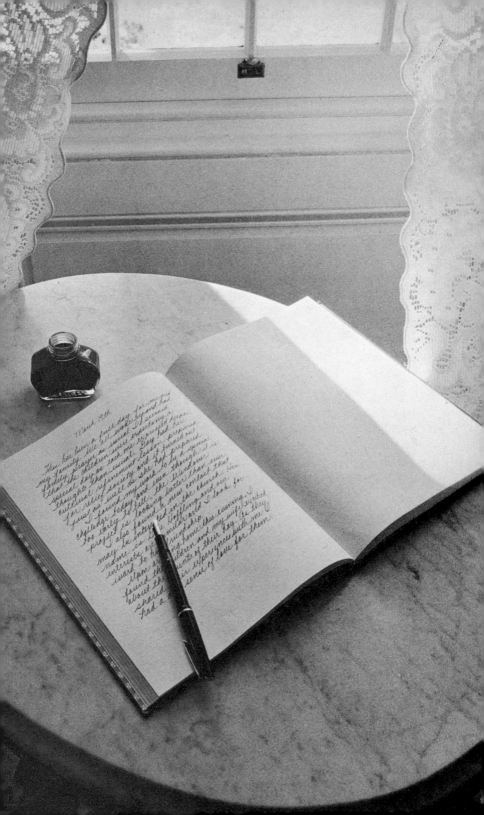

SIGNS OF
THE SECOND COMING

JESUS CHRIST WILL RETURN TO THE EARTH

The Savior told Joseph Smith: "I will reveal myself from heaven with power and great glory . . . and dwell in righteousness with men on earth a thousand years, and the wicked shall not stand" (D&C 29:11; see also this manual, chapters 43 and 44, "The Second Coming of Jesus Christ" and "The Millennium"). Jesus had told us that certain signs and events would warn us that the time of his second coming was near. This second coming is also called "the great and dreadful day of the Lord."

Read Acts 1:9-11.
What great truth did the two angels tell the Apostles?

SIGNS WILL TELL US OF JESUS' COMING

For thousands of years followers of Jesus have looked forward to the Second Coming as a time of peace and joy. But before he comes, the peoples of the earth will experience great trials and calamities. Our Heavenly Father wants us to be prepared for the troubles that will surely come. He also expects us to be spiritually ready when the Lord comes in his glory. Therefore, God has given us signs, which are occurrences or events that will tell us when the Savior's second coming is near. Throughout the ages God has revealed these signs to his prophets. He has said that all faithful followers of Christ will know what the signs are and will be watching for them (see D&C 45:39). If we are obedient and faithful, we will study the scriptures and know of the signs.

There are many signs that the second coming of Jesus Christ is near.

Why is it important to know the signs of the Second Coming?
How may we know these signs?

WHAT ARE THE SIGNS FORETELLING JESUS CHRIST'S COMING?

Many signs foretell the second coming of Jesus Christ. Some have already been or are now being fulfilled. Others will be fulfilled in the future.

WICKEDNESS, WAR, AND TURMOIL

Many of the signs are terrifying and dreadful. The prophets have warned us that the earth will experience great turmoil, wickedness, war, and suffering. The prophet Daniel said that this would be a time of trouble such as the earth has never known (see Daniel 12:1). The Lord said: "The love of men shall wax cold, and iniquity shall abound" (D&C 45:27). "And all things shall be in commotion," and people shall be afraid (see D&C 88:91). We can expect earthquakes, disease, and famines (see Matthew 24:7), and great storms, lightnings, and thunder (see D&C 88:90). Hailstorms will destroy the crops of the earth (D&C 29:16).

Jesus told his disciples that war would fill the earth. He said: "Ye shall hear of wars and rumours of wars. . . . For nation shall rise against nation, and kingdom against kingdom" (Matthew 24:6–7). These wars will continue until a great and final war, the most destructive the world has known. In the midst of this war the Savior will appear (see Bruce R. McConkie, *Mormon Doctrine,* p. 732).

We can see that many of these signs are being fulfilled. Wickedness is everywhere. Nations are constantly at war. Earthquakes and other calamities are occurring. Many people now suffer from devastating storms, drought, and hunger. We can be certain that these calamities will become more severe until the Lord comes.

However, not all the events preceding the Second Coming will be dreadful. Many of them will bring joy to the world.

THE RESTORATION OF THE GOSPEL

Prophets of old foretold the restoration of the gospel. The Lord said: "light shall break forth among them that sit in darkness, and it shall be the fulness of my gospel" (D&C 45:28). The Apostle John saw that the gospel would be restored by an angel (see Revelation 14:6–7). In fulfillment of this prophecy, the angel Moroni and other heavenly visitors brought the gospel of Jesus Christ to Joseph Smith.

THE COMING FORTH OF THE BOOK OF MORMON

The Lord told the Nephites of another sign: the Book of Mormon would come to their descendants (see 3 Nephi 21). In Old Testament times the prophets Isaiah and Ezekiel foresaw the coming of the Book of Mormon (see Ezekiel 37:16–20). These prophecies are now being fulfilled. The Book of Mormon is being taken to all the world.

THE GOSPEL PREACHED TO ALL THE WORLD

Another sign of Jesus' coming is that the "gospel of the kingdom shall be preached in all the world for a witness unto all nations" (Matthew 24:14). All people will hear the fulness of the gospel in their own language (see D&C 90:11). Ever since the restoration of the Church, missionaries have preached the gospel. The missionary effort has increased over the years until thousands of missionaries now preach to many countries of the world in many languages. Before the Second Coming the Lord will provide a way to bring the truth to *all* nations.

THE COMING OF ELIJAH

The prophet Malachi predicted that before Christ came the second time, the prophet Elijah would visit the earth. He would restore to men the sealing powers so that families could be sealed together. He would also inspire people to be concerned about their ancestors and descendants (see Malachi 4:5–6; D&C Section 2). The prophet Elijah came to Joseph Smith in April 1836. At that time people were not very interested in genealogy. People's interest in genealogy has rapidly grown in the years that have followed. Since Elijah's coming, we are also able to perform sealing ordinances in the temples for the living and the dead.

THE LAMANITES WILL BECOME A GREAT PEOPLE

The Lord said that when his coming was near, the Lamanites would become a righteous and respected people. He said: "Before the great day of the Lord shall come, . . . the Lamanites shall blossom as the rose" (D&C 49:24). This sign is coming to pass as great numbers of Lamanites in Central and South America and the South Pacific receive the blessings of the gospel.

BUILDING OF THE NEW JERUSALEM

Near the time of the coming of Jesus, the faithful Saints will build a righteous city, a city of God, called the New Jerusalem. Jesus Christ himself will rule there (see 3 Nephi 21:23–25). Although this city is not yet built, the Lord has said that it would be built in the state of Missouri, in the United States (see D&C 84:3–4).

These are only a few of the signs that the Lord has given us. The scriptures describe many more.

List some of the signs of Jesus' Second Coming. Discuss each one.

KNOWING THE SIGNS OF THE TIMES SHOULD HELP US

No one except our Heavenly Father knows exactly when the Lord will come (see Matthew 24:36). However, we can tell that the end is near because many of the signs are already being fulfilled. The Savior taught this with the parable (story) of the fig tree. He said that when we see the fig tree putting forth leaves, we can tell that summer will soon come. Likewise, when we see the signs, we can know that his coming is near at hand (Matthew 24:32–33).

The Lord gave us these signs to help us. We can put our lives in order and prepare ourselves and our families for those things yet to come. We do not need to worry about the calamities, but can look forward to the coming of the Savior and be glad. The Lord said, "Be not troubled, for, when all these things [the signs] shall come to pass, ye may know that the promises which have been made unto you shall be fulfilled" (see D&C 45:35). He goes on to say that those who are righteous when he comes will not be destroyed, "but shall abide the day, and the earth shall be given them for an inheritance; . . . and their children shall grow up without sin . . . for the Lord shall be in their midst, and his glory shall be upon them, and he will be their king and their lawgiver" (D&C 45:57–59).

How can knowing the signs of the Second Coming help us?
Why do we need to know when his coming is near?

ADDITIONAL SCRIPTURES
Acts 1:9–11 (Jesus will come again)
1 Corinthians 15:22–28 (the end cometh; death done away)
1 Thessalonians 5:1–6 (signs of a woman in childbirth)
Matthew 16:1–4 (discern signs of times)
Matthew 24 (signs of the second coming)
D&C 38:30 (prepare that we might not fear)
D&C 68:11 (we can know the signs)
D&C 88:111–15 (earth's final war)

SUGGESTED SONG
"Now Let Us Rejoice"

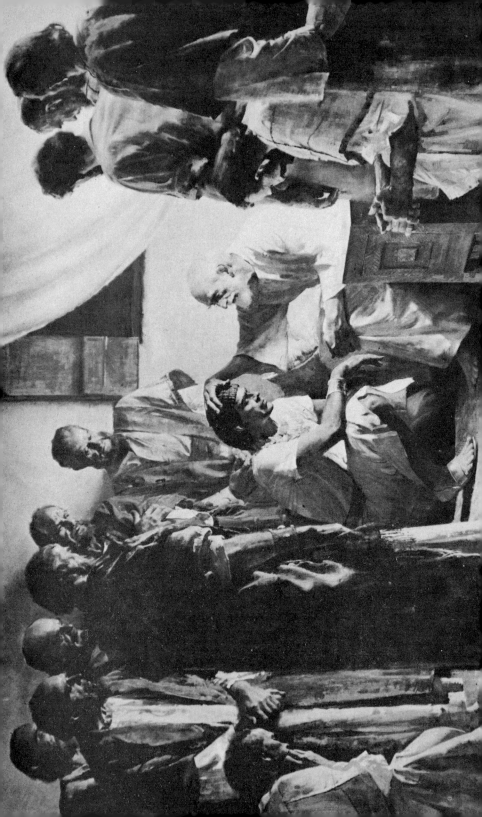

THE GATHERING OF THE HOUSE OF ISRAEL

THE HOUSE OF ISRAEL BECOMES GOD'S CHOSEN PEOPLE

Jacob was a great prophet who lived hundreds of years before the time of Christ. Because Jacob was so faithful, the Lord gave him the special name of Israel, which means "a prince of God" (see Genesis 32:28). Jacob (Israel) had twelve sons. These sons and their families became known as the Twelve Tribes of Israel, or Israelites (see Genesis 49:28).

Jacob was a grandson of Abraham. The Lord made an everlasting covenant with Abraham which was renewed with Jacob (Israel) and his children (see Deuteronomy 32:7-9; see also this manual, chapter 15, "The Lord's Covenant People"). God promised that the Israelites would be his chosen people as long as they would obey his commandments (see Deuteronomy 28:9-10). As his chosen people, the Israelites would be a blessing to all the nations of the world by taking the gospel and the priesthood to them. Thus, they would keep their covenant with the Lord and he would keep his covenant with them.

Discuss the promise of the Lord to make the Israelites his chosen people.

THE HOUSE OF ISRAEL WAS SCATTERED

Again and again prophets of the Lord warned the house of Israel what would happen if they were wicked. Moses prophesied: "And the Lord shall scatter thee among all people, from the one end of the earth even unto the other" (Deutero-

Jacob, whose name was changed by the Lord to Israel, blessed his sons and prophesied what would befall their descendants in the last days.

nomy 28:64). Gradually, the Israelites began to break the commandments of God. They fought among themselves and split into two kingdoms: The Northern Kingdom, called the kingdom of Israel, and the Southern Kingdom, called the kingdom of Judah. Ten of the twelve tribes of Israel lived in the Northern Kingdom. During a war they were conquered by their enemies and were carried away into captivity. Some of them later escaped into the lands of the north and became lost to the rest of the world.

About one hundred years after the capture of the Northern Kingdom, the Southern Kingdom of Judah was conquered. At about that time (600 B.C.) Lehi and his family left Jerusalem and settled on the American continent. The Lamanites are descendants of Lehi's people. The capital city of Jerusalem was destroyed in 586 B.C. and the remaining two tribes of Israel were taken captive. Later some of them returned and rebuilt Jerusalem. After the time of Christ, Jerusalem was again destroyed, this time by the Roman soldiers. The Jews were scattered over much of the world. Today Israelites are found in all countries of the world. Many of them do not know that they are descended from the ancient house of Israel.

Have members list the important events that led to and occurred at the scattering of the house of Israel.

THE HOUSE OF ISRAEL MUST BE GATHERED

The Lord promised that the Israelites, his chosen people, would someday be gathered: "I will gather the remnant of my flock out of all countries whither I have driven them" (Jeremiah 23:3).

The Lord has some important reasons for gathering his people, the Israelites. The people of Israel need to learn the teachings of the gospel and prepare themselves to meet the Savior when he comes again. The Israelites have the responsibility of building temples and performing sacred ordinances in the temples for their ancestors who died without having this opportunity. The chosen people of God must take the gospel to all nations. They must fulfill the covenant to be a blessing to all the world.

The power and authority to direct the work of gathering the house of Israel was given to Joseph Smith by the prophet Moses in 1836 in the Kirtland Temple (see D&C 110:11). Since that time, each latter-day prophet has held the keys for the gathering of the house of Israel. The work of gathering the scattered Israelites has continued as an important part of the work of Christ's true church. The house of Israel is now being gathered as they accept the restored gospel and serve the God of Abraham, Isaac, and Jacob (see Deuteronomy 30:1–5).

List some of the reasons why the house of Israel must be gathered.

HOW WILL THE HOUSE OF ISRAEL BE GATHERED?

The Israelites are to be gathered first spiritually and then physically. They are gathered spiritually when they join The Church of Jesus Christ of Latter-day Saints. This spiritual gathering began during the time of the Prophet Joseph Smith and has continued to grow since that time. Thousands of people all over the world are joining the Church each year. These converts are Israelites either by blood or adoption. They belong to the family of Abraham and Jacob (see Abraham 2:9–11; Galatians 3:26–29).

President Joseph Fielding Smith said: "There are many nations represented in the . . . Church. . . . They have come because the Spirit of the Lord rested upon them; . . . receiving the *spirit of gathering*, they have left everything for the sake of the gospel" (*Doctrines of Salvation*, 3:256).

The physical gathering of Israel means that the Israelites will be "gathered home to the lands of their inheritance, and . . . established in all their lands of promise" (see 2 Nephi 9:2). The tribes of Ephraim and Manassah will be gathered to the land of America. The tribe of Judah will be returned to the city of Jerusalem and the area surrounding it. The ten lost tribes will receive from the tribe of Ephraim (in America) their promised blessings (see D&C 133).

Gathering is occurring throughout the world wherever the pure in heart are found.

"Every stake on earth is the gathering place for the lost sheep of Israel who live in its area.

"The gathering place for Peruvians is in the stakes of Zion in Peru, or in the places which soon will become stakes. The gathering place for Chileans is in Chile; for Bolivians it is in Bolivia; for Koreans it is in Korea; and so it goes through all the length and breadth of the earth. Scattered Israel in every nation is called to gather to the fold of Christ, to the stakes of Zion, as such are established in their nations" (Bruce R. McConkie, *Ensign,* May 1977, p. 118).

It will not be long until this great work of gathering will be complete. However, the physical gathering of Israel will not be complete until the second coming of the Savior (see Joseph Smith 1:37; 1 Nephi 14:12). Then the Lord's promise will be fulfilled:

"Behold, the days come saith the Lord, that it shall no more be said, The Lord liveth, that brought up the children of Israel out of the land of Egypt; But, the Lord liveth, that brought up the children of Israel from the land of the north, and from all the lands whither he had driven them; and I will bring them again into their land that I gave unto their fathers" (Jeremiah 16:14-15).

In what two ways will the house of Israel be gathered? Discuss each of these.

ADDITIONAL SCRIPTURES
Genesis 17:1-8 (God's covenant with Abraham)
2 Kings 17 (Northern Kingdom taken captive)
2 Chronicles 36:11-20 (Southern Kingdom taken captive)
James 1:1 (twelve tribes scattered abroad)
1 Nephi 10:12-13 (Nephite migration part of scattering)
Deuteronomy 30:1-6 (Israel to come from all nations)
Jeremiah 3:14-18 (one from a city, two from a family)
Jeremiah 31:7-14 (lost tribes to come from the north countries)
Ezekiel 20:33-36 (Israel gathered from all countries)
3 Nephi 20:29-46 (covenanted Jews to Jerusalem)
3 Nephi 21:26-29 (starts with restoration of the gospel)
D&C 133:26-34 (ten tribes to return from the north)
Isaiah 11:11-13 (the Lord will recover his people)
Revelation 18:4-8 (a voice will proclaim the gathering)
D&C 110:11 (keys restored for the gathering)
D&C 133:6-15 (gentiles to Zion, Jews to Jerusalem)

SUGGESTED SONG
"Redeemer of Israel"

Chapter 43

THE SECOND COMING OF JESUS CHRIST

Forty days after his resurrection, Jesus and his Apostles were gathered together on the Mount of Olives. The time had come for him to leave the earth. He had completed all the work that he had to do at that time. He was to return to our Heavenly Father until the time of his second coming.

After he had instructed his Apostles, Jesus ascended into heaven. While the Apostles gazed up into the heavens after him, two angels stood beside them and said: "Ye men of Galilee, why stand ye gazing up into heaven? this same Jesus, which is taken up from you into heaven, shall so come in like manner as ye have seen him go" (Acts 1:11).

From that time until the present day, the followers of Jesus Christ have looked forward to his second coming.

Why is it important for us to know about the Second Coming?

WHY IS JESUS CHRIST COMING AGAIN?

Jesus Christ is coming again to the earth for several reasons:

1. He is coming to cleanse the earth. When Jesus comes again to the earth, he will come in power and great glory. At that time, the wicked will be destroyed. All things that are corrupt will be burned, and the earth will be cleansed by fire (D&C 101:24–25).

2. He is coming to judge his people (see this manual, chapter 46, "The Last Judgment"). When Jesus comes again, he will judge the nations and will divide the righteous from the wicked (Matthew 25:31–46). John the Revelator wrote about

265

this judgment: "I saw thrones, and they sat upon them, and judgment was given unto them: and I saw the souls of them that were beheaded for the witness of Jesus, and for the word of God . . . and they lived and reigned with Christ a thousand years." The wicked he saw, "lived not again until the thousand years were finished" (Revelation 20:4–5; see also D&C 88:95–98).

3. He is coming to usher in the Millennium. The Millennium is the 1,000-year period when Jesus will reign on the earth. At the beginning of this period of time, the righteous will be caught up to meet Jesus at his coming. His coming will begin the millennial reign (see this manual, chapter 44, "The Millennium").

Brigham Young said:

"In the Millennium, when the Kingdom of God is established on the earth in power, glory and perfection, and the reign of wickedness that has so long prevailed is subdued, the Saints of God will have the privilege of building their temples, and of entering into them, becoming, as it were, pillars in the temples of God, and they will officiate for their dead . . . And we will have revelations to know our forefathers clear back to Father Adam and Mother Eve, and we will enter into the temples of God and officiate for them. Then man will be sealed to man until the chain is made perfect back to Adam, so that there will be a perfect chain of Priesthood from Adam to the winding-up scene" (John A. Widtsoe, comp., *Discourses of Brigham Young,* p. 116).

4. At his coming many will be resurrected. Those who have earned the right to come forth in the resurrection of the just will rise from their graves. They will be caught up to meet him as he comes down from heaven.

After Jesus Christ rose from the dead, other righteous people who had died were also resurrected. They appeared in Jerusalem and also on the American continent (see Matthew 27:52–53; 3 Nephi 23:9). This was the beginning of the first resurrection. Some people have been resurrected since

then. Those who already have been resurrected and those who will be resurrected at the time of his coming will all inherit the glory of the celestial kingdom (see D&C 76:50–70).

After the beginning of the Millennium, those who have earned a terrestrial glory will be resurrected (see D&C 88:99; D&C 76:71–80). When all of these people have been resurrected, then the first resurrection will be completed.

The wicked who are living at the time of the second coming of the Lord will be destroyed in the flesh. They, along with the wicked who are already dead will have to wait until the end of the Millennium before they can come forth from their graves. At the end of the Millennium, the "second" resurrection will take place. All of the remaining dead will rise to meet God. They will either inherit the telestial kingdom or be cast into outer darkness with Satan (see D&C 76:81–112; 76:32–33).

5. The Savior will take his rightful place as king of heaven and earth. When Jesus comes, he will establish his government on the earth. The Church will become part of that kingdom. He will rule all the peoples of the earth in peace for 1,000 years.

When Jesus Christ first came to the earth, he did not come in glory. He was born in a lowly stable and laid in a manger of hay. He did not come with great armies as the Jews had expected their Savior to do. Instead, he came saying: "Love your enemies, . . . do good to them that hate you, and pray for them which despitefully use you" (Matthew 5:44). Because of this, he was rejected and crucified. But he will not be rejected at his second coming, "for every ear shall hear it, and every knee shall bow, and every tongue shall confess" that Jesus is the Christ (D&C 88:104). He will be greeted as "Lord of Lords and King of Kings." He will be called "Wonderful, Counselor, The Mighty God, The Everlasting Father, The Prince of Peace" (Isaiah 9:6).

Have members discuss some of the reasons for the second coming of the Lord. (To cleanse the earth, judge the people, begin the Millennium, complete the resurrection, reign as king.)

HOW SHALL WE KNOW WHEN JESUS' COMING IS NEAR?

When Jesus was born, very few people knew that the Savior of the world had come. When he comes again, there will be no doubt who he is. No one knows the exact time that the Savior will come again. "Of that day and hour knoweth no man, no, not the angels of heaven, but my Father only" (Matthew 24:36). He has given us an idea by using a parable. He said: "Now learn a parable of the fig tree; When her branch is yet tender, and putteth forth leaves, ye know that summer is near: So ye in like manner, when ye shall see these things come to pass, know that it is nigh, even at the doors" (Mark 13:28–29). He did, however, give us some signs to let us know when his coming is near (see this manual, chapter 41, "Signs of the Second Coming"). After telling the signs, he cautioned: "Watch therefore: for ye know not what hour your Lord doth come. . . . Be ye also ready; for in such an hour as ye think not the Son of man cometh" (Matthew 24:42–44).

Read Mark 13:1–29. How can we tell when his coming is near?

WE CAN BE READY WHEN THE SAVIOR COMES

The best way we can be ready for his coming is to accept the teachings of the gospel and make them a part of our lives. We should live each day the best we can, just as Jesus taught when he was on the earth. We can look to his prophet for guidance and follow his counsel. We must live worthy to have the Holy Ghost guide us. Then we will look forward to our Savior's coming with happiness in our hearts and not with fear. The Lord said: "Fear not, little flock, the kingdom is yours until I come. Behold, I come quickly. Even so. Amen" (D&C 35:27).

Read Matthew 25:1–13. What are some things we can do to be ready when the Savior (the bridegroom) comes again?

ADDITIONAL SCRIPTURES
John 14:2–3; Matthew 26:64 (Jesus to prepare a place and come again)
Malachi 3:2–4; 4:1; D&C 64:23–25 (earth to be burned)
D&C 133:41–51 (wicked to be destroyed)
Matthew 13:40–43 (the Judgment predicted)

Matthew 25:31–46; Romans 2:6–9; Revelation 20:12–13 (the Judgment)
1 Corinthians 15:40–42; D&C 76; D&C 88:17–35 (degrees of glory)
2 Corinthians 12:2 (men caught up to third heaven)
D&C 43:29–30; D&C 29:11 (his coming ushers in Millennium)
Tenth article of faith (Jesus to reign)
Alma 11:43–44; Alma 40 (resurrection explained)
Helaman 14:25 (dead to rise)
Zechariah 14:9; Revelation 11:15; 1 Nephi 22:24–26 (Jesus to reign as King)

SUGGESTED SONG
"We'll Sing All Hail to Jesus' Name"

Chapter 44

THE MILLENNIUM

A thousand years of peace, love, and joy will begin upon the earth at the second coming of Jesus Christ. This thousand years is called the Millennium. It will be the final thousand years of the earth's temporal existence. The scriptures and the prophets help us understand what it will be like to live on the earth during the Millennium.

What is the Millennium?

WHO WILL BE ON EARTH DURING THE MILLENNIUM?

Only righteous people will continue to live on the earth during the Millennium. They will be those who have lived virtuous and honest lives. These people will inherit either the terrestrial or celestial kingdom.

During the Millennium, mortals will still live on earth, and they will continue to have children as we do now (see D&C 45:58). Joseph Smith said that immortal beings will frequently visit the earth. These resurrected beings will help with the government and other work (see *Teachings of the Prophet Joseph Smith,* p. 268).

Brigham Young taught that there will be nonmembers of The Church of Jesus Christ of Latter-day Saints as well as members. People will still have their agency, and for a time many will continue to believe their false religions and ideas. Eventually, everyone will accept Jesus Christ as the Savior (see Daniel H. Ludlow, ed., *Latter-day Prophets Speak,* pp. 261–62).

During the Millennium, Jesus Christ will "reign personally upon the earth" (tenth article of faith). Joseph Smith explained that Jesus Christ and the resurrected Saints would probably not live on the earth all the time but would visit whenever they pleased or when necessary to help in the governing of the earth (see *Teachings of the Prophet Joseph Smith,* p. 268).

Who will be on the earth during the Millennium?

WHAT WILL BE DONE DURING THE MILLENNIUM?

There will be two great works for members of the Church during the Millennium—temple work and missionary work.

Some ordinances are necessary for exaltation. These include baptism, the laying on of hands for the gift of the Holy Ghost, and such temple ordinances as the endowment, temple marriage, and the sealing together of family units. Many people have died without receiving these ordinances. People on the earth must perform these ordinances for them. This work is now being done in the temples of the Lord. Because there is too much work to finish before the Millennium begins, it will be completed during that time. Resurrected beings will help us correct the mistakes we have made in doing research concerning our dead ancestors. They will also help us find the information we need to complete our records.

The other great work during the Millennium will be missionary work. The gospel will be taught with great power to all people. Eventually, there will be no need to teach others the first principles because "they shall all know me, from the least of them unto the greatest of them, saith the Lord" (Jeremiah 31:34). However, there will always be things to be taught.

Discuss the great works to be done during the Millennium.

CONDITIONS DURING THE MILLENNIUM

The earth will again be as it was when Adam and Eve lived in the Garden of Eden (see tenth article of faith). The whole earth will be a delightful garden. There will not be different continents as we have now, but the land will all be gathered in one place as it was in the beginning (see D&C 133:23–24).

SATAN BOUND

During the Millennium, Satan will be bound. This means that he will not have power to tempt those who are living at that time (see D&C 101:28). The "children shall grow up without sin unto salvation" (D&C 45:58). "Because of the righteousness of his people, Satan has no power; wherefore, he cannot be loosed for the space of many years; for he hath no power over the hearts of the people, for they dwell in righteousness, and the Holy One of Israel reigneth" (1 Nephi 22:26).

PEACE ON THE EARTH

During the Millennium, there will be no war. People will live in peace and harmony together. Everything that had been used for war will be turned to useful purposes. "They shall beat their swords into plowshares, and their spears into pruning-hooks: nation shall not lift up sword against nation, neither shall they learn war any more" (Isaiah 2:4).

GOVERNMENT

Jesus Christ will not only lead the Church during the Millennium, but he will also be in charge of the political government. This government will be based on principles of righteousness and will preserve the basic rights and freedoms of all people. Mortals, both members of the Church and nonmembers, will hold government positions (see Brigham Young, *Journal of Discourses*, 2:310). They will receive help from resurrected beings. At this time, there will be two capitals in the world, one in Jerusalem, the other in America (see Joseph Fielding Smith, *Doctrines of Salvation*, 3:66–72). "For out of Zion shall go forth the law, and the word of the Lord from Jerusalem" (Isaiah 2:3).

NO DISEASE OR DEATH

Even though there will be mortal men on the earth during the Millennium, they will not have diseases as we do now. There will be no death as we know it. When people have lived to an old age, they will not die and be buried. Instead, they will be changed from their mortal condition to an immortal condition in an instant (see D&C 63:51; 101:29–31).

ALL THINGS REVEALED

Some truths have not been revealed to us. These will be revealed during the Millennium. The Lord has said that he would "reveal all things—things which have passed, and hidden things which no man knew, things of the earth, by which it was made, and the purpose and the end thereof—Things most precious, things that are above, and things that are beneath, things that are in the earth, and upon the earth, and in heaven" (D&C 101:32–34).

CHANGES IN ANIMAL KINGDOM

The animal kingdom will also be at peace. All animals, even those which are now enemies, will live together in harmony. Those animals which now eat flesh will eat grass and grain (see Isaiah 11:6–7).

OTHER MILLENNIAL ACTIVITIES

In many ways, life will be much as it is now, except that everything will be done in righteousness. People will eat and drink and will wear clothing (see *Discourses of Brigham Young,* p. 115). People will continue to plant and harvest crops and build houses (Isaiah 65:21).

Have several people discuss the conditions that will exist during the Millennium. Ask them to use the scriptural reference listed for each condition.

ONE FINAL STRUGGLE AFTER THE MILLENNIUM

At the end of the thousand years, Satan will be set free for a short time. Some people will turn away from Heavenly Father. Satan will gather his armies, and Michael (Adam) will gather the hosts of heaven. In this great struggle, Satan and his followers will be cast out forever. After this will come the final judgment, and all people will be assigned to the kingdoms they have earned by the way they have lived. The earth will be changed into a celestial kingdom (see D&C 29:22–29; 88:110–115; 88:17–20).

ADDITIONAL SCRIPTURES
Zechariah 14:4-9; 1 Nephi 22:24-26 (Jesus to reign on the earth)
Daniel 7:27 (Saints to be given the kingdom)
D&C 88:87-116 (conditions during the Millennium)
Revelation 20:1-3; 2 Nephi 30:10-18 (Satan bound)
D&C 101:22-31 (enmity to cease; no death; Satan to have no power to tempt)
Isaiah 11:1-9 (wolf and lamb to dwell together)
D&C 43:31; Revelation 20:7-10 (Satan loosed to gather forces)

THE POST-EARTHLY SPIRIT WORLD

As part of our Heavenly Father's plan for our salvation, he sent us from his presence to live on earth and receive mortal bodies of flesh and bones. Eventually our mortal bodies will die, and our spirits will go to the spirit world. The spirit world is a place of waiting, working, learning, and resting from care and sorrow. Here, our spirits will live until we are ready for our resurrection. Then our mortal bodies will once more unite with our spirits, and we will receive the degree of glory which we have earned (see this manual, chapter 46, "The Last Judgement").

Many of us have wondered what the spirit world is like. The scriptures and Latter-day Saint prophets have given us information about the spirit world.

What is the purpose of the spirit world?

WHERE IS THE SPIRIT WORLD?

In a funeral sermon, Joseph Smith declared that the spirits of righteous people who have died "are not far from us, and know and understand our thoughts, feelings, and emotions, and are often pained therewith" (*Teachings of the Prophet Joseph Smith*, p. 326). Other latter-day prophets have made similar statements. Elder Ezra Taft Benson, an apostle, said: "Sometimes the veil between this life and the life beyond becomes very thin. Our loved ones who have passed on are not far from us" (Conference Report, Apr. 1971, p. 18). President Brigham Young said: "Where is the spirit world? It

We will join our families and loved ones in the spirit world after death.

is right here" (John A. Widtsoe, comp., *Discourses of Brigham Young,* p. 376).

Where is the spirit world?

WHAT ARE SPIRITS LIKE?

Spirit beings have the same bodily form as mortals except that the spirit body is in perfect form (see Ether 3:16). Spirits carry with them from earth their same attitudes of devotion or antagonism toward things of righteousness (see Alma 34:34). They have the same appetites and desires that they had when they lived on earth.

All spirits are in adult form. They were adults before their mortal existence, and they are in adult form after death, even if they die as infants or children (see Joseph F. Smith, *Gospel Doctrine,* p. 455).

Read Ether 3:16. What do spirit bodies look like?

ARE THERE DIVISIONS IN THE SPIRIT WORLD?

The prophet Alma in the Book of Mormon teaches about two divisions or states in the spirit world:

"The spirits of those who are righteous are received into a state of happiness, which is called paradise, a state of rest, a state of peace, where they shall rest from all their troubles and from all care, and sorrow.

"And then shall it come to pass, that the spirits of the wicked, yea, who are evil—for behold, they have no part nor portion of the Spirit of the Lord; for behold, they chose evil works rather than good; therefore the spirit of the devil did enter into them, and take possession of their house—and these shall be cast out into outer darkness: there shall be weeping, and wailing, and gnashing of teeth, and this because of their own iniquity, being led captive by the will of the devil.

"Now this is the state of the souls of the wicked, yea, in darkness, and a state of awful, fearful looking for the fiery indignation of the wrath of God upon them; thus they remain in this state, as well as the righteous in paradise, until the time of their resurrection" (Alma 40:12–14).

The spirits are classified according to the purity of their lives and their obedience to the will of the Lord while on earth. The righteous and the wicked are separated (see 1 Nephi 15:28–30), but the spirits may progress from one level to another as they learn gospel principles and live in accordance with them (see Bruce R. McConkie, *Mormon Doctrine,* p. 762).

What divisions are there in the spirit world?

·PARADISE

According to the prophet Alma, the righteous spirits rest from earthly care and sorrow. Nevertheless, they are occupied in doing the work of the Lord. President Joseph F. Smith saw in a vision that immediately after Jesus Christ was crucified he visited the righteous in the spirit world. He appointed messengers, clothed with power and authority. He commissioned them to "carry the light of the gospel to them that were in darkness, even to all the spirits of men" (Pearl of Great Price, Joseph F. Smith—Vision of the Redemption of the Dead 30).

The Church is organized in the spirit world, with each prophet standing at the head of his own generation (see Joseph Smith *History of the Church of Jesus Christ of Latter-day Saints,* 4:209). Members of the priesthood continue their responsibilities in the spirit world. President Wilford Woodruff taught: "The same Priesthood exists on the other side of the veil. . . . every Apostle, every Seventy, every Elder, etc., who has died in the faith as soon as he passes to the other side of the veil, enters into the work of the ministry" (*Journal of Discourses* 22:333–34).

Family relationships are also important. President Jedediah M. Grant, a counselor to Brigham Young, described the organization that exists: "He said that the people he there saw were organized in family capacities. . . . he said, 'when I looked at families, there was a deficiency in some, . . . for I saw families that would not be permitted to come and dwell together, because they had not honored their calling here' " (Heber C. Kimball, *Journal of Discourses* 4:135–36).

What do the spirits in paradise do?
Why are some families incomplete in paradise?

SPIRIT PRISON

The Apostle Peter referred to the spirit world as a "prison," which it is for some (see 1 Peter 3:18-20). For many spirits, it is a place of learning and waiting; for some it is a place of suffering (see Alma 40:14). In the spirit prison are those who have not yet received the gospel of Jesus Christ. These spirits have agency and may be enticed by both good and evil.

Missionaries from paradise visit the spirit prison to teach the gospel. There are three classes of spirits to whom the gospel is preached: those who have never heard the gospel (Pearl of Great Price, Joseph Smith—Vision of the Celestial Kingdom 7-9); honorable people who rejected the gospel while on earth because of being blinded by the "craftiness of men" (D&C 76:75); and the wicked and disobedient who "rejected the prophets" (Pearl of Great Price, Joseph F. Smith—Vision of the Redemption of the Dead 29-32). These last include those described by the Apostle Peter as being disobedient during the time of Noah (see 1 Peter 3:18-20).

After spirits in prison accept the gospel and the ordinances performed for them in the temples, they may prepare themselves to leave the spirit prison and dwell in paradise.

Those who reject the gospel after it is preached to them in the spirit prison suffer in a condition known as hell. They remove themselves from the mercy of Jesus Christ, who said: "Behold, I, God, have suffered these things for all, that they might not suffer if they would repent; But if they would not repent they must suffer even as I; Which suffering caused myself, even God, the greatest of all, to tremble because of pain, and to bleed at every pore, and to suffer both body and spirit" (D&C 19:16–18). After suffering in full for their sins, they will be allowed to inherit the lowest degree of glory, which is the telestial kingdom.

The hell in the spirit world will not continue forever. Even the spirits there who have sinned the greatest sins will have suffered sufficiently by the end of the Millennium (see Acts 2:25–27). They will then be resurrected.

What are some of the activities that go on in the spirit world?

THE SPIRIT WORLD COMES TO AN END

After the resurrection, there is no more need for a spirit world. All of God's children will have been assigned to one of four places prepared for them, depending on their obedience to the laws and ordinances of the gospel. These places are known as the celestial, terrestrial, and telestial kingdoms of glory, and outer darkness. These are discussed in detail in chapters 46 and 47.

When will the spirit world come to an end?

ADDITIONAL SCRIPTURES
1 Peter 4:6 (gospel preached to the dead)
Moses 7:37–39 (spirit prison prepared for wicked)
D&C 76 (revelation concerning salvation for man)
Luke 16:19–31 (fate of beggar and rich man in spirit world)

SUGGESTED SONG
"Let Us All Press On"

THE LAST JUDGMENT

JUDGMENTS OF GOD

We are often told in the scriptures that the day will come when we stand before God and be judged. We need to understand how judgment takes place so that we can be better prepared for this important event.

The scriptures teach that all men will be judged according to their works (see Revelation 20:12; D&C 76:111; 1 Nephi 15:32; Abraham 3:25–28).

"And I saw the dead, small and great, stand before God; and the books were opened: and another book was opened, which is the book of life: and the dead were judged out of those things which were written in the books, according to their works" (Revelation 20:12).

In this scripture John the Revelator is referring to the "final judgment." This judgment is the last in a long series of judgments. In the premortal life all men who were judged worthy were allowed to receive a body and come to earth. Here on earth we are often judged as to our worthiness to receive opportunities within the kingdom of God. At the time we are baptized we are judged worthy to receive this ordinance. When we are called to serve in the Church or interviewed for a priesthood advancement or a temple recommend we are judged.

Alma taught that the spirits of all men at the time of death are then assigned to a state of happiness or of misery (see Alma 40:11–15). This is a partial judgment.

Name some of the judgments we have and will receive.

All men will be brought before Christ to be judged.

OUR WORDS, WORKS, AND THOUGHTS JUDGE US

The prophet Alma testified: "Our words will condemn us, yea all our works will condemn us; . . . and our thoughts will also condemn us" (Alma 12:14).

The Lord himself said: "Every idle word that men shall speak, they shall give account thereof in the day of judgment. For by thy words thou shalt   justified, and by thy words thou shalt be condemned" (Matthew 12:36–37).

To help us prepare for the judgment, we should learn to control our thoughts. We can replace evil thoughts with good. We can avoid people, places, literature, and situations that encourage unworthy or unrighteous thoughts. We can speak kindly of others.

Ask each person to imagine hearing all his words and thoughts revealed at the judgment. Then have each silently think what he can do to improve his thoughts and words.

WE WILL BE JUDGED BY RECORDS

The Prophet Joseph Smith said that the dead will be judged out of records which are kept on earth. We will also be judged out of the "book of life" which is kept in heaven (see D&C 128:6–7).

"We are going to be judged out of the things written in books, out of the revelations of God, out of the temple records, out of those things which the Lord has commanded us to keep. . . . there will be the record in heaven which is a perfect record" (Joseph Fielding Smith, *Doctrines of Salvation,* 2:200).

There is another record that will be used to judge us. The Apostle Paul taught that man himself is the most complete record of his life (see Romans 2:15; 2 Corinthians 3:1–3). Stored in our body and mind is a complete history of everything we have done. President John Taylor taught this truth: "[the individual] tells the story himself, and bears witness against himself. . . . That record that is written by the man himself in the tablets of his own mind—that record that cannot lie—will in that day be unfolded before God and angels, and those who sit as judges" (Daniel H. Ludlow, comp., *Latter-day Prophets Speak,* pp. 56–57).

What are three records from which we will be judged?
How do our daily thoughts and actions influence these records?

THOSE WHO WILL JUDGE

The Apostle John informed us that "the Father judgeth no man, but hath committed all judgment unto the Son" (John 5:22). The Son, in turn, will call upon others to assist in the judgment. The Twelve who were with him in his ministry will judge the twelve tribes of Israel (see Matthew 19:28; Luke 22:30). The Nephite twelve will judge the Nephite and Lamanite people (see 1 Nephi 12:9–10; Mormon 3:18–19). President John Taylor said that the First Presidency and the Twelve Apostles in our own dispensation will judge us (see John Taylor, *Mediation and Atonement,* p. 157).

Read John 5:22.
Who is at the head of the judgment of all men?
Who will help judge the people living in our day?

ASSIGNMENT TO GLORIES

At the final judgment we will be assigned to the kingdom we have earned. We will be sent to one of four places: the celestial kingdom, which is the highest degree of glory; the terrestrial kingdom, the middle degree; the telestial kingdom, which is the lowest degree of glory; outer darkness, which is the kingdom of the devil and is *not* a degree of glory.

In a revelation to Joseph Smith (D&C 76) the Lord described several ways we can choose to live our earth life. The Lord explained that our choices would earn for us one of the four kingdoms. We learn from this revelation that even members of the Church will earn different kingdoms because they will not be equally valiant in keeping the commandments.

The following are the kinds of lives that we can choose to live and the kingdoms that our choices will earn for us.

CELESTIAL

"They are they who received the testimony of Jesus, and believed on his name and were baptized . . . That by keeping the commandments they might be washed and cleansed from all their sins, and receive the Holy Spirit." These are they who overcome the world by their faith. These are they who are just and true so that the Holy Ghost can seal their blessings upon them (see D&C 76:51-53). Those who inherit the highest degree of the celestial kingdom, who become gods, must also have been married for eternity in the temple (see D&C 131:1-4). All who inherit the celestial kingdom will live with our Heavenly Father and Jesus Christ forever and ever (see D&C 76:62).

TERRESTRIAL

These are they who rejected the gospel on earth, but afterwards received it in the spirit world. These are they who are honorable people on the earth, but who were blinded to the gospel of Jesus Christ by the craftiness of men. These are also they who did receive the gospel and a testimony of Jesus, but afterwards were not valiant. They will be visited by Jesus Christ, but not by our Heavenly Father (see D&C 76:73-79). They will not be part of an eternal family; they will live separately and singly forever and ever (see D&C 131:1-4).

TELESTIAL

These did not receive the gospel or the testimony of Jesus either on earth or in the spirit world. These are they who suffer for their own sins in hell until after the Millennium, when they will be resurrected. "These are they who are liars, and sorcerers, and adulterers, and whoremongers, and whosoever loves and makes a lie." These are as numerous as the stars in heaven and the sand on the seashore. They will be visited by the Holy Ghost, but not the Father or the Son, Jesus Christ (see D&C 76:81-85, 103-106).

OUTER DARKNESS

These are they who had testimonies of Jesus through the Holy Ghost and had known the power of the Lord, but allowed Satan to overcome them. They denied the truth and defied the power of the Lord. It would have been better for them if they had never been born. There is no forgiveness for them. They denied the Holy Spirit after having received it. They will not have a kingdom of glory. They will live in eternal darkness, torment, and misery with Satan and his angels forever and ever (see D&C 76:28–35; 44–48).

Have someone tell about the three degrees of glory and outer darkness and who will go to each (see D&C 76:50–88).

WE SHOULD PREPARE NOW FOR JUDGMENT

In reality, every day is a day of judgment. Our words, our thoughts, our actions are performed according to a celestial, terrestrial, or a telestial law. Our daily actions determine which kingdom we will inherit.

We have the restored gospel of Jesus Christ in its fulness. The gospel is the law of the celestial kingdom. All the priesthood ordinances necessary for our progression have been revealed. We have entered the waters of baptism and have made a covenant to live Christlike lives. If we are faithful and keep the covenants we have made, the Lord has told us what our judgment will be. He will say unto us: "Come, ye blessed of my Father, inherit the kingdom prepared for you from the foundation of the world" (Matthew 25:34).

What must we do to be ready for the final judgment?
Ask the members to think how they would feel about hearing the words recorded in Matthew 25:34 spoken to them.

ADDITIONAL SCRIPTURES
D&C 88:98–102 (sounding of the trumps of judgment)
Matthew 25:31–46 (the Second Coming)
Mormon 7:6; Alma 11:41, 45; 32:22; Mormon 9:13–14 (dead rise to be judged in immortal, spiritual body)
2 Nephi 29:11; 3 Nephi 27:23–26 (books used in judgment)
D&C 128:6–8 (records of earth life, book of life—heaven's record)
Romans 2:15; 2 Corinthians 3:1–3 (record written on your heart)
Alma 41:2–7 (judged by self as to works, desires of heart, repentance, enduring to end)
Mormon 3:22 (repent, prepare to stand before judgment seat)
Luke 12:47–48; D&C 82:3 (of whom much is given, much is required)
D&C 88:16–33 (each to receive that of which he is worthy)

SUGGESTED SONG
"Now Let Us Rejoice"

EXALTATION

When we lived with our Heavenly Father, he explained a plan for progression to us, his spirit children. We could become like him, an exalted being. The plan required that we be separated from our Heavenly Father and come to the earth. This separation was necessary to prove whether we would obey our Father's commandments even though we were no longer in his presence. The plan provided that when earth life was ended, we would be judged and rewarded according to the degree of our obedience. We would then be assigned the place we had earned for our eternal home.

Jesus taught: "In my father's house are many mansions" (John 14:2). From the scriptures we learn there are three degrees or kingdoms of glory in heaven. The Apostle Paul mentioned that he knew a man who was "caught up to the third heaven" (2 Corinthians 12:2). Paul names two of the kingdoms in heaven—the celestial and the terrestrial (see 1 Corinthians 15:40–42). The celestial is the highest and the terrestrial is second. Through latter-day revelation we learn the name of the third kingdom. It is the telestial kingdom (see D&C 76:81). We also learned that there are three heavens or degrees within the celestial kingdom (see D&C 131:1).

Have someone tell about our Heavenly Father's plan for exaltation.

WHAT IS EXALTATION?

Exaltation is eternal life, the kind of life that God lives. He lives in great glory. He is perfect. He possesses all knowl-

Those who are faithful to the end will be exalted with Heavenly Father and Jesus Christ.

Print Courtesy of Monkmeyer Press Photo Service

edge and all wisdom. He is the father of spirit children. He is a creator. We can become Gods like our Heavenly Father. This is exaltation.

If we prove faithful and obedient to all the commandments of the Lord, we will live in the highest degree of the celestial kingdom of heaven. We will become exalted, just like our Heavenly Father. Exaltation is the highest reward that our Heavenly Father can give his children. The Lord has said that exaltation is the greatest gift of all the gifts of God (see D&C 14:7).

What is exaltation?

BLESSINGS OF EXALTATION

Our Heavenly Father is perfect. However, he is not jealous of his wisdom and perfection. He glories in the fact that it is possible for his children to become like him. He has said: "This is my work and my glory—to bring to pass the immortality and eternal life of man" (Moses 1:39).

Those who live the commandments of the Lord and receive eternal life (exaltation) in the celestial kingdom will receive special blessings. The Lord has said: "All [things] are theirs" (D&C 76:59). These are some of the special blessings given to exalted persons:

1. They will live eternally in the presence of our Heavenly Father and Jesus Christ (see D&C 76).

2. They will become gods.

3. They will have their righteous family members with them and will be able to have spirit children also. These spirit children will have the same relationship to them as we do to our Heavenly Father. They will be an eternal family.

4. They will receive a fullness of joy.

5. They will have everything that our Heavenly Father and Jesus Christ have, all power, glory, dominion, and knowledge. President Joseph Fielding Smith wrote: "The Father has promised through the Son that all that he has shall be given to those who are obedient to his commandments. *They*

shall increase in knowledge, wisdom, and power, going from grace to grace, until the fullness of the perfect day shall burst upon them" (*Doctrines of Salvation,* 2:36).

List some of the blessings that will be given to those who earn exaltation.

REQUIREMENTS FOR EXALTATION

Latter-day Saints are taught that now is the time to fulfill the requirements for exaltation (see Alma 34:32–34). President Joseph Fielding Smith said, "In order to obtain the exaltation we must accept the gospel and all its covenants; and take upon us the obligations which the Lord has offered; and walk in the light and understanding of the truth; and 'live by every word that proceedeth forth from the mouth of God' " (*Doctrines of Salvation,* 2:43).

There are specific ordinances we must have received to be exalted:

1. We must be baptized and confirmed a member of the Church of Jesus Christ.

2. We must receive the Holy Ghost.

3. We must receive the temple endowment.

4. We must be married for time and all eternity.

In addition to the required ordinances, there are also many laws we have to obey to qualify for exaltation. We must—

1. Love God and worship him.

2. Have faith in Jesus Christ.

3. Live the law of chastity.

4. Repent of our wrong doings.

5. Pay honest tithes and offerings.

6. Be honest in our dealings with others and with the Lord.

7. Speak the truth always.

8. Obey the Word of Wisdom.

9. Search out our kindred dead and perform the saving ordinances of the gospel for them.

10. Keep the Sabbath day holy.

11. Attend our Church meetings as regularly as possible to renew our baptismal covenants. This is done as we partake of the sacrament.

12. Love and strengthen our family members in the ways of the Lord.

13. Have family and individual prayers every day.

14. Honor our parents.

15. Teach the gospel to others by word and example.

16. Study the scriptures.

17. Listen to and obey the words of the prophets of the Lord.

18. Develop true charity in our lives.

In other words, each person must endure in faithfulness, keeping all the Lord's commandments until the end of his life on earth.

What specific ordinances must we accept in order to become exalted?
What laws do we need to obey to enjoy exaltation?

AFTER WE HAVE ENDURED TO THE END

What happens when we have endured to the end and have been faithful? The Lord has said: "If you keep my commandments and endure to the end you shall have eternal life, which gift is the greatest of all the gifts of God" (D&C 14:7). President Joseph Fielding Smith said: "If we will continue in God; that is, keep his commandments, worship him and live his truth; then the time will come when we shall be bathed in the fulness of truth, which shall grow brighter and brighter until the perfect day" (*Doctrines of Salvation,* 2:36).

The Prophet Joseph Smith taught: "*When you climb up a ladder, you must begin at the bottom, and ascend step by step, until you arrive at the top; and so it is with the principles of the Gospel—you must begin with the first, and go on until you learn all the principles of exaltation. But it will be a great while after you have passed through the veil* [died] *before you will have learned them. It is not all to be comprehended in this world; it will be a great work to learn our salvation and exaltation even beyond the grave"* (*Teachings of the Prophet Joseph Smith,* pp. 347–48).

This is the way our Heavenly Father became a God. Joseph Smith taught, "It is the first principle of the Gospel to know for a certainty the character of God . . . he was once a man like us; . . . God himself, the Father of us all, dwelt on an earth, the same as Jesus Christ himself did" (*Teachings of the Prophet Joseph Smith,* pp. 345–46).

Our Heavenly Father knows our trials, our weaknesses, and mistakes. He has compassion and mercy on us. He wants us to succeed even as he did.

Imagine what joy each of us will have when we return to our Heavenly Father if we can say: "Father, I did what you wanted me to do. I have been faithful and have kept all thy commandments. I am happy to be home again." Then we will hear him say: "Well done . . . thou hast been faithful over a few things, I will make thee ruler over many things. Enter thou into the joy of thy Lord" (Matthew 25:23).

Describe how you might feel to hear the Savior's words in Matthew 25:23.
What must we do to endure to the end?

ADDITIONAL SCRIPTURES
D&C 132:3–4, 16–26, 37 (pertaining to exaltation)
D&C 131:1–4 (eternal marriage key to exaltation)
D&C 76:59–70 (blessings of celestial glory explained)

SUGGESTED SONGS
"I Am a Child of God," "O My Father"

HYMNS

REDEEMER OF ISRAEL

Adapted by
William W. Phelps

Freeman Lewis

Steadily ♩ = 84

1. Re - deem - er of Is - rael, Our on - ly de - light, On
2. We know he is com - ing To gath - er his sheep And
3. As chil - dren of Zi - on, Good ti - dings for us: The

whom for a bless - ing we call, Our shad - ow by day, And our
lead them to Zi - on in love; For why in the val - ley Of
to - kens al - read - y ap - pear. Fear not, and be just, For the

pil - lar by night, Our King, our De - liv - er - er, our all!
death should they weep Or in the lone wil - der - ness rove?
king - dom is ours. The hour of re - demp - tion is near.

COME, COME, YE SAINTS

William Clayton
Resolutely ♩ = 66

Old English Tune

1. Come, come, ye Saints, no toil nor la-bor fear, But with joy wend your way. Though hard to you this jour-ney may ap-pear, Grace shall be as your day. 'Tis bet-ter far for us to strive Our use-less cares from us to drive; Do this, and joy your hearts will swell— All is well! all is well!

2. Why should we mourn or think our lot is hard? 'Tis not so; all is right. Why should we think to earn a great re-ward, If we now shun the fight? Gird up your loins; fresh cour-age take; Our God will nev-er us for-sake; And soon we'll have this tale to tell— All is well! all is well!

3. We'll find the place which God for us pre-pared, Far a-way in the West, Where none shall come to hurt or make a-fraid; There the Saints will be blessed. We'll make the air with mu-sic ring, Shout prais-es to our God and King; A-bove the rest these words we'll tell— All is well! all is well!

4. And should we die be-fore our jour-ney's through, Hap-py day! all is well! We then are free from toil and sor-row, too; With the just we shall dwell! But if our lives are spared a-gain To see the Saints their rest ob-tain, O how we'll make this cho-rus swell— All is well! all is well!

rit.

HOW FIRM A FOUNDATION

Kirkham

Stately ♩ = 104

1. How firm a foun - da - tion, ye Saints of the Lord, Is
2. In ev - ery con - di - tion, in sick - ness, in health, In
3. Fear not, I am with thee, O be not dis - mayed, For

laid for your faith in his ex - cel - lent word! What
pov - er - ty's vale or a - bound - ing in wealth, At
I am thy God and will still give thee aid; I'll

more can he say than to you he hath said, ____ You
home or a - broad, on the land or the sea, ____ As thy
strength - en thee, help thee, and cause thee to stand, ____ Up -

who un - to Je - sus, you who un - to Je - sus, You
days may de - mand, as thy days may de - mand, As thy
held by my righ - teous, up - held by my righ - teous, Up -

who un - to Je - sus for ref - uge have fled?
days may de - mand, so thy suc - cor shall be.
held by my righ - teous, om - nip - o - tent hand.

COME, YE CHILDREN OF THE LORD

James H. Wallis

Spanish Melody

1. Come, ye chil-dren of the Lord, Let us sing with one ac-cord;
2. O how joy-ful it will be, When our Sav-ior we shall see!
3. All ar-rayed in spot-less white, We will dwell 'mid truth and light;

Let us raise a joy-ful strain To our Lord who soon will reign
When in splen-dor he'll de-scend, Then all wick-ed-ness will end.
We will sing the songs of praise; We will shout in joy-ous lays.

On this earth, when it shall be Cleansed from all in-iq-ui-ty;
O what songs we then will sing To our Sav-ior, Lord and King!
Earth shall then be cleansed from sin. Ev-'ry liv-ing thing there-in

When all men from sin will cease, And will live in love and peace.
O what love will then bear sway, When our fears shall flee a-way!
Shall in love and beau-ty dwell; Then with joy each heart will swell.

WHEN UPON LIFE'S BILLOWS

J. Oatman, Jr.
Brightly ♩ = 88

E. O. Excell

1. When up - on life's bil - lows you are tem - pest - tossed,
2. Are you ev - er bur - dened with a load of care?
3. So a - mid the con - flict, wheth - er great or small,

When you are dis - cour - aged, think - ing all is lost,
Does the cross seem heav - y you are called to bear?
Do not be dis - cour - aged; God is o - ver all.

Count your man - y bless - ings; name them one by one,
Count your man - y bless - ings; ev - ery doubt will fly,
Count your man - y bless - ings; an - gels will at - tend,

And it will sur - prise you what the Lord has done.
And you will be sing - ing as the days go by.
Help and com - fort give you to your jour - ney's end.

Copyright renewal Hope Publishing Co., owner. Used by permission.

LET US ALL PRESS ON

Evan Stephens

Evan Stephens

With marked accent ♩ = 104

1. Let us all press on in the work of the Lord,
2. We will not re - treat, though our num-bers may be few,
3. If we do what's right we have no need to fear,

That when life is o'er we may gain a re - ward;
When com - pared with the op - po - site host in view;
For the Lord, our help - er, will ev - er be near;

In the fight for right let us wield a sword,
But an un - seen pow - er will aid me and you
In the days of tri - al his Saints he will cheer,

The might - y sword of truth.
In the glo - rious cause of truth.
And pros - per the cause of truth.

Fear not, though the en - e - my de - ride,
Fear not cour - age, though the en - e - my de - ride, We must

Cour - age, for the Lord is on our side; We will
be vic - to - rious, for the Lord is on our side; We'll not

heed not what the wick - ed may say, But the
fear the wick - ed or give heed to what they say, But the

Lord a - lone we will o - bey.
Lord, our Heaven - ly Fa - ther, him a - lone we will o - bey.

SWEET IS THE WORK

Isaac Watts

John J. McClellan

Worshipfully ♩ = 84

1. Sweet is the work, my God, my King, To praise thy
2. Sweet is the day of sa - cred rest. No mor - tal
3. My heart shall tri - umph in my Lord. And bless his
4. But, oh, what tri - umph shall I raise To thy dear

name, give thanks and sing, To show thy love by
care shall seize my breast. O may my heart in
works and bless his word. Thy works of grace, how
name through end - less days, When in the realms of

morn - ing light And talk of all thy truths at night.
tune be found Like Da - vid's harp of sol - emn sound!
bright they shine! How deep thy coun - sels, how di - vine!
joy I see Thy face in full fe - lic - i - ty.

I NEED THEE EVERY HOUR

Annie S. Hawkes

Robert Lowery

Tenderly ♩ = 60

1. I need thee ev - 'ry hour, Most gra - cious Lord;
2. I need thee ev - 'ry hour, Stay thou near by;
3. I need thee ev - 'ry hour, Most ho - ly One;

No ten - der voice like thine Can peace af - ford.
Temp - ta - tions lose their power When thou art nigh.
O make me thine in - deed, Thou bless - ed Son!

I need thee, O I need thee; Ev - 'ry hour I need thee!

O bless me now, my Sav - ior; I come to thee!

303

OH, HOW LOVELY WAS THE MORNING

George Manwaring
Cheerfully ♩ = 84

A. C. Smyth

1. Oh, how love-ly was the morn-ing! Ra-diant beamed the sun a-
2. Hum-bly kneel-ing, sweet ap-peal-ing— 'Twas the boy's first ut-tered
3. Sud-den-ly a light de-scend-ed, Bright-er far than noon-day
4. "Jo-seph, this is my be-lov-ed; Hear him!" Oh, how sweet the

bove. Bees were hum-ming, sweet birds sing-ing, Mu-sic
prayer When the powers of sin as-sail-ing Filled his
sun, And a shin-ing glo-rious pil-lar O'er him
word! Jo-seph's hum-ble prayer was an-swered, And he

ring-ing through the grove, When with-in the shad-y
soul with deep de-spair; But un-daunt-ed, still he
fell, a round him shone, While ap-peared two heaven-ly
list-ened to the Lord. Oh, what rap-ture filled his

wood-land Jos-eph sought the God of love; When with
trust-ed In his Heaven-ly Fa-ther's care; But un-
be-ings, God the Fa-ther and the Son; While ap-
bos-om, For he saw the liv-ing God; Oh, what

in the shad-y wood-land, Jos-eph sought the God of love;
daunt-ed, still he trust-ed In his Heaven-ly Fa-ther's care.
peared two heaven-ly be-ings, God the Fa-ther and the Son.
rap-ture filled his bos-om, For he saw the liv-ing God.

304

HOW GREAT THE WISDOM AND THE LOVE

Eliza R. Snow

Thomas McIntyre

Calmly ♩ = 66

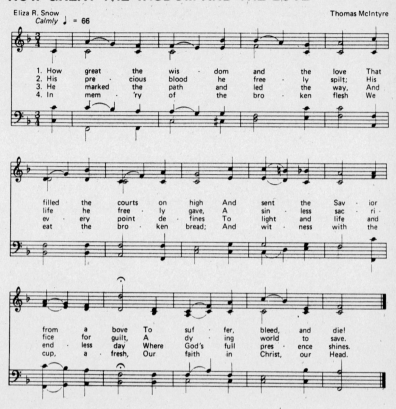

1. How great the wis - dom and the love That
2. His pre - cious blood he free - ly spilt; His
3. He marked the path and led the way, And
4. In mem - 'ry of the bro - ken flesh We

filled the courts on high And sent the Sav - ior
life he free - ly gave, A sin - less sac - ri -
ev - ery point de - fines To light and life and
eat the bro - ken bread; And wit - ness with the

from a - bove To suf - fer, bleed, and die!
fice for guilt, A dy - ing world to save.
end - less day Where God's full pres - ence shines.
cup, a - fresh, Our faith in Christ, our Head.

305

BEHOLD THE GREAT REDEEMER DIE

Eliza R. Snow

George Careless

1. Be - hold the great Re - deem - er die, A bro - ken
2. Al - though in ag - o - ny he hung, No mur - muring
3. He lives he lives, we hum - bly now, A - round these

law to sat - is - fy. He dies a sac - ri -
word es - caped his tongue. His high com - mis - sion
sac - red sym - bols bow And seek, as Saints of

fice for sin; He dies a sac - ri - fice for
to ful - fil, His high com - mis - sion to ful -
lat - ter days, And seek, as Saints of lat - ter

sin, That man may live _____ and ___ glo - ry win.
fil, He mag - ni - fied _____ his ___ Fa - ther's will.
days, To do his will _____ and ___ live his praise.

O GOD, THE ETERNAL FATHER

William W. Phelps

Felix Mendelssohn

With simplicity ♩ = 69

1. O God, th'E-ter-nal Fa-ther, Who dwells a-mid the sky,
2. That sa-cred ho-ly of-fering By man least un-der-stood,
3. How in-fi-nite that wis-dom, The plan of ho-li-ness,

In Je-sus' name we ask thee, To bless and sanc-ti-fy,
To have our sins re-mit-ted, And take his flesh and blood;
That made sal-va-tion per-fect And veiled the Lord in flesh;

If we are pure be-fore thee, This bread and cup of wine,
That we may ev-er wit-ness The suf-fering of thy Son;
To walk up-on his foot-stool, And be like man, al-most,

That we may all re-mem-ber That of-fer-ing di-vine;
And al-ways have his Spir-it, To make our hearts as one.
In his ex-alt-ed sta-tion, And die or all was lost.

307

GOD, OUR FATHER, HEAR US PRAY

Annie Malin

Arr. from Louis Gottschalk

Worshipfully ♩ = 72

1. God, our Fa - ther, hear us pray; Send thy grace this ho - ly day; As we take of em - blems blest, On our Sav - ior's love we rest.

2. Grant us, Fa - ther, grace di - vine; May thy smile up - on us shine; As we eat the bro - ken bread, Thine ap - prov - al on us shed.

3. As we drink the wa - ter clear, Let thy Spir - it lin - ger near; Par - don faults, O Lord, we pray; Bless our ef - forts day by day.

JESUS, ONCE OF HUMBLE BIRTH

Parley P. Pratt

From "English Chorister"

Solemnly ♩ = 69

1. Je - sus, once of hum - ble birth, Now in glo - ry comes to earth. Once he suf - fered grief and pain; Now he comes on earth to reign; Now he comes on earth to reign.

2. Once a meek and low - ly Lamb, Now the Lord, the great I Am; Once up - on the cross he bowed, Now his char - iot is the cloud; Now his char - iot is the cloud.

3. Once he groaned in blood and tears; Now in glo - ry he ap - pears; Once re - ject - ed by his own, Now their King he shall be known; Now their King he shall be known.

I STAND ALL AMAZED

Charles H. Gabriel

Charles H. Gabriel

Thoughtfully ♩ = 88
mf Unison

1. I stand all a - mazed at the love Je - sus of - fers me, Con -
2. I mar - vel that he would de - scend from his throne di - vine To
3. I think of his hands pierced and bleed - ing to pay the debt! Such

fused at the grace that so ful - ly he prof - fers me; I
res - cue a soul so re - bel - lious and proud as mine; That
mer - cy, such love, and de - vo - tion can I for - get? Oh,

trem - ble to know that for me he was cru - ci - fied, That
he should ex - tend his great love un - to such as I, Suf -
no, I will praise and a - dore at the mer - cy seat, Un -

for me, a sin - ner, he suf - fered, he bled and died.
fi - cient to own, to re - deem, and to jus - ti - fy.
til at the glo - ri - fied throne I kneel at his feet.

Sop, Alto

Oh, it is won - der - ful that he should care for me, E - nough to

Tenor, Bass

won - der - ful!

310

die for me! Oh, it is won-der-ful, won-der-ful to me!

won - der - ful!

Copyright 1926 by Chas. H. Gabriel. Renewal, Homer A. Rodeheaver, owner. Used by permission.

THERE IS A GREEN HILL

Cecil Frances Alexander

John H. Gower

Simply ♩ = 88

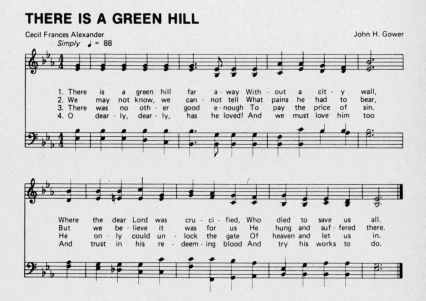

1. There is a green hill far a - way With - out a cit - y wall,
2. We may not know, we can - not tell What pains he had to bear,
3. There was no oth - er good e - nough To pay the price of sin.
4. O dear - ly, dear - ly, has he loved! And we must love him too

Where the dear Lord was cru - ci - fied, Who died to save us all.
But we be - lieve it was for us He hung and suf - fered there.
He on - ly could un - lock the gate Of heaven and let us in.
And trust in his re - deem - ing blood And try his works to do.

311

WE'LL SING ALL HAIL TO JESUS' NAME

R. Alldridge

Joseph Coslett

Fervently ♩ = 80

1. We'll sing all hail to Je - sus' name And praise and hon - or give To him who bled on Cal - vary's hill And died that we might live.

2. He passed the por - tals of the grave; Sal - va - tion was his song; He called up - on the sin - bound soul To join the heav'n - ly throng.

3. The bread and wa - ter rep - re - sent His sac - ri - fice for sin; Ye Saints par - take and tes - ti - fy Ye do re - mem - ber him.

IN HUMILITY, OUR SAVIOR

Mabel Jones Gabbott

Rowland H. Prichard

Simply ♩ = 80

1. In hu - mil - i - ty, our Sav - ior, Grant thy Spir - it here, we pray;
2. Fill our hearts with sweet for - giv - ing; Teach us tol - er - ance and love;

As we bless the bread and wa - ter In thy name, this ho - ly day.
Let our prayers find ac - cess to thee In thy ho - ly courts a - bove.

Let me not for - get, O Sav - ior, Thou didst bleed and die for me
Then, when we have prov - en wor - thy Of thy sac - ri - fice di - vine,

When thy heart was stilled and bro - ken On the cross at Cal - va - ry.
Lord, let us re - gain thy pres - ence; Let thy glo - ry round us shine.

THE SPIRIT OF GOD LIKE A FIRE

William W. Phelps

With exultation ♩ = 100

1. The Spir - it of God like a fire is burn - ing!
2. The Lord is ex - tend - ing the Saints' un - der - stand - ing,
3. How bless - ed the day when the lamb and the li - on

The lat - ter day glo - ry be - gins to come forth; The
Re - stor - ing their judg - es and all as at first. The
Shall lie down to - geth - er with - out an - y ire, And

vi - sions and bless - ings of old are re - turn - ing, And
knowl - edge and pow - er of God are ex - pand - ing, The
Eph - raim be crowned with his bless - ing in Zi - on, As

an - gels are com - ing to vis - it the earth.
veil o'er the earth is be - gin - ning to burst.
Je - sus de - scends with his char - iot of fire!

314

We'll sing and we'll shout with the ar - mies of heav - en, Ho - san - na, ho - san - na to God and the Lamb! Let glo - ry to them in the high - est be giv - en, Hence - forth and for - ev - er A - men and a - men!

HIGH ON THE MOUNTAIN TOP

Joel H. Johnson

EbenezerBeesley

Not too fast ♩ = 60

1. High on the moun - tain top A ban - ner is un - furled;
2. For God re - mem - bers still His prom - ise made of old
3. For there we shall be taught The law that will go forth,

Ye na - tions, now look up; It waves to all the world!
That he on Zi - on's hill Truth's stan - dard would un - fold!
With truth and wis - dom fraught, To gov - ern all the earth;

In Des - er - et's sweet, peace - ful land
Her light should there at - tract the gaze
For ev - er there his ways we'll tread,

On Zi - on's mount be - hold it stand!
Of all the world in lat - ter days.
And save our - selves with all our dead.

316

OH SAY, WHAT IS TRUTH?

John Jaques

Sturdily ♩ = 76

Ellen Knowles Melling

1. Oh say, what is truth? 'Tis the fair - est gem That the rich - es of worlds can pro - duce, And price - less the val - ue of truth will be when The proud mon - arch's cost - li - est di - a - dem Is count - ed but dross and ref - use.

2. Yes, say, what is truth? 'Tis the bright - est prize To which mor - tals or Gods can as - pire; Go search in the depths where it glit - ter - ing lies Or as - cend in pur - suit to the lof - tiest skies: 'Tis an aim for the no - blest de - sire.

3. Then say, what is truth? 'Tis the last and the first, For the lim - its of time it steps o'er. Though the heav - ens de - part and the earth's foun - tains burst, Truth, the sum of ex - ist - ence, will weath - er the worst, E - ter - nal, un-changed, ev - er - more.

317

NOW LET US REJOICE

William W. Phelps
Cheerfully ♩ = 104

1. Now let us re - joice in the day of sal - va - tion. No
2. We'll love one an - oth - er and nev - er dis - sem - ble, But
3. In faith we'll re - ly on the arm of Je - ho - vah To

long - er as stran - gers on earth need we roam. Good
cease to do e - vil and ev - er be one. And
guide through these last days of trou - ble and gloom; And

ti - dings are sound - ing to us and each na - tion, And
when the un - god - ly are fear - ing and trem - ble, We'll
af - ter the scourg - es and har - vest are o - ver, We'll

short - ly the hour of re - demp - tion will come, When
watch - for the day when the Sav - ior will come, When
rise with the just when the Sav - ior doth come. Then

all that was prom - ised the Saints will be giv - en, And
all that was prom - ised the Saints will be giv - en, And
all that was prom - ised the Saints will be giv - en, And

none will mo - lest them from morn un - til ev'n, And
none will mo - lest them from morn un - til ev'n, And
they will be crowned with the an - gels of heav'n And

earth will ap - pear as the gar - den of E - den, And
earth will ap - pear as the gar - den of E - den, And
earth will ap - pear as the gar - den of E - den, And

Je - sus will say to all Is - rael, "Come home."
Je - sus will say to all Is - rael, "Come home."
Christ and his peo - ple will ev - er be one.

DO WHAT IS RIGHT

E. Kaillmark

1. Do what is right; the day-dawn is break-ing,
2. Do what is right; the shack-les are fall-ing;
3. Do what is right; be faith-ful and fear-less;

Hail-ing a fu-ture of free-dom and light;
Chains of the bonds-men no long-er are bright;
On-ward, press on-ward, the goal is in sight;

An-gels a-bove us are si-lent notes tak-ing
Light-ened by hope soon they'll cease to be gall-ing;
Eyes that are wet now ere long will be tear-less;

Of ev-'ry ac-tion; do what is right!
Truth go-eth on-ward; do what is right!
Bless-ings a-wait you in do-ing what's right!

Do what is right; let the con - se - quence fol - low;
Bat - tle for free - dom in spir - it and might;
And with stout hearts look ye forth till to - mor - row;
God will pro - tect you; then do what is right!

WE THANK THEE, O GOD, FOR A PROPHET

William Fowler
Brightly ♩ = 76

Caroline S. Norton

1. We thank thee, O God, for a proph - et To guide us in
2. When dark clouds of trou - ble hang o'er us And threat - en our
3. We'll sing of his good - ness and mer - cy. We'll praise him by

these lat - ter days. We thank thee for send - ing the gos - pel
peace to de - stroy, There is hope smil - ing bright - ly be - fore us,
day and by night, Re - joice in his glo - ri - ous gos - pel

To light - en our minds with its rays. We thank thee for ev - e - ry
And we know that de - liv - erance is nigh. We doubt not the Lord nor his
And bask in its life giv - ing light. Thus on to e - ter - nal per -

bless - ing Be - stowed by thy boun - te - ous hand. We feel it a
good - ness. We've proved him in days that are past. The wick - ed who
fec - tion The hon - est and faith - ful will go, While they who re -

pleas - ure 'to serve thee, And love to o - bey thy com - mand.
fight a - gainst Zi - on Will sure - ly be smit - ten at last.
ject this glad mes - sage Shall nev - er such hap - pi - ness know.

I KNOW THAT MY REDEEMER LIVES

Samuel Medley

Lewis D. Edwards

Unison With conviction ♩ = 60

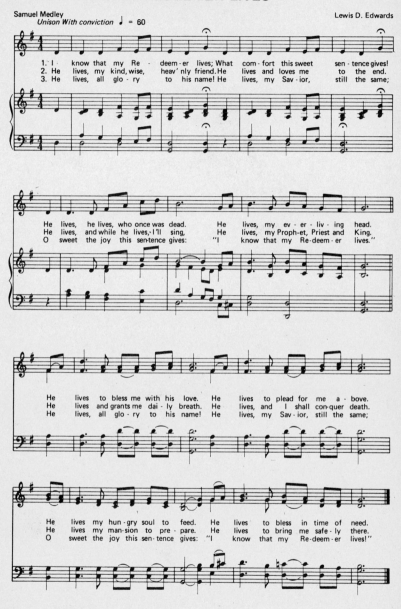

1. I know that my Re-deem-er lives; What com-fort this sweet sen-tence gives!
2. He lives, my kind, wise, heav'n-ly friend. He lives and loves me to the end.
3. He lives, all glo-ry to his name! He lives, my Sav-ior, still the same;

He lives, he lives, who once was dead. He lives, my ev-er-liv-ing head.
He lives, and while he lives, I'll sing, He lives, my Proph-et, Priest and King.
O sweet the joy this sen-tence gives: "I know that my Re-deem-er lives."

He lives to bless me with his love. He lives to plead for me a-bove.
He lives and grants me dai-ly breath. He lives, and I shall con-quer death.
He lives, all glo-ry to his name! He lives, my Sav-ior, still the same;

He lives my hun-gry soul to feed. He lives to bless in time of need.
He lives my man-sion to pre-pare. He lives to bring me safe-ly there.
O sweet the joy this sen-tence gives: "I know that my Re-deem-er lives!"

GOD BE WITH YOU

J. E. Rankin

W. G. Tomer

Firmly ♩ = 66

1. God be with you till we meet a - gain;
2. God be with you till we meet a - gain;
3. God be with you till we meet a - gain;

By his coun - sels guide, up - hold you;
When life's per - ils thick con - found you;
Keep love's ban - ner float - ing o'er you;

With his sheep se - cure - ly fold you;
Put his arms un - fail - ing round you;
Smite death's threat - 'ning wave be - fore you;

God be with you till we meet a - gain.
God be with you till we meet a - gain.
God be with you till we meet a - gain.

Till we meet, till we meet, Till we
Till we meet, till we meet; till we meet,

meet at Je - sus' feet. Till we
till we meet; Till we

meet, till we meet,
Till we meet, meet, till we meet,

God be with you till we meet a - gain.

O MY FATHER

Eliza R. Snow

James McGranahan

With contemplation ♩. = 42

1. O my Fa-ther, thou that dwell-est In the high and glo-rious
2. For a wise and glo-rious pur-pose Thou hast placed me here on
3. I had learned to call thee Fa-ther, Through thy Spir-it from on
4. When I leave this frail ex-ist-ence, When I lay this mor-tal

place, When shall I re-gain thy pres-ence, And a-
earth, And with-held the rec-ol-lec-tion Of my
high; But un-til the key of knowl-edge Was re-
by, Fa-ther, Moth-er, may I meet you In your

gain be-hold thy face? In thy ho-ly hab-i-
for-mer friends and birth, Yet oft-times a se-cret
stored, I knew not why. In the heavens are par-ents'
roy-al courts on high? Then, at length, when I've com-

In thy ho-ly hab-i-

ta-tion, Did my spir-it once re-side? In my
some-thing Whis-pered, "You're a stran-ger here," And I
sin-gle? No; the thought makes rea-son stare! Truth is
plet-ed All you sent me forth to do, With your

ta-tion, Did my spir-it once re-side?

first pri-me-val child-hood, Was I nur-tured near thy side?
felt that I had wan-dered From a more ex-alt-ed sphere.
rea-son, truth e-ter-nal Tells me I've a moth-er there.
mu-tual ap-pro-ba-tion Let me come and dwell with you.

In my first pri-me-val child-hood, Was I nurtured near thy side?

326

THERE IS BEAUTY ALL AROUND

John Hugh McNaughton

Fervently ♩ = 96

1. There is beau-ty all a-round When there's love at home; There is joy in
2. In the cot-tage there is joy When there's love at home; Hate and en-vy
3. Kind-ly heav-en smiles a-bove When there's love at home; All the world is

ev-ery sound When there's love at home. Peace and plen-ty here a-bide,
ne'er an-noy When there's love at home. Ros-es bloom be-neath our feet;
filled with love When there's love at home. Sweet-er sings the brook-let by;

Smil-ing sweet on ev-ery side. Time doth soft-ly, sweet-ly glide
All the earth's a gar-den sweet, Mak-ing life a bliss com-plete
Bright-er beams the az-ure sky; Oh, there's One who smiles on high

When there's love at home. Love at home; love at home;
When there's love at home. Love at home; love at home;
When there's love at home. Love at home; love at home;

Time doth soft-ly, sweet-ly glide When there's love at home.
Mak-ing life a bliss com-plete When there's love at home.
Oh, there's One who smiles on high When there's love at home.

327

IT MAY NOT BE ON THE MOUNTAIN HEIGHT

Mary Brown

Carrie E. Rounsefell

Earnestly ♩. = 54

1. It may not be on the moun - tain height Or o - ver the storm - y sea; It may not be at the bat - tle's front My Lord will have need of me; But if, by a still, small voice he calls, To paths that I do not know, I'll an - swer, dear Lord, with my

2. There's sure - ly some - where a low - ly place In earth's har - vest fields so wide, Where I may la - bor through life's short day For Je - sus, the Cru - ci - fied; So trust - ing my all to thy ten - der care, And know - ing thou lov - est me, I'll do thy will with a

hand in thine: I'll go where you want me to go.
heart sin - cere; I'll be what you want me to be.

I'll go where you want me to go, dear Lord, O - ver

moun - tain, or plain, or sea; I'll say what you want me to

say, dear Lord; I'll be what you want me to be.

ERE YOU LEFT YOUR ROOM THIS MORNING

Mrs. M. A. Kidder

W. O. Perkins

Sincerely ♩ = 72

1. Ere you left your room this morn - ing, Did you think to pray?
2. When your heart was filled with an - ger, Did you think to pray?
3. When sore tri - als came up - on you, Did you think to pray?

In the name of Christ, our Sav - ior, Did you sue for lov - ing
Did you plead for grace, my broth - er, That you might for - give an -
When your soul was full of sor - row, Balm of Gil - ead did you

fav - or As a shield to - day?
oth - er Who had crossed your way?
bor - row At the gates of day?

O how pray - ing rests the

wea - ry! Prayer will change the night to day;

So when life gets dark and drear - y, Don't for - get to pray.

PRAISE TO THE MAN

William W. Phelps
Brightly ♩ = 76

1. Praise to the man who com - muned with Je - ho - vah!
2. Praise to his mem - ory, he died as a mar - tyr;
3. Great is his glo - ry and end - less his priest - hood:

Je - sus a - noint - ed that Proph - et and Seer.
Hon - ored and blest be his ev - er great name!
Ev - er and ev - er the keys he will hold.

Bless - ed to o - pen the last dis - pen - sa - tion,
Long shall his blood, which was shed by as - sas - sins,
Faith - ful and true, he will en - ter his king - dom,

Kings shall ex - tol him, and na - tions re - vere.
Plead un - to heaven while the earth lauds his fame.
Crowned in the midst of the proph - ets of old.

Hail to the Proph-et, as-cend-ed to heav-en!

Trait-ors and ty-rants now fight him in vain.

Min-gling with Gods, he can plan for his breth-ren;

Death can-not con-quer the he-ro a-gain.

FAR, FAR AWAY ON JUDEA'S PLAINS

J. Macfarlane

J. Macfarlane

Joyously ♩ = 100

1. Far, far a - way on Ju - de - a's plains,
2. Lord, with the an - gels we too would re - joice;
3. Has - ten the time when, from ev - 'ry clime,

Shep - herds of old heard the joy - ous strains:
Help us to sing with the heart and voice:
Men shall u - nite in the strains sub - lime:

Glo - ry to God, Glo - ry to God,
Glo - ry to God in the
Glo - ry to God in the high - est

Glo - ry to God in the high - est; Peace on earth, good -
high - est,

will to men, Peace on earth, Good - will to men!

SILENT NIGHT

Joseph Mohr

Franz Gruber

Quietly ♪ = 112

1. Si - lent night! Ho - ly night! All is calm;
2. Si - lent night! Ho - ly night! Shep - herds quake
3. Si - lent night! Ho - ly night! Son of God,

all is bright Round yon vir - gin moth - er and Child,
at the sight! Glo - ries stream from heav - en a - far;
love's pure light Ra - diant beams from thy ho - ly face,

Ho - ly In - fant, so ten - der and mild. Sleep in heav - en - ly
Heaven - ly hosts sing Al - le - lu - ia; Christ, the Sav - ior, is
With the dawn of re - deem - ing grace, Je - sus, Lord, at thy

peace; Sleep in heav - en ly peace.
born! Christ, the Sav - ior, is born!
birth, Je - sus, Lord, at thy birth.

335

CHRIST THE LORD IS RISEN TODAY

Charles Wesley

Henry Carey

With exultation ♩ = 104

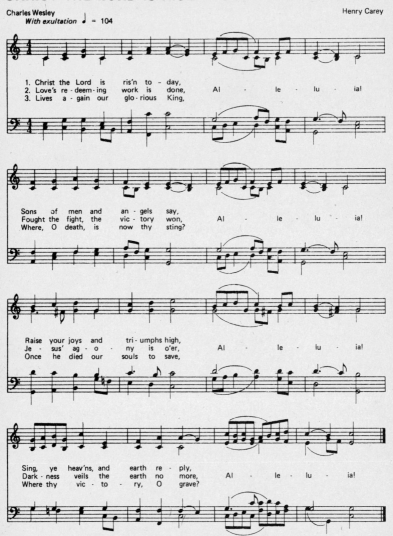

1. Christ the Lord is ris'n to - day,
2. Love's re - deem - ing work is done,   Al - le - lu - ia!
3. Lives a - gain our glo - rious King,

Sons of men and an - gels say,
Fought the fight, the vic - tory won,   Al - le - lu - ia!
Where, O death, is now thy sting?

Raise your joys and tri - umphs high,
Je - sus' ag - o - ny is o'er,   Al - le - lu - ia!
Once he died our souls to save,

Sing, ye heav'ns, and earth re - ply,
Dark - ness veils the earth no more,   Al - le - lu - ia!
Where thy vic - to - ry, O grave?

HE IS RISEN

Cecil Alexander
Stately ♩ = 92

Joachim Neander

1. He is ris - en; he is ris - en! Tell it out with
2. Come with high and ho - ly hymn - ing, Chant our Lord's tri -
3. He is ris - en; he is ris - en! He hath o - pened

joy - ful voice: He has burst his three days' pris - on;
um - phant lay; Not one dark - some cloud is dim - ming
heav - en's gate: We are free from sin's dark pris - on,

Let the whole wide earth re - joice: Death is con - quered,
Yon - der glo - rious morn - ing ray, Break - ing o'er the
Ris - en to a ho - lier state; And a bright - er

man is free; Christ has won the vic - to - ry.
pur - ple east, Sym - bol of our Eas - ter feast.
Eas - ter beam On our long - ing eyes shall stream.

337

CHILDREN'S SONGS

I KNOW MY FATHER LIVES

Reid Nibley

Reverently

Reid Nibley

1. I know my Fa - ther lives and loves me too; The Spi - rit whis - pers this to me and tells me it is true, and tells me it is true.
2. He sent me here to earth By faith to live his plan; The Spi - rit whis - pers this to me and tells me that I can, and tells me that I can.

I AM A CHILD OF GOD

Naomi W. Randall

Mildred T. Pettit

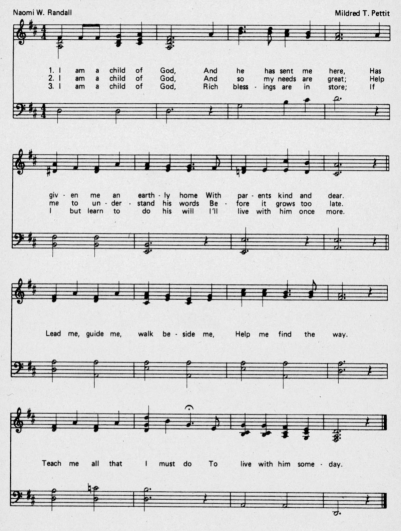

1. I am a child of God, And he has sent me here, Has given me an earthly home With parents kind and dear.

2. I am a child of God, And so my needs are great; Help me to understand his words Before it grows too late.

3. I am a child of God, Rich blessings are in store; If I but learn to do his will I'll live with him once more.

Lead me, guide me, walk beside me, Help me find the way.

Teach me all that I must do To live with him someday.

I THANK THEE, DEAR FATHER

George Careless

Simply

1. I thank thee, dear Father in heaven a - bove,
2. Help me to be good, kind, and gen - tle to - day,

For thy good - ness and mer - cy, thy kind - ness and love,
And mind what my fa - ther and moth - er shall say;

I thank thee for home, friends, and par - ents so dear,
In the dear name of Je - sus, so lov - ing and mild,

And for ev - 'ry bless - ing that I en - joy here.
I ask thee to bless me and keep me thy child.

I THINK WHEN I READ THAT SWEET STORY

Jemima Luke

Leah A. Lloyd

1. I think when I read that sweet sto - ry of old, When Je - sus was here a - mong men, How he called lit - tle chil - dren like lambs to his fold, I should like to have been with him then.

2. I wish that his hands had been placed on my head, That his arms had been thrown a - round me, That I might have seen his kind look when he said, "Let the lit - tle ones come un - to me."

3. Yet still to his foot - stool in prayer I may go, And ask for a share in his love; And if I thus ear - nest - ly seek him be - low, I shall see him and hear him a - bove.

TEACH ME TO WALK IN THE LIGHT

Clara McMaster

Clara McMaster

In a reverent mood

(Child) Teach me to walk in the light of his love,
(Parent) Come, lit - tle child, and to - geth - er we'll learn
(Both) Fa - ther in hea - ven, we thank thee this day

Teach me to pray to my Fa - ther a - bove,
Of his com - mand - ments, that we may re - turn
For lov - ing gui - dance to show us the way.

Teach me to know of the things that are right,
Home to his pres - ence, to live in his sight—
Grate - ful, we praise thee with songs of de - light!

Teach me, teach me to walk in the light.
Al - ways, al - ways to walk in the light.
Glad - ly, glad - ly we'll walk in the light.

342

THE LORD GAVE ME A TEMPLE

Donnell Hunter
Sweetly

Darwin Wolford

The Lord gave me a tem-ple to live with-in on earth. Once in Heav-en I was spir-it, but I left my home at birth. I'll make my tem-ple bright-er; I'll keep my spir-it free. My bod-y is the tem-ple my Fa-ther gave to me.

KINDNESS BEGINS WITH ME

Clara W. McMaster   Clara W. McMaster

I want to be kind to ev - 'ry one, For that is right you see. So I say to my - self: "Re - mem - ber this, Kind - ness be - gins with me."

DARE TO DO RIGHT

A. C. Smyth, arr.

Not too fast

1. Dare to do right! dare to be true! You have a work that no
2. Dare to do right! dare to be true! Oth-er men's fail-ures can

oth-er can do; Do it so brave-ly, so kind-ly, so well,
nev-er save you, Stand by your con-science, your hon-or, your faith,

An-gels will has-ten the sto-ry to tell.
Stand like a he-ro and bat-tle till death.

Dare, dare, dare to do right, Dare, dare,

dare to be true, Dare to be true, Dare to be true.

THE GOLDEN PLATES

Rose Thomas Graham

J. Spencer Cornwall

Articulately

1. The gold - en plates lay hid - den
2. A rec - ord made by Ne - phi,

Deep in a moun - tain side, Un - til God found one
A god - ly man of old, Now, in the Book of

faith - ful, In whom he could con - fide.
Mor - mon, The sto - ry is re - told.

FAMILY PRAYER

DeVota M. Peterson

Reverently

DeVota M. Peterson

1. Let us gath - er in a cir - cle, And kneel in fam - 'ly pray'r, To thank our Heav'n - ly Fa - ther For the bless - ings which we share.

2. Let us thank him for our meal - time, For clothes we dai - ly wear, For par - ents, homes, and church - es, For his kind and lov - ing care.

3. Oh, ____ may we al - ways serve him, In thought and ac - tion too, And hum - bly kneel at pray'r time, As so man - y fam - 'lies do.

347

GLOSSARY

AARONIC PRIESTHOOD: The lesser of the two divisions in the priesthood in the Church. It includes the offices of deacon, teacher, priest, and bishop.

ADAM: The first man. The father of the human race. Before his earth life, he was known as Michael. He led the righteous in the war in heaven. He helped in the creation of the earth.

ADMINISTER THE SACRAMENT: To bless the sacrament.

ADMINISTER TO THE SICK: To annoint and bless the sick by the power of the priesthood.

ADULTERY: Sexual intercourse between a married man and someone other than his wife or between a married woman and someone other than her husband.

ADVERSARY: Enemy; one of Satan's names.

AFFLICTION: Anything causing pain or suffering.

AGENCY: The ability and freedom to choose good or evil.

AGE OF ACCOUNTABILITY: A time when a person is held responsible for his actions. In most cases a person begins to be responsible for his actions when he becomes eight years old.

ALTAR: 1. Anciently, a raised place on which sacrifices were offered. 2. In LDS temples today, a place where covenants are made and couples or families are sealed together for time and eternity.

ANCESTOR: One from whom a person is descended.

ANGEL: In a general sense, a messenger sent from God.

ANNOINT: To place a few drops of oil on the head, usually as part of the procedure of a priesthood blessing.

APOSTASY: Turning away from or leaving the true gospel teachings.

APOSTLE: A person called and appointed to be a special witness for Christ. An office in the Melchizedek Priesthood.

ARTICLES OF FAITH: Thirteen statements written by the Prophet Joseph Smith telling some of the basic teachings and ordinances of The Church of Jesus Christ of Latter-day Saints.

ASCEND: To move upward toward heaven.

ATONEMENT: The sacrifice of Jesus Christ who had no sin, but suffered and died to free all men from the effects of both physical death and spiritual death.

AUTHORITY: The right to function in certain capacities in the Church.

BAPTISM BY IMMERSION: An ordinance in which a person is put under water and brought up out of the water. Part of the ordinance necessary to become a member of The Church of Jesus Christ of Latter-day Saints.

BAPTISM FOR THE DEAD: Baptism by immersion of a living person acting for one who is dead. This ordinance is performed in LDS temples.

BESTOW: To give a gift.

BIBLE: One of the standard works of the Church. It includes the Old and the New Testaments.

BISHOP: The presiding officer in the Aaronic Priesthood. Also, a man who has been ordained and set apart as the presiding high priest for a ward. He has the responsibility for the temporal and spiritual well-being of all his ward members.

Glossary

BOOK OF MORMON: An account of God's dealings with the people of the American continents from about 2200 years before the birth of Jesus Christ to 421 years after Jesus Christ lived on the earth. It was translated from gold plates by Joseph Smith and contains the fulness of the gospel.

BORN IN THE COVENANT: Children born to parents who have been sealed in the temple.

BRETHREN: Brothers; sometimes used to refer to the General Authorities.

BROKEN HEART AND CONTRITE SPIRIT: A deep, godly sorrow for our sins; humility.

CALLED: To be asked or assigned to a duty or position in the Church.

CELESTIAL KINGDOM: The highest kingdom of glory, where one is in the presence of our Heavenly Father and Jesus Christ.

CHARITY: Love, compassion, kindness, concern, interest in and sympathy for others; the pure love of Christ.

CHASTITY: Personal righteousness, particularly avoidance of sexual relations with anyone except one's legal mate by marriage or of any improper sexual experiences.

COMFORTER, THE: The Holy Ghost.

COMMANDMENTS: Directions given by God to his children to prepare them for eternal life in the world to come.

COMMITMENT: An agreement or pledge to do something.

CONFIRMATION: An ordinance following baptism through which a person is confirmed a member of The Church of Jesus Christ of Latter-day Saints by the laying on of hands. At the same time he has the Holy Ghost conferred or given to him.

CONVERT: One who has accepted the gospel of Jesus Christ through baptism and confirmation into the Church. Usually applied to those who join the Church after eight years of age.

CORRUPTIBLE: Able to be destroyed.

COUNCIL IN HEAVEN: The grand meeting in heaven in which the Father announced his plan of salvation and redemption and in which he chose Jesus Christ as our Redeemer.

COVENANT: A binding and solemn agreement, contract or promise between God and a person or group of persons.

CREATE: To organize elements that already exist into a new form.

CRUCIFIXION: A method of execution used in the days of the Savior. The act of putting a person to death by nailing or tying the hands and feet to a cross.

CUT OFF: To end, send away, excommunicate.

DEATH: Separation of a person's spirit from his physical body.

DEVIL: A spirit son of God who rebelled against the Father and tried to destroy the agency of man. Also known as Lucifer, Satan. He is the author of sin.

DISCIPLE: Follower.

DISCERNMENT: Spirit, gift, or power to know the difference between two things, such as good and evil.

DISPENSATION: A period of time in which truth from heaven is given to men on earth.

DIVINE: Coming from God, godlike.

DOCTRINE: Something that is taught; teachings of the gospel.

DOCTRINE AND COVENANTS: A book containing revelations given to Joseph Smith and other presidents of the Church. One of the standard works of the Church.

ENDOWMENT: A special spiritual blessing given to worthy and faithful members of the Church in the temple.

ENDURING TO THE END: Obedience to God's laws to the end of mortal life.

ENTICE: To attract by offering a reward.

ESTABLISH: To set up; to make firm.

ETERNAL: Everlasting, without beginning or end.

ETERNITY: Time without end.

EVE: Adam's wife, mother of human race.

EVERLASTING: Lasting or enduring forever.

EVIL: The opposite of good. That which is morally bad, wicked, unrighteous. Disobedience to God's laws.

EXALTATION: The continuation of the family unit in eternity; an inheritance in the highest of the three heavens within the celestial kingdom. "All [that] the Father hath," (D&C 84:38).

EXHORT: To ask strongly. To advise or warn earnestly.

EXTERNAL: On the outside.

FALL OF ADAM: Change to mortality that occurred when Adam ate the forbidden fruit.

FAMINE: Little or no food.

FAST: To abstain from food and drink for spiritual reasons.

FAST OFFERING: Contribution of food or money saved by fasting for two consecutive meals.

FIRST PRESIDENCY: A quorum made up of the President of the Church and his counselors.

FOREORDAIN: To appoint in the premortal world.

FOREORDINATION: A calling by our Heavenly Father to come to earth at a particular time and place to help with the Lord's work in a particular way.

FOREVER: Always, no end, eternal.

FORNICATION: Sexual intercourse by an unmarried person.

FREEDOM: Liberty.

FULFILL: To finish or complete.

FULL TITHEPAYER: A person who pays one tenth of his annual increase to the Lord.

GAIN: To win; to get.

GATHERING OF ISRAEL: The eventual bringing together of all the peoples of Israel in the latter days.

GENEALOGY: A study of family wherein ancestors are identified.

GENERATION: A period of time between parents, children, and grandchildren.

GENTILE: A person of non-Israelite or non-Jewish faith. Sometimes used to refer to persons who are not members of The Church of Jesus Christ of Latter-day Saints.

GIFT OF THE HOLY GHOST: The right, received by the laying on of hands, to enjoy the constant companionship of the Holy Ghost when we are worthy.

GIFTS OF THE SPIRIT: Certain spiritual blessings given to those who are faithful to obey the commandments of God.

GLORIFIED: Heavenly, having great spiritual beauty.

GOD: The Eternal Father. The Father of Jesus Christ and of the spirits of all men.

GODHEAD: The Father, the Son, and the Holy Ghost.

GOSPEL: In a general sense, the plan of salvation, embracing all that is necessary to save and exalt mankind. In a special sense, the good news that Jesus is the Christ.

HELL: That part of the spirit world where wicked spirits await the day of their resurrection. In a general sense the place where Satan and his followers dwell.

HOLY GHOST: Third member of the Godhead; a personage of spirit.

HOUSE OF ISRAEL: Natural or adopted descendants of the sons of Jacob who was given the name of Israel by the Lord.

HUMBLE: Willing to learn, teachable.

IMAGE: Likeness; having the same appearance.

IMMERSE: To put under water.

IMMORTALITY: Beyond the power of death. If a person is immortal he cannot die.

INIQUITIES: Sins.

INSPIRATION: Divine guidance that comes from the promptings of the Holy Ghost.

ISRAEL: 1. The name given to Jacob of the Old Testament. 2. The name given to the descendants of Jacob's twelve sons. 3. The modern nation to which many Jews have gathered today.

JESUS CHRIST: Our Lord, the Only Begotten of the Father in the flesh and the firstborn in the spirit; our Redeemer and Savior.

JEW: One belonging to the tribe of Judah, to the ancient kingdom of Judah, or to the Jewish religion.

KINGDOM OF GOD: The Church of Jesus Christ of Latter-day Saints as it is now. In the eternal sense, the celestial kingdom.

LAST DAYS: Near the end of the world or the second coming of the Savior.

LATTER-DAY SAINTS: Members of The Church of Jesus Christ of Latter-day Saints.

LAYING ON OF HANDS: The act by a priesthood holder of placing hands on the head of a person to bless, anoint, confirm, ordain, or heal him.

LITERAL: Actual, real.

LORD: God, master. Often refers to Jesus.

LUCIFER: Satan, the devil.

MERCY: Love, forgiveness.

MILLENNIUM: One thousand years of peace when Jesus Christ will reign personally on the earth.

MESSIAH: Jesus Christ, the Anointed One.

MISSION: A period of time during which a person who has been called and set apart preaches the gospel; a task or assignment.

MISSIONARY: A member of the Church who is called to preach the gospel to the people of the world.

MORTAL: Able to die; pertaining to this life.

MORTALITY: Earthly existence in a body that is subject to death.

NONMEMBER: Used to refer to persons who are not members of The Church of Jesus Christ of Latter-day Saints.

OBEY: To do what one is commanded to do.

OFFICIATE: To perform a ceremony or duty.

ONLY BEGOTTEN SON: Jesus Christ, the only person of whom God the Father was the father of his mortal body.

OPPRESSION: Physical or mental distress.

ORDAIN: To give man a priesthood office by the laying on of hands.

ORDINANCES: Sacred rites and ceremonies that are necessary for eternal progression. God's laws and commandments.

OUTER DARKNESS: The dwelling place of the devil and his followers.

PARADISE: The part of the spirit world where righteous spirits go to await the day of their resurrection.

PARTAKE: To eat and drink the emblems of the sacrament.

PATRIARCHAL BLESSING: An inspired blessing declaring a person's lineage and giving inspired counsel and insight about his life.

PEARL OF GREAT PRICE: A volume of latter-day scripture, one of the standard works of the Church.

PERSECUTED: To be troubled constantly by others; to be treated wrongfully.

PLAN OF SALVATION: Our Heavenly Father's program for his children by which they can overcome sin and death and gain eternal life.

PRAYER: Communication with the Lord.

PREMORTAL EXISTENCE (LIFE): The period between the birth of spirit children of God and their birth into mortal life.

PRESIDE: To take charge of; to be in authority.

PRIESTHOOD: The power and the authority of God given to men on earth to act in all things for the salvation of men.

PRINCIPLE: Basic law or doctrine; rule of behavior.

PROGRESS: To grow; to go ahead.

PROPHECY: Inspired words of a prophet about a future event before it happens.

PROPHESY: To tell something before it happens.

PROPHET: One who has been called of the Lord to be a special witness of the divinity of Jesus Christ. *The Prophet* refers to the President of The Church of Jesus Christ of Latter-day Saints.

PROSPER: To do well.

PUNISH: To make someone pay for doing wrong.

QUARREL: To fight with words.

QUORUM: An organized unit of the priesthood.

RAIMENT: Clothing.

RECOMMEND: A certificate to identify persons as members of the Church and to certify their worthiness to receive certain ordinances or blessings.

REDEEM: To free from the results of sins from which a person has repented. To free from the effects of physical death.

REDEEMER: The Savior, Jesus Christ.

REJECTED: Refused.

REMISSION: Forgiveness.

REPENTANCE: The act of turning from sin and changing the course of one's life to follow the Savior's teachings.

RESTITUTION: Making good or giving repayment for a sin.

RESTORATION: To make as it was; to re-establish. To bring back.

RESURRECTED: Raised from the dead with an immortal body.

RESURRECTION: Reuniting of body and spirit, never to be separated again.

REUNITE: To come together again.

REVELATION: The making known of divine truths by communication from God.

RIGHTEOUS: Good, worthy.

SABBATH DAY: A day of rest from daily work and activities. A day of worship observed by the members of the Church on Sunday, the first day of the week.

SACRAMENT: An ordinance in which bread and water are blessed and passed to members of the Church. The bread and water are emblems of the body and blood sacrificed by the Savior.

SACRED: Entitled to reverence and respect.

SACRIFICE: To offer to God something precious; to forsake all things for the gospel of Jesus Christ.

SALVATION: Inseparable connection of body and spirit brought about through the Savior's atonement and resurrection; eternal life.

SANCTIFY: To make clean, pure, and spotless; to make free from the blood and sins of this world.

SATAN: Name of the devil, who opposes the plan of salvation.

SAVIOR: Jesus Christ who has saved us from physical death and made it possible for us to be saved from spiritual death.

SCRIPTURES: Words, both written and spoken, by holy men of God when moved upon by the Holy Ghost.

SEALING: An ordinance performed in the temple eternally uniting a husband and wife or children and their parents.

SECOND DEATH: Spiritual death; death as to things of righteousness.

SEED: In one sense, children or descendants.

SET APART: To authorize one, by the laying on of hands, to act in a specific calling.

SIN: Breaking of laws of God.

SON OF GOD: The Savior, Jesus Christ.

SONS OF PERDITION: The spirit hosts of heaven who followed Lucifer. Those who having gained a perfect knowledge of the divinity of the Savior turn from him and follow after Satan.

SPIRITUAL DEATH: Separation from the Spirit of God and from his presence.

STANDARD WORKS: The volumes of scripture officially accepted by the Church—Bible, Book of Mormon, Doctrine and Covenants, and Pearl of Great Price.

SUPREME: Highest in power and authority.

SUSTAIN: To give support; to accept.

TELESTIAL KINGDOM: The lowest kingdom of glory.

TEMPLE: A place of worship and prayer. The house of the Lord prepared and dedicated for sacred gospel ordinances.

TEMPLE ORDINANCE WORK: Sacred ordinances of the gospel performed in the temples by those who are living for themselves and for those who are dead. These ordinances include baptisms, endowments, marriages, and sealings.

TERRESTRIAL KINGDOM: The middle kingdom of glory.

TESTIFY: To declare what one knows; to bear witness.

TESTIMONY: Knowledge, received by revelation from the Holy Ghost, of the divinity of the Savior and of gospel truths.

TITHE: One-tenth of one's annual increase paid to the Lord.

TRANSGRESSION: Violation or breaking of a commandment or law; sin.

VISION: An appearance of spiritual personages or scenes, revealed by the power of the Holy Ghost.

WORD OF WISDOM: A revelation concerning health practices, given to Joseph Smith in 1833; section 89 of the Doctrine and Covenants.

WORSHIP: Reverence, honor, or devotion to God.

WORTHY MEMBER: A Church member who obeys the commandments of God to the best of his ability.

ZION: The name given by the Lord to those who obey his laws. The name of the place where the righteous live.

BOOKS CITED

Grant, Heber J. *Gospel Standards.* Compiled by A. Homer Durham, Salt Lake City: Improvement Era, 1941.

Hinckley, Bryant S. *The Faith of Our Pioneer Fathers.* Salt Lake City: Bookcraft, 1956.

Kimball, Spencer W. *Faith Precedes the Miracle.* Salt Lake City: Deseret Book Company, 1972.

Kimball, Spencer W. *The Miracle of Forgiveness.* Salt Lake City: Bookcraft, 1969.

Lee, Harold B. *Stand Ye in Holy Places.* Salt Lake City: Deseret Book Company, 1974.

McConkie, Bruce R. *Mormon Doctrine.* 2nd ed. Salt Lake City: Bookcraft, 1966.

McKay, David O. *True to the Faith.* Compiled by Llewelyn R. McKay. Salt Lake City: Bookcraft, 1966.

Principles of the Gospel. Salt Lake City: The Church of Jesus Christ of Latter-day Saints, 1976.

Smith, Joseph. *History of the Church of Jesus Christ of Latter-day Saints.* 7 vols. 2nd ed. rev. Edited by B. H. Roberts. Salt Lake City: The Church of Jesus Christ of Latter-day Saints, 1932–51.

Smith, Joseph. *Lectures on Faith.* Compiled by N. B. Lundwall. Salt Lake City: N. B. Lundwall, n. d.

Smith, Joseph. *Teachings of the Prophet Joseph Smith.* Selected by Joseph Fielding Smith. Salt Lake City: Deseret Book Company, 1938.

Smith, Joseph Fielding. *Answers to Gospel Questions.* 5 vols. Compiled by Joseph Fielding Smith, Jr. Salt Lake City: Deseret Book Company, 1957–66.

Smith, Joseph Fielding. *Doctrines of Salvation.* 3 vols. Compiled by Bruce R. McConkie. Salt Lake City: Bookcraft, 1954–56.

Talmage, James E. *Jesus the Christ.* 3rd ed. Salt Lake City: The Church of Jesus Christ of Latter-day Saints, 1916.

Young, Brigham. *Discourses of Brigham Young.* Selected by John A. Widtsoe. Salt Lake City: Deseret Book Company, 1941.

COMMENTS AND SUGGESTIONS

Your comments and suggestions about this manual are appreciated. Please submit them to—

Curriculum Planning and Development
Floor 24
50 East North Temple Street
Salt Lake City, Utah 84150
USA

Identify yourself by name, address, ward, and stake. Then identify the name of the manual, how you used it, your feelings regarding its strengths and weaknesses, and any recommended improvements.